# Wander: Exploring LACMA's David Geffen Galleries

Los Angeles County Museum of Art

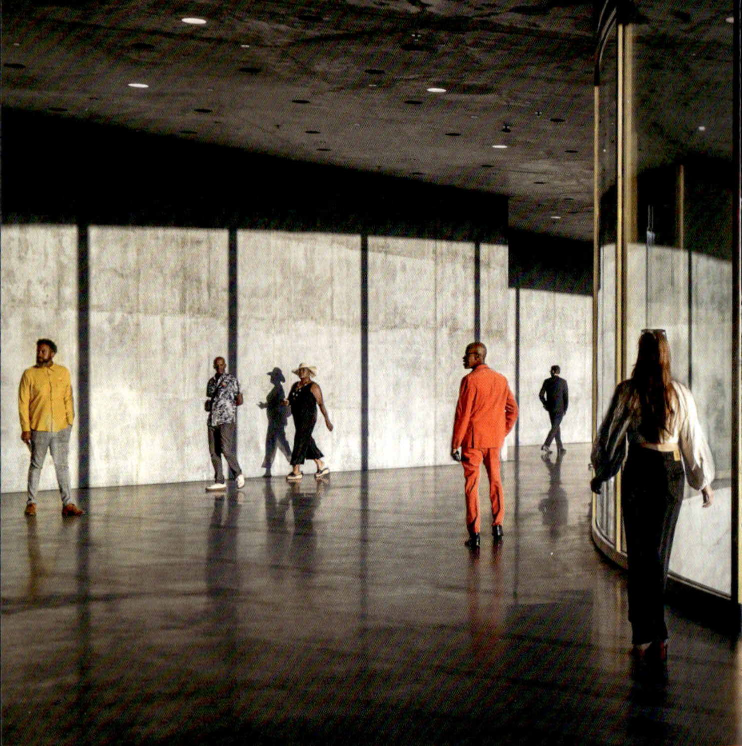

# Contents



Visitors in the David Geffen Galleries

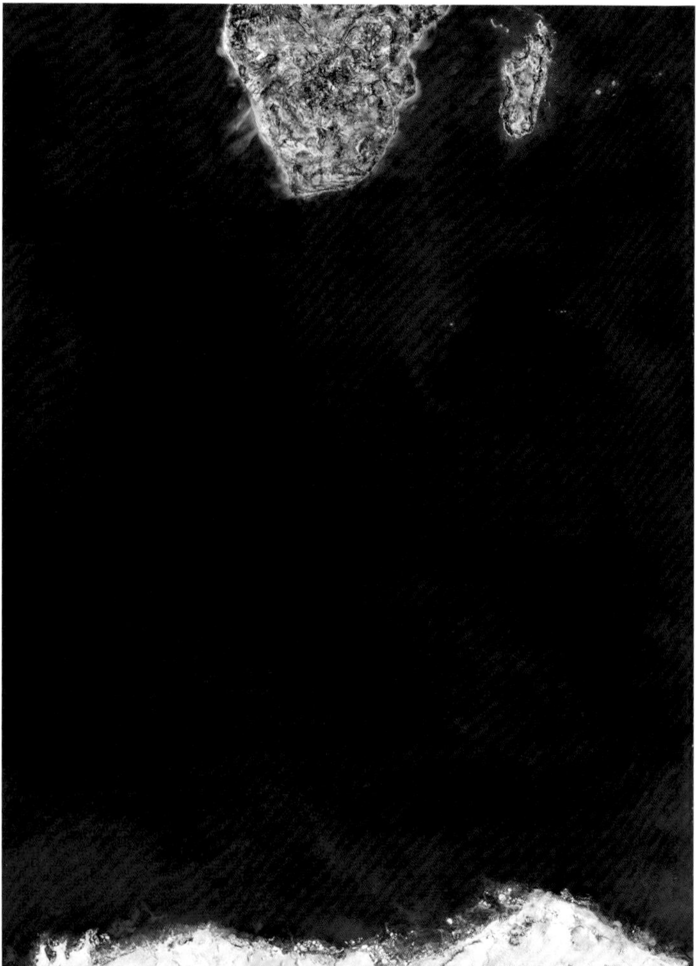

# Welcome

The opening of LACMA's Peter Zumthor–designed David Geffen Galleries is the capstone of a two-decade planning and building process that transformed the campus into a place of outdoor space, public sculpture, and exhibition buildings—including the Broad Contemporary Art Museum (BCAM) and the Lynda and Stewart Resnick Exhibition Pavilion, both designed by Renzo Piano, and Bruce Goff's landmark Pavilion for Japanese Art. The Geffen Galleries will serve as the anchor of the campus and a showcase for LACMA's art: though our encyclopedic collection is exhibited in all four exhibition spaces, the galleries were imagined as an extensive, immersive experience of world culture through art—one as diverse and open as modern-day Los Angeles itself.

The brief to Peter Zumthor was to create a museum of galleries on a single floor, without hierarchies, featuring natural light and transparency to the outside. My dream was of visitors wandering through art and ideas as one might meander through a park, choosing their own paths and engaging their own interests. I have always been skeptical of describing history as linear and progressive: there are so many stories to tell, and so many ways to arrange artworks to tell

Andreas Gursky, *Ocean IV*, 2010
(See inside front flap for more information about this work)

them. LACMA's talented curatorial team has chosen to explore these stories through the lens of the oceans and seas that have connected cultures—by trade, by migration, and by force—over millennia. If museums were originally conceived in the eighteenth and nineteenth centuries to preserve and order knowledge into clearly defined categories, we are more interested in how multiple origin stories and traditions have become intertwined through the interaction of peoples and how artworks reflect that complexity. Here, traditional categories of geography, chronology, and medium expand into more multifaceted thematic groupings.

Please wander through the many artworks and art histories woven into this installation of the Geffen Galleries. Trust your own curiosity and interests. This guidebook highlights some of the artworks that demonstrate the diversity and quality of LACMA's collections, but each visitor will have different favorites. As you return over months and years, you will also experience the ebb and flow of new presentations. Drawn from more than 150,000 works spanning world history, these arrangements tell endless stories shaped by ongoing, collaborative research and discussion among curators, scholars, and educators. As the world and its concerns change, so will we.

As we celebrate the opening of the David Geffen Galleries, I offer profound gratitude to the literally thousands of artists, donors, civic leaders, builders, craftspeople, and staff who have shared in the making of the galleries, this guide, and the many related programs that expand access to our art collections. Very special thanks are due to David Geffen and to Tony Ressler and the late Elaine Wynn, our board co-chairs through more than a decade of the process. The Geffen Galleries are the fruit of the long-term public-private partnership between Los Angeles County and the museum. Our programs and collections continue to grow through the generosity of our communities and supporters; notably, the commitment to building new galleries has inspired some of the most significant gifts of art in the museum's history. Indeed, all of LACMA is a gift—of art, facilities, thought, and people—directed toward the public in the hope of delight, learning, and inspiration toward the future. Art isn't static, nor is its impact. Every person who views a work of art adds to its story. Thank you to all who make up LACMA, including those who visit and take part in the power of art to lift our world.

Michael Govan
CEO and Wallis Annenberg Director
Los Angeles County Museum of Art

# The David Geffen Galleries

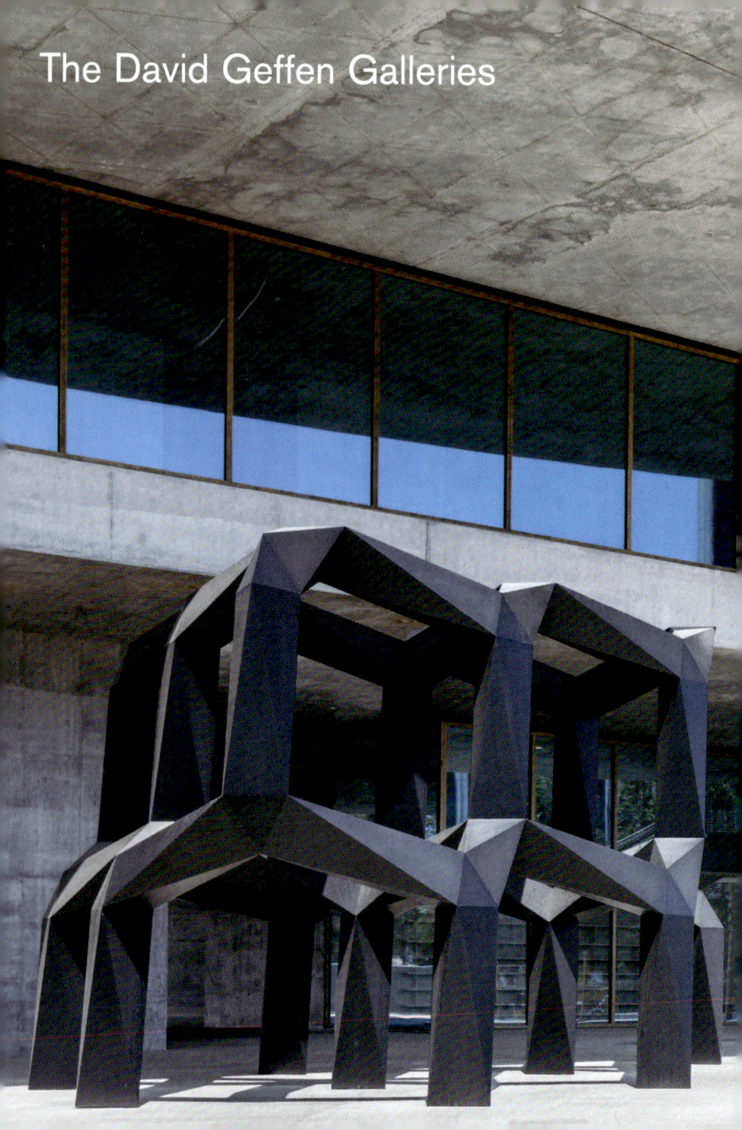

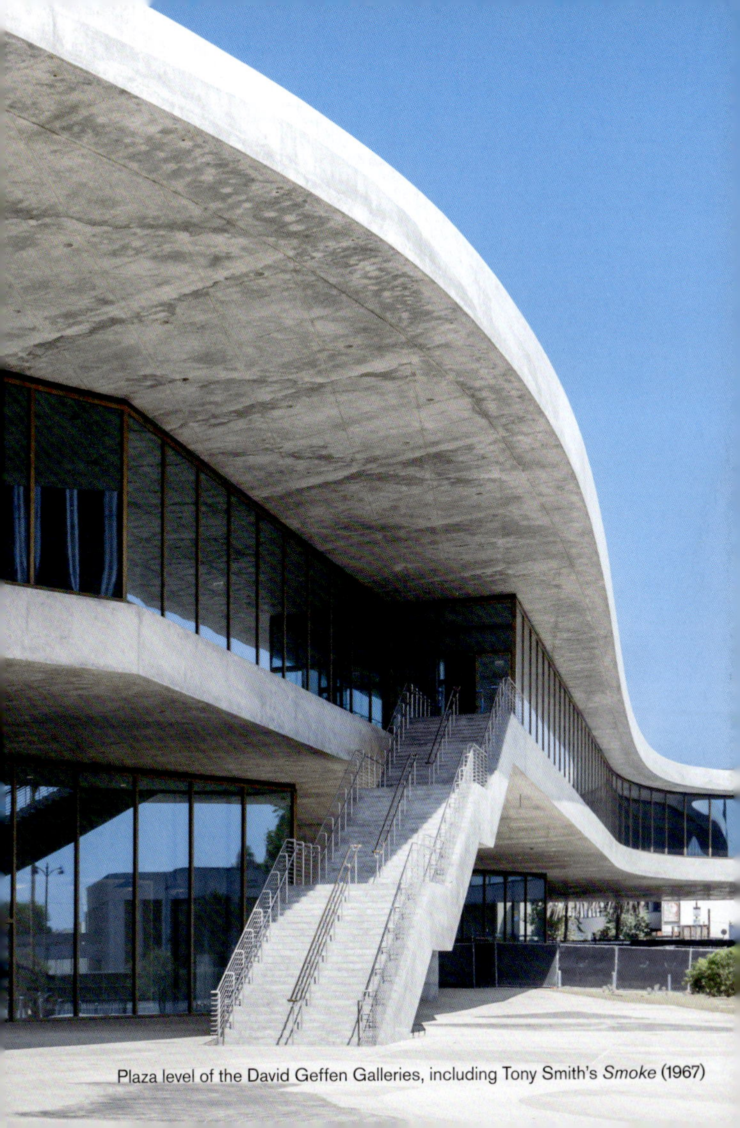

Plaza level of the David Geffen Galleries, including Tony Smith's *Smoke* (1967)

# Space

The David Geffen Galleries—LACMA's new home for its permanent collection—rise above Hancock Park, adjacent to the La Brea Tar Pits. Crafted from architectural concrete and glass, the building's organic form spans Wilshire Boulevard—a sculptural whole that embraces the neighbor-hood. Outside, its elevated gallery floor creates 3.5 acres of shaded public space below. Inside, visitors encounter airy terrace galleries with floor-to-ceiling windows, plaza-like courtyard galleries where stories converge, and intimate interior galleries that encourage contemplation.



Aerial view of the David Geffen Galleries and the Pavilion for Japanese Art

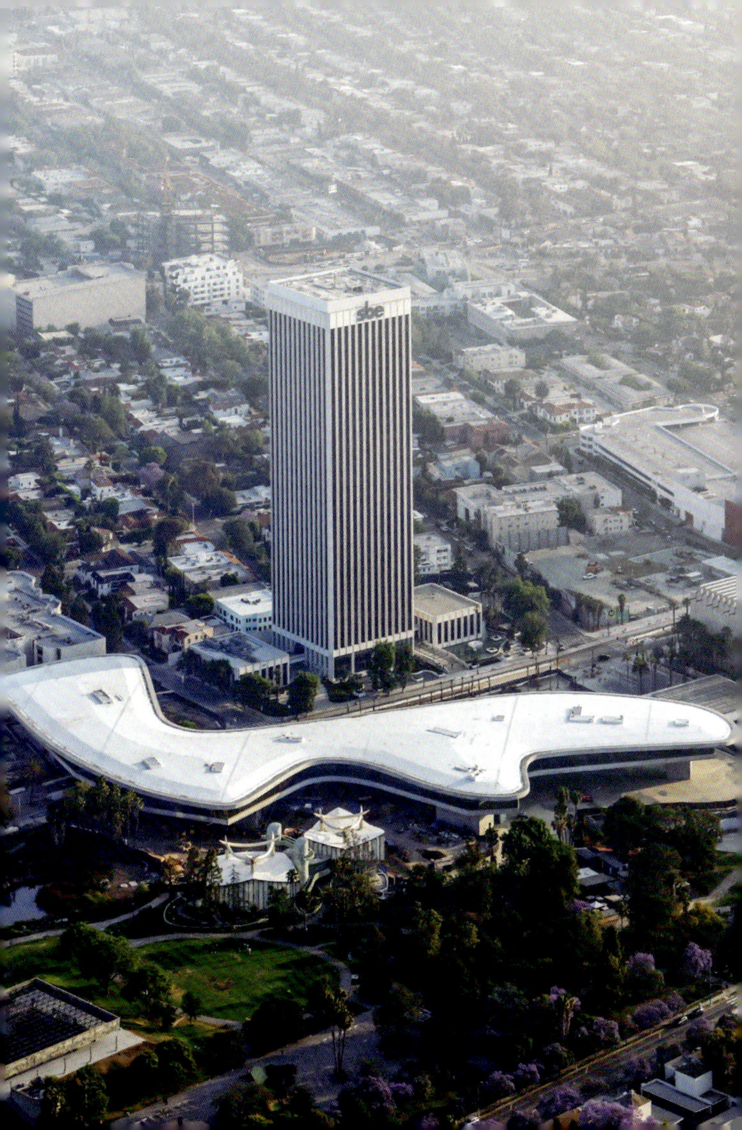
sbe

# Light

Rather than providing uniform illumination, architect Peter Zumthor designed the galleries to allow light and shadow to work in dialogue. Southern California's clear, warm sunlight enters from the sides—providing what Zumthor calls "the most noble light" for viewing art and people. Shadow, light's counterpart, is cast by the building's overhang and transforms the galleries throughout the day. Metallic curtains by textile designer Reiko Sudō add further dimension to the building's landscape of light and shadow while providing protection for delicate works. Because the building is curved, it reflects itself in the glass, creating an ever-changing interplay between interior and exterior. No two visits are alike; the building responds to the weather, season, and time of day.



View of the David Geffen Galleries from the plaza level

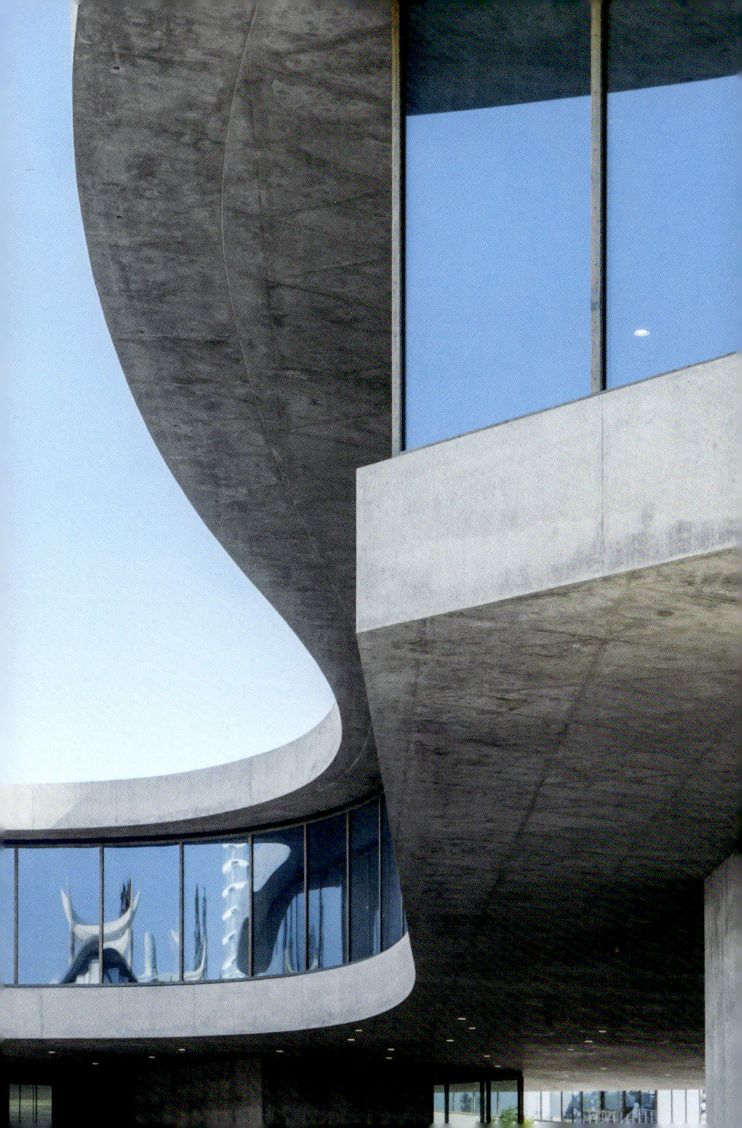

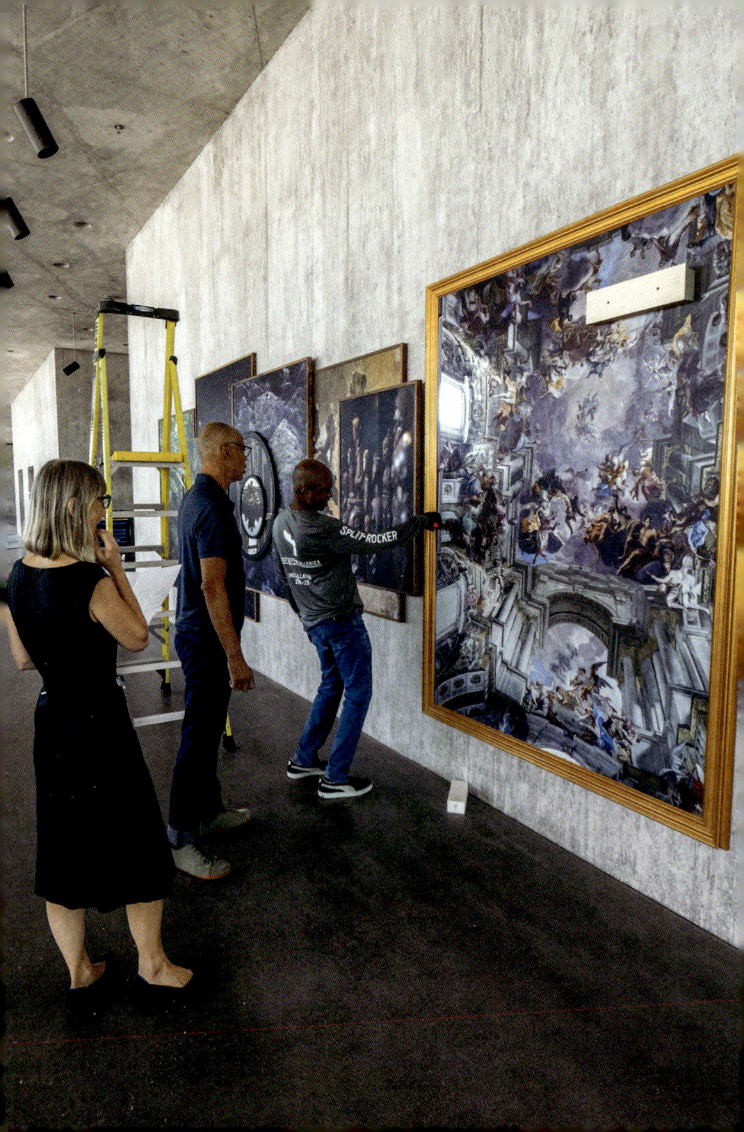
SPLIT-ROCKER

# Oceans

Inspired by an oceanic framework, the galleries explore networks of exchange around the Atlantic Ocean, Mediterranean Sea, Indian Ocean, and Pacific Ocean. This arrangement creates unexpected encounters—a seventeenth-century Dutch painting beside twentieth-century photography, African textiles near American quilts—inviting you to discover visual and thematic connections across time and geography. With a nonhierarchical layout of more than eighty presentations comprising nearly three thousand objects, you'll discover new works as well as rediscover familiar pieces in entirely new contexts.

Todd Gray's *Octavia's Gaze* (2025) being installed in the David Geffen Galleries

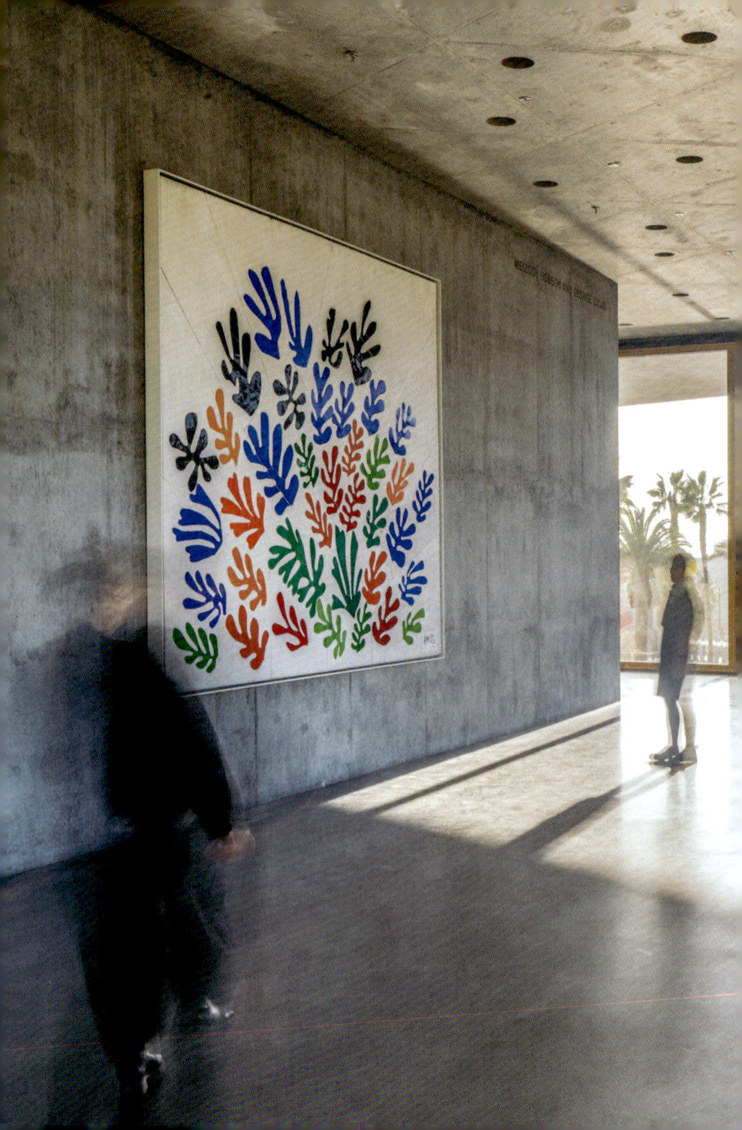

# Visiting the Galleries

The David Geffen Galleries have no front or back—you may enter from north of Wilshire Boulevard into the Pacific galleries, or from the south into the Atlantic galleries. Once inside, you'll move freely through a single exhibition floor where different gallery spaces connect and flow into one another.

This guidebook highlights more than two hundred of the works on view in our opening presentation, beginning with the Pacific galleries, followed by Indian and Mediterranean, and concluding with Atlantic. The artworks appear in an order that roughly reflects gallery adjacencies, with the gallery name shown at the bottom of each entry.

The organization of the book suggests just one possible route through the building, but the galleries were designed for wandering. Discover your own path through the collection. Use this guidebook as a companion on your journey, whether you choose to traverse the entire length of the building, concentrate your visit within a particular space, or stroll the perimeter to take in the views of the city. Visit often—new works and new presentations will appear regularly, transforming what you find both inside and out.

Henri Matisse, *La Gerbe*, 1953
(See inside front flap for more information about this work)

# Pacific Ocean

1. Pacific Connections in the Ancient Americas
2. Keepers of the Cosmos in Mesoamerican Art
3. *Indigenismo* in Latin America
4. Spanish America at the Center of the World
5. Textiles of the Andes
6. Modern Silver in Mexico and Peru
7. The Silver That Moved the World
8. Polynesia: "Our Sea of Islands"
9. Navigating Pacific Asia
10. Netsuke: Japanese Carvings, Foreign Connections
11. Blue-and-White Porcelain of East Asia
12. Ultramodern: Kyoto Ceramics
13. Japan: Living Landscapes, Flowing Waters
14. L.A. Printmaking: June Wayne
15. Car Culture
16. Photo Experimentation
17. The Stuff of Alchemy: Plastic in Art
18. In This Light
19. Henri Matisse: *La Gerbe*
20. Earth and Water
21. Picturing the American West
22. rafa esparza: *...we are the mountain*
23. Kimsooja: *A Needle Woman*

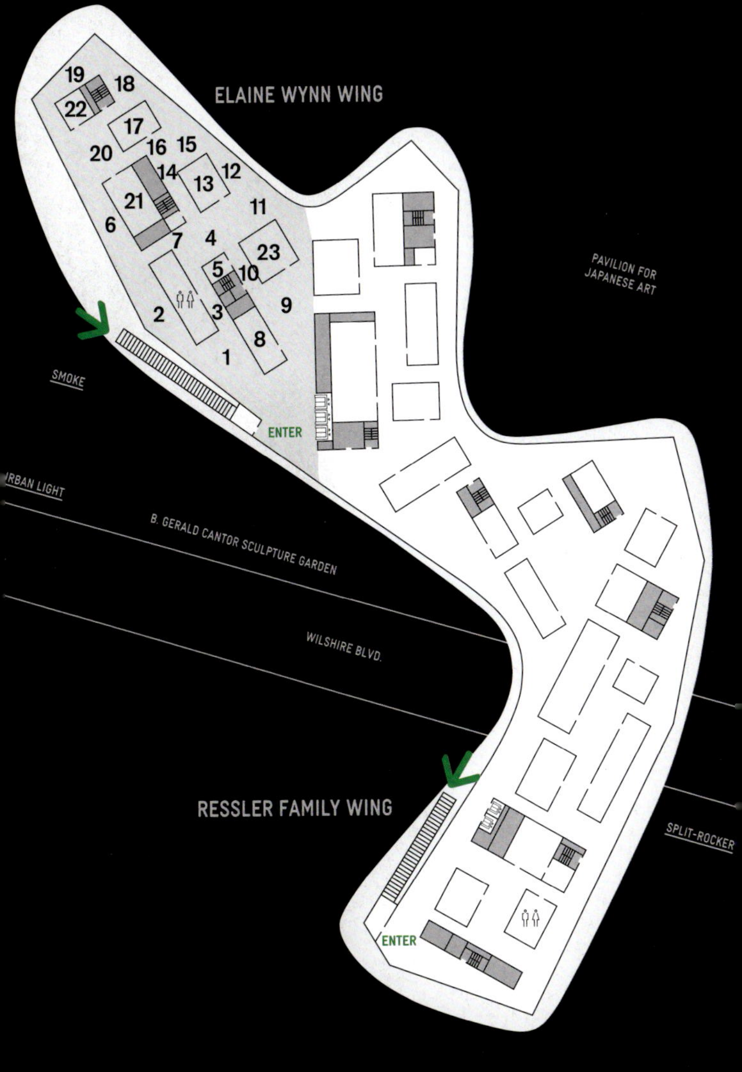
ELAINE WYNN WING
19
18
22
17
20
16
15
14
13
12
21
11
6
7
4
23
5
10
9
2
3
8
1
SMOKE
ENTER
PAVILION FOR JAPANESE ART
URBAN LIGHT
B. GERALD CANTOR SCULPTURE GARDEN
WILSHIRE BLVD.
RESSLER FAMILY WING
SPLIT-ROCKER
ENTER

# Pacific Ocean

The Pacific Ocean covers thirty percent of Earth's surface—165 million square kilometers of open water. Movement and trade flourished within its various regions for thousands of years. But rather than connecting cultures like a highway, the Pacific has functioned as an archipelago of separate artistic traditions, divided by distances too vast for regular contact until the 1500s, when Spanish expeditions accomplished transpacific navigation.

Four major regions—each with its own material resources, forms of knowledge, and religious traditions—developed their own approaches to making art along the ocean's rim: the Pacific Americas (from Alaska through Mexico and Peru to Chile), East Asia (China, Korea, Japan), Maritime Southeast Asia (Philippines, Indonesia, Malaysia), and Oceania (Polynesia, Melanesia, Micronesia, Australasia). Chinese potters learned to fire porcelain at temperatures exceeding 1300°C in the fourteenth century; Andean textile weaving achieved thread counts of 300 to 500 per inch using special weaving techniques and llama and alpaca fibers; and Polynesian and Southeast Asian craftspeople responded to severe resource constraints by making sophisticated use of organic materials—each achieving technical mastery unknown to the others.

The Pacific Ocean galleries display artworks from these major regions, in many cases demonstrating the continuation of ancient traditions into modern times despite colonial disruption or oppression. Here you will encounter ancient and modern porcelains from East Asia, selections from LACMA's outstanding collection of Mesoamerican sculpture, works that reflect the interests of Spanish colonists, paintings by Mexican modernists, photographs, contemporary sculpture by artists from California and beyond, plus more.

Artists working in the Colima tradition (Mexico)
Old Dog, made c. 200 BCE–500 CE
Slip-painted earthenware; 16½ × 7¾ × 19½ in.
The Proctor Stafford Collection, purchased with funds provided by Mr. and Mrs. Allan C. Balch, M.86.296.152

In ancient West Mexico, dogs held spiritual significance as companions and guides for the deceased into the afterlife. The artist rendered this Xoloitzcuintli—a hairless breed still favored today—with remarkable naturalism, capturing the protruding spine and sagging skin of an old dog rather than an idealized form. Nonetheless, the alert posture suggests a vigilant guardian. The size and carefully observed details of this hollow sculpture, whose only venthole is the dog's mouth, demonstrate both keen observation and mastery of ceramic technique.

Pacific Connections in the Ancient Americas

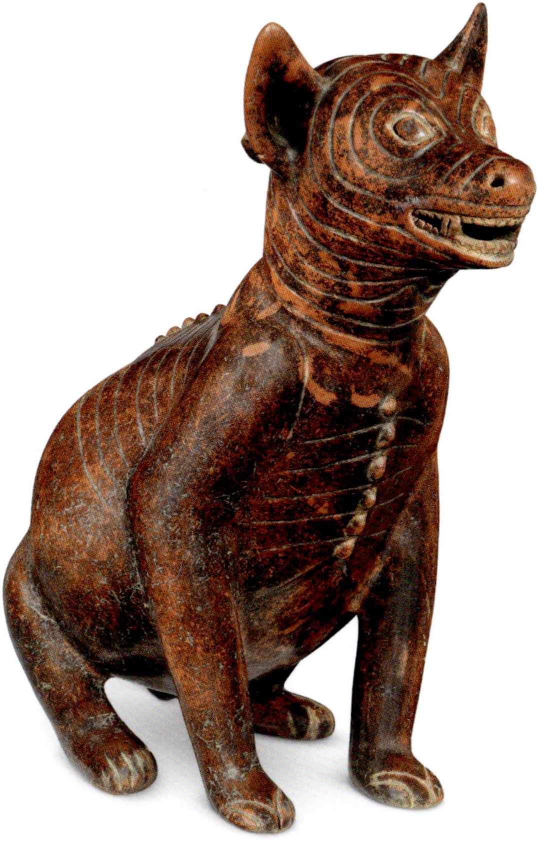

Artists working in the Tlatilco style (Mexico)
Woman with Bulbous Legs, made c. 1400–1100 BCE
Earthenware with postfire pigment; 3¼ × 1¾ × ¾ in.
Gift of Ann Ziff, M.2019.45.73

Artists working in the Tlatilco style (Mexico)
Dancer, made c. 1400–1100 BCE
Earthenware with postfire pigment; 3⅝ × 1½ × ⅞ in.
Gift of Ann Ziff, M.2019.44.5

Artists working in the Tlatilco style (Mexico)
Two-Headed Woman, made c. 1400–1100 BCE
Earthenware with postfire pigment; 3¾ × 2¼ × ⅞ in.
Gift of Ann Ziff, M.2019.45.57

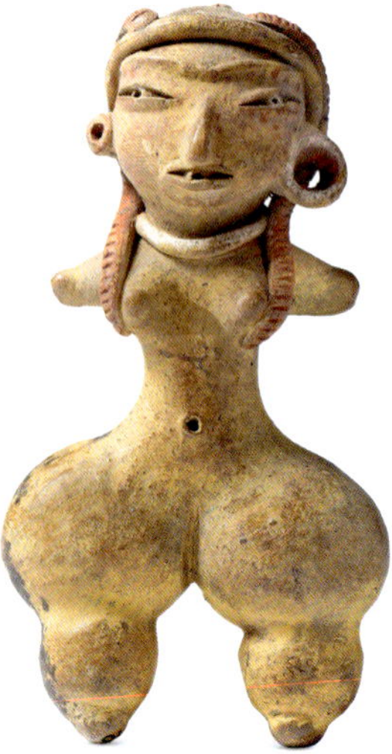

One of Mesoamerica's oldest artistic traditions, Tlatilco figurines feature delicately modeled bodies, elaborate coiffures, and evocative expressions, all while fitting in the palm of your hand. Remarkable details reveal personages whose stories are now lost to us: women with exaggerated, bulbous thighs, dancers in ruffled skirts, and two-headed women, among others. Caches of similar figurines have accompanied the burials of Tlatilco women and children, yet little else is known about their role in early Mesoamerican society.

Pacific Connections in the Ancient Americas

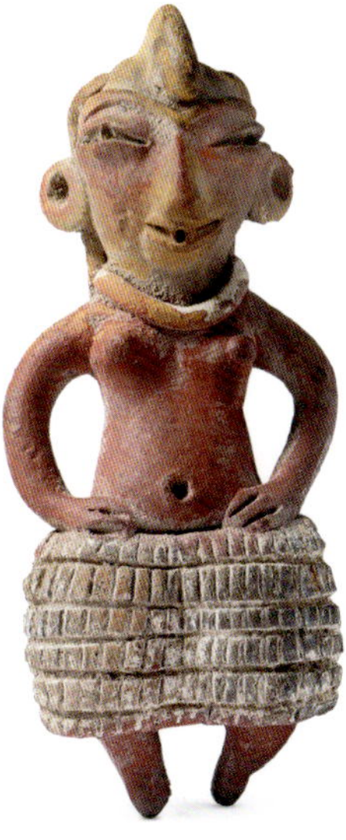

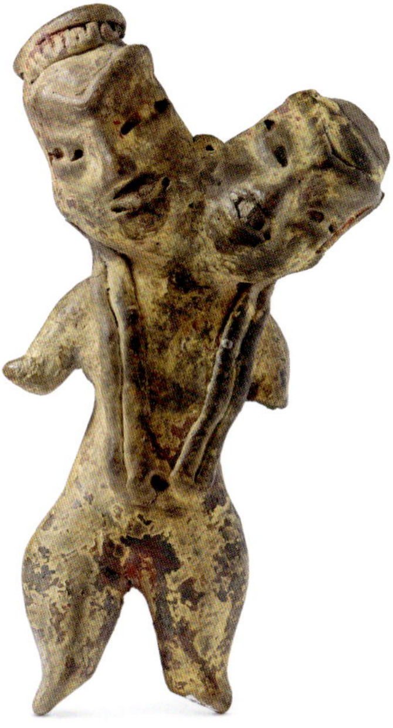

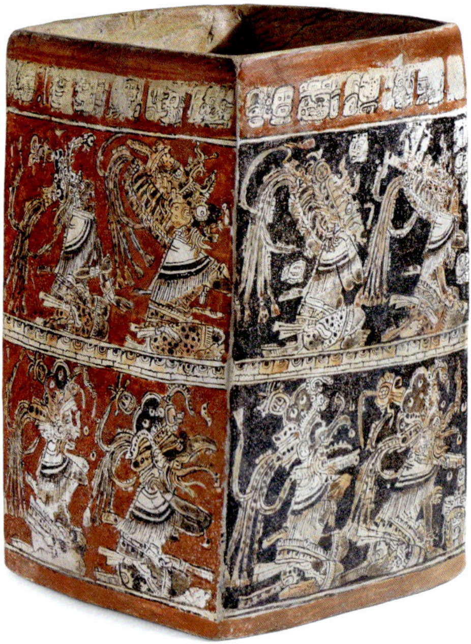

Lo' Took' Akan Xok (Maya, Sa'aal, active 8th century)
*Drinking Cup for Cacao of K'ahk' Ukalaw Chan Chahk* (Vase of the Eleven Gods), made c. 755–80 CE
Engobe-painted earthenware with postfire stucco; 9⅝ × 6½ × 6⅜ in.
Anonymous gift, M.2010.115.14

This squared drinking cup depicts on its four sides a consequential convening. An old cigar-smoking deity associated with the night presides over the ordering of ten celestial and earthly deities, gathered before him in primordial darkness on the day that time began. As described in the glyphic text, the vessel was painted by Lo' Took' Akan Xok and commemorates a rite early in the reign of K'ahk' Ukalaw Chan Chahk, the Holy Lord of Sa'aal and owner of the vessel.

Keepers of the Cosmos in Mesoamerican Art

Maya artists (Lakamha' or vicinity, now Palenque, Mexico)
Pair of Solar Deity Censer Stands, made c. 770–850 CE
Earthenware with postfire pigment; 42½ × 24 × 8½ in., 46 × 23 × 8½ in.
Anonymous gift, M.2010.115.426–.427

Each of these two censer stands—cylindrical chimneys for the smoke of burning incense—depicts a solar deity with an array of aquatic features: a protruding shark tooth, catfish barbels, *Spondylus* shell ear ornaments, and a finned jawline. These are attributes of the sun at dawn, when he emerges from the sea following his nightly transit of the watery underworld. He is one of three patron deities of the Classic Maya city of Lakamha' (now Palenque).

Keepers of the Cosmos in Mesoamerican Art

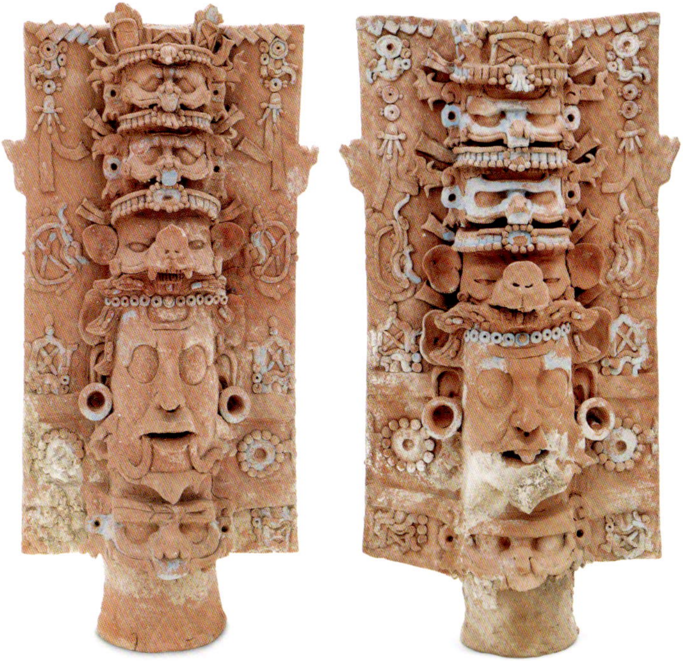

Diego Rivera (Mexico, 1886–1957)
*Flower Day*, 1925
Oil on canvas; 58 × 47½ in.
Los Angeles County Fund, 25.7.1

This is one of Diego Rivera's most iconic paintings of a calla lily vendor. When Rivera returned to Mexico in 1921, after spending several years in Europe, he devoted many works to historic, revolutionary, and Indigenous themes. The blocklike figures reflect his interest in Mesoamerican sculpture, while the aerial view of the flowers is indebted to his earlier Cubist works. Acquired in 1925, *Flower Day* is Rivera's first major painting to enter a public collection in the United States.

*Indigenismo* in Latin America

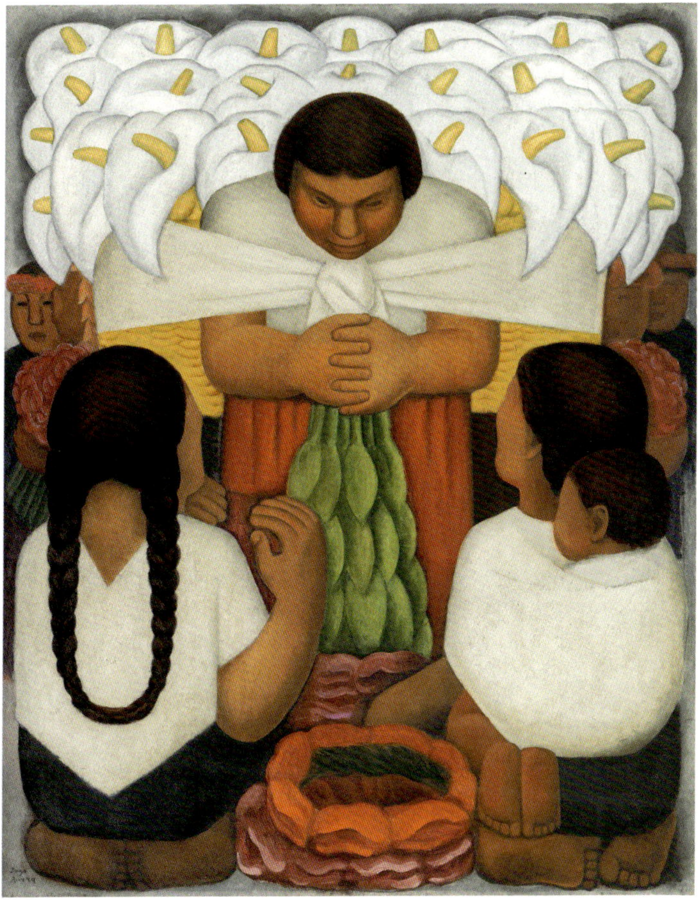

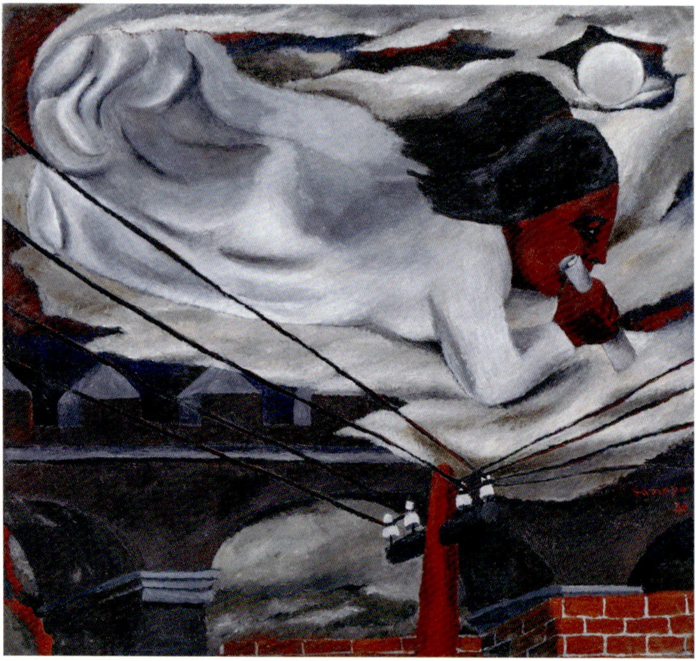

Rufino Tamayo (Mexico, 1899–1991)
*Messengers in the Wind*, 1931
Oil on canvas; 31 × 34⅛ in.
The Bernard and Edith Lewin Collection of Mexican Art, AC1997.LWN.36

This painting embodies Rufino Tamayo's interest in combining the dreamlike and the commonplace. Two Indigenous women fly through an imaginary urban sky, their white robes melding into the evening clouds. They bear a pressing message, like those traveling through the telephone wires below. Tamayo's strategic use of reddish brown for the woman's face, telephone pole, and brick rooftop links the Indigenous subjects to the built environment, underscoring the tension between Mexico's rich past and the capital city's progressive modernization.

*Indigenismo* in Latin America

Felipe Santiago Gutiérrez (Mexico, 1824–1904)
*Indigenous Indian Woman with Marigolds*, 1876
Oil on canvas; 26¾ × 22¼ in.
Gift of Ronald A. Belkin, Long Beach, California, M.2013.130.2

This allegorical portrait of a pregnant Indigenous woman wearing a *huipil* (a loose blouse with origins in the pre-Conquest period) is emblematic of Felipe Santiago Gutiérrez's interest in *costumbrista* images (scenes of everyday life). The figure is captured in an intimate moment, gazing at *cempasúchiles* (marigolds), flowers widely associated with death in Mexico. Trained at the National Academy of San Carlos, Gutiérrez was one of Mexico City's most salient nineteenth-century academic artists.

*Indigenismo* in Latin America

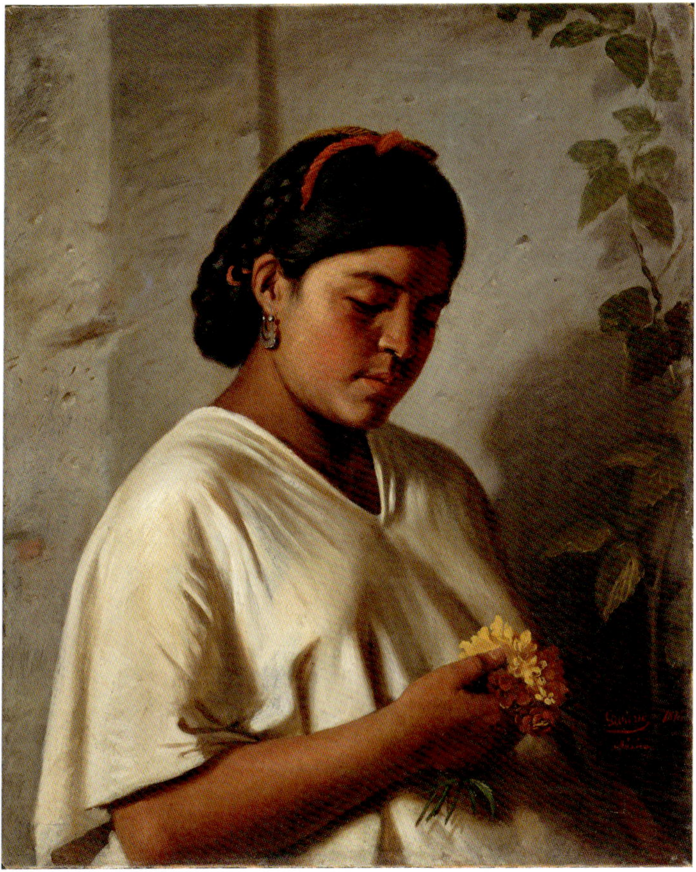

Vicente Albán (Ecuador, active 1769–96)
*Noble Woman with Her Black Slave*, c. 1783 (detail)
Oil on canvas; 32 × 41¾ in.
Purchased with funds provided by the Bernard and Edith Lewin Collection of Mexican Art Deaccession Fund, M.2014.89.1

This painting of Ecuadorian racial types presents richly dressed figures next to giant tropical fruits to symbolize the abundance of the land. The Spanish woman wears a luxurious regional ensemble, including a petticoat (*pollera*) decorated with gold and (now tarnished) silver elements, finely embroidered silk stockings, pearls (associated with the Americas), and a crucifix to signal her faith. The Black woman beside her is more modestly bedecked and portrayed barefoot to emphasize the differences in their social status.

Spanish America at the Center of the World

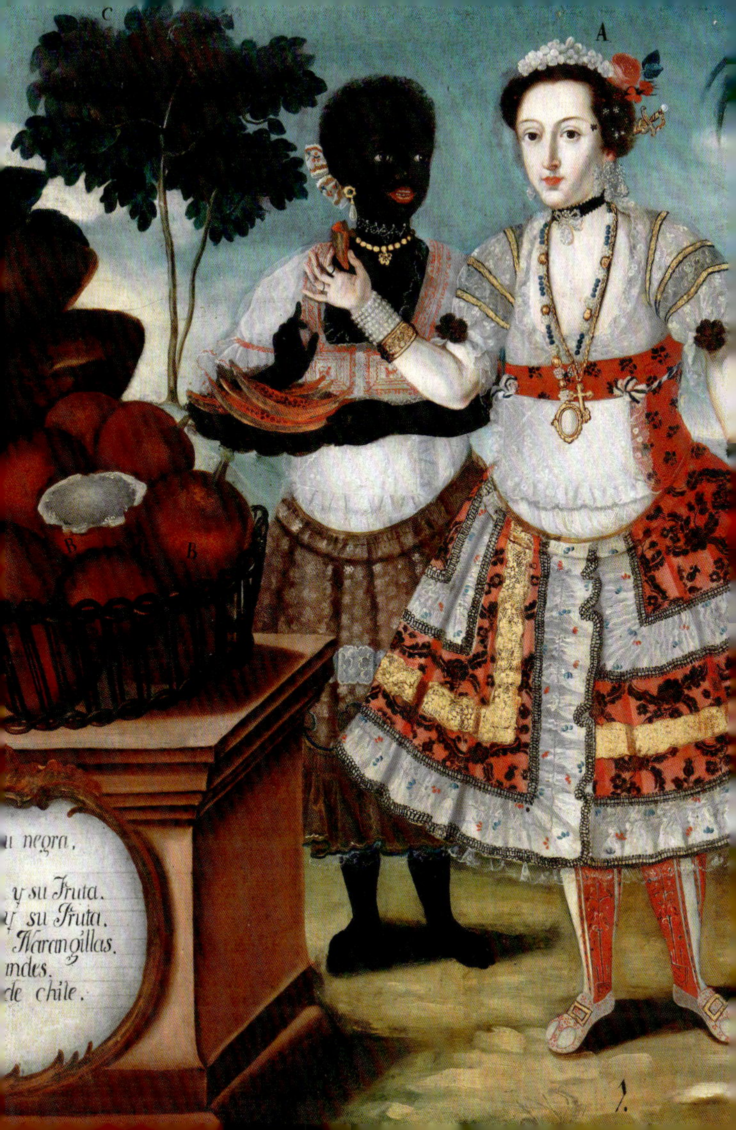
C
A
B
B
a negra,
y su Fruta.
y su Fruta.
Narangillas.
ndes.
de chile.
1.

Miguel Cabrera (Mexico, c. 1710–1768)
*6. From Spaniard and Morisca, Albino Girl*, 1763
Oil on canvas; 54¾ × 44¼ in.
Purchased with funds provided by Kelvin Davis in honor of the museum's 50th anniversary and partial gift of Christina Jones Janssen in honor of the Gregory and Harriet Jones Family, M.2014.223

This family scene belongs to an important set of *casta* paintings, a complex pictorial genre invented in Mexico to document racial mixing among Natives, Spaniards, and Africans. *Casta* paintings depict figures dressed in distinctive local and foreign attire, engaged in particular activities, and often next to local products—in this case tobacco. The mother wears a Mexican *rebozo* (shawl) and the father a leather coat used by soldiers. The canvas still preserves its original Asian-inspired traveling scroll case.

Spanish America at the Center of the World

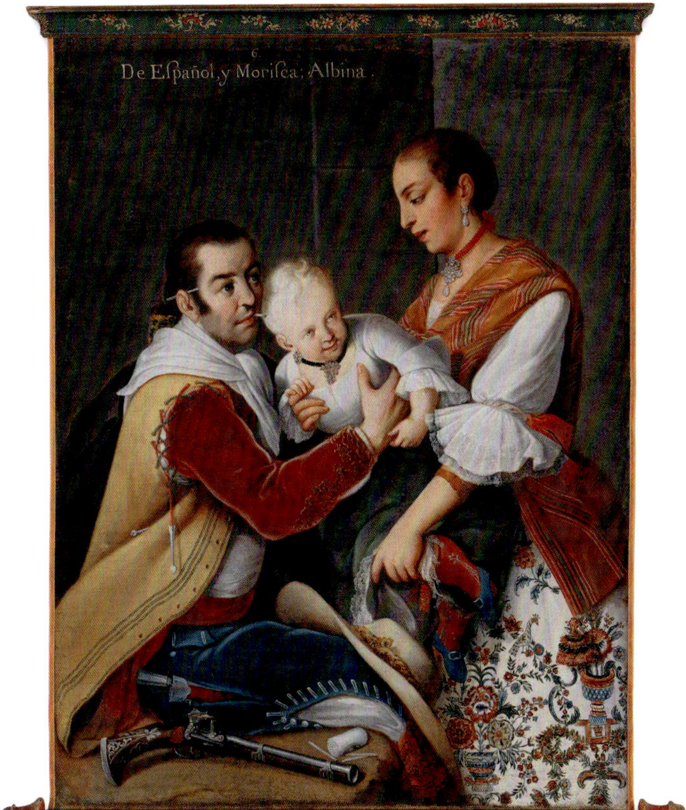
6.
De Española, y Morisca; Albina.

Unidentified artist (Mexico)
Folding Screen with Indian Wedding, *Mitote*, and Flying Pole, c. 1660–90
Oil on canvas; 66 × 120 in.
Purchased with funds provided by the Bernard and Edith Lewin Collection of Mexican Art Deaccession Fund, M.2005.54a–d

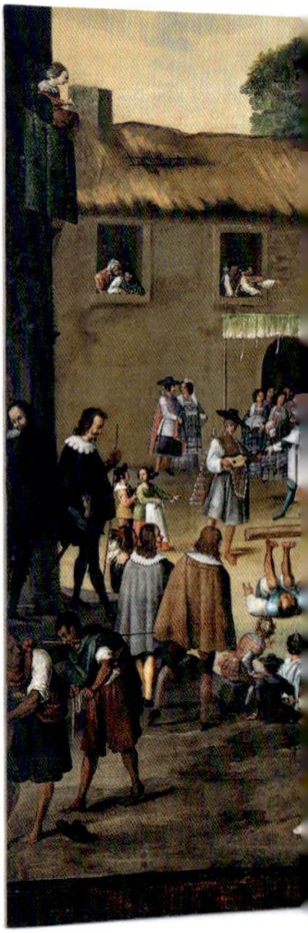

This folding screen depicts an Indigenous wedding in Iztacalco, outside of Mexico City. The pre-Hispanic performances include a *mitote* dance (with a figure impersonating the Aztec emperor Motecuzoma), a *juego de palo* (with a man tossing a log in the air), and an aerial *palo volador* (flying pole). Diplomacy,

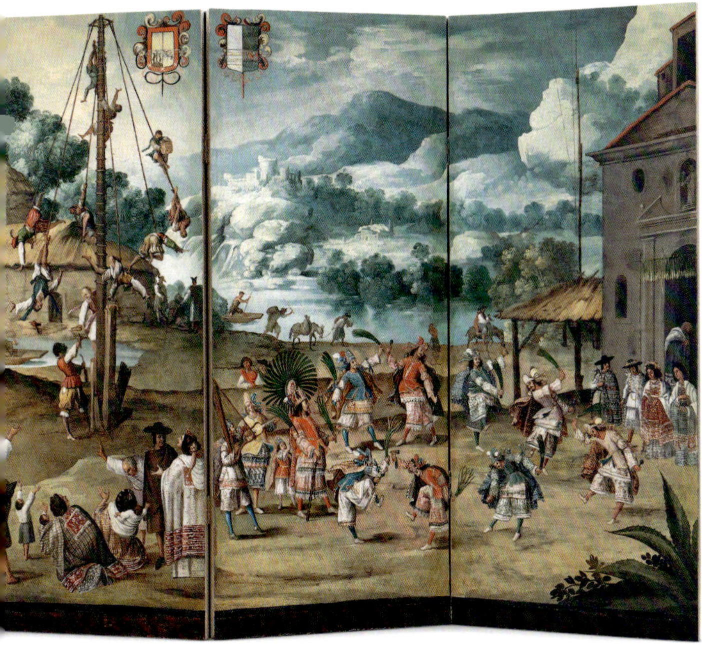

missionaries, and trade brought screens from Asia to Mexico beginning in the sixteenth century. Local artists created their own versions; some showcased local traditions and landmarks.

Spanish America at the Center of the World

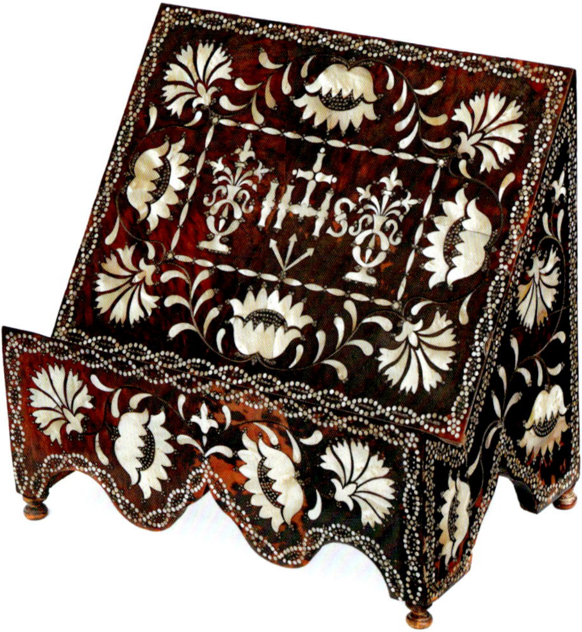
IHS

Unidentified makers (possibly Guatemala)
Missal Stand, 18th century
Wood, inlaid with tortoiseshell and mother-of-pearl; brass and silver;
13¼ × 14½ × 9¼ in.
Purchased with funds provided by the Bernard and Edith Lewin Collection of Mexican Art Deaccession Fund, M.2019.264.3

This luxurious missal stand is veneered in tortoiseshell and mother-of-pearl designs. It likely originated in Guatemala, where the prized materials were harvested locally. Such furnishings were exported to Mexico and Peru to serve elite consumers in their homes or in ecclesiastical contexts. The central panel is decorated with the Jesuit monogram IHS, symbolizing Christ. Enhanced with shimmering silver beadings, the intricate designs draw on a range of European and Asian sources, which local artists ingeniously reinvented.

Spanish America at the Center of the World

Unidentified artists, Bolivia (Potosí)
Eucharistic Urn in the Form of a Pelican, c. 1760
Silver and glass; 42¼ × 35½ × 18½ in.
Purchased with funds provided by the Bernard and Edith Lewin Collection of Mexican Art Deaccession Fund in honor of Julian Sands, M.2024.154

This imposing Eucharistic pelican was created in Bolivia, part of the Viceroyalty of Peru. Pelicans symbolized Christ's sacrifice for humanity, and containers such as this were used to store the consecrated host or a chalice. This sculpture stands out for its refined craftmanship and extravagant use of silver, abundantly mined in the town of Potosí. The life-size fowl resembles a large South American southern screamer (*chajá*), demonstrating how traditional Western symbols were ingeniously refashioned in the Andes.

The Silver That Moved the World

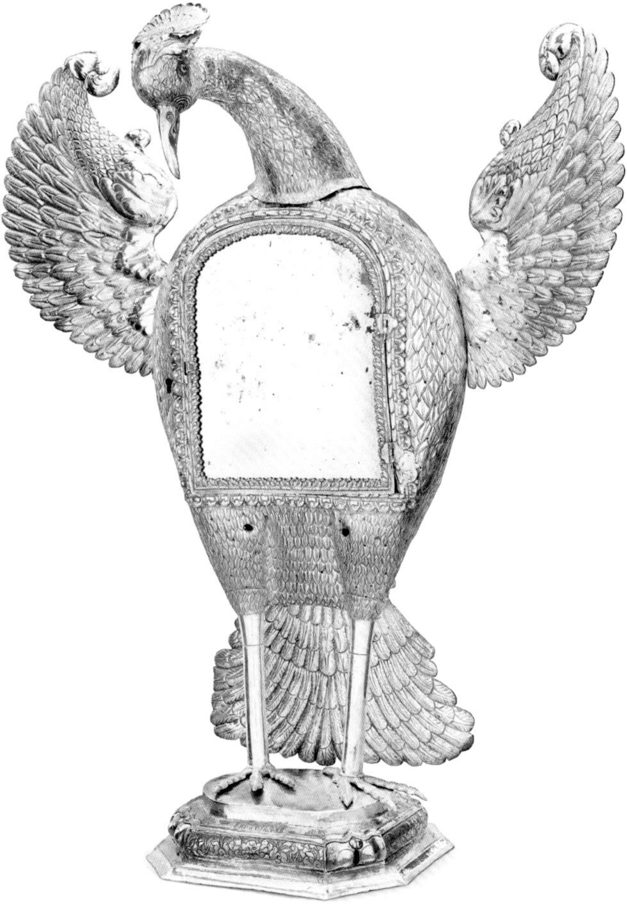

Peru, South Coast, Wari culture
Man's Tunic, 600–850 (detail)
Camelid fiber and cotton, tapestry weave; 37⅝ × 42¼ in.
Los Angeles County Fund, 70.3.1

The colors of this extraordinary tunic have retained their vibrancy well after a thousand years. Indigo appears blue only after a complex chemical process of fermentation and oxidation, making it both a testament to the dyer's skill and a sign of prestige for the wearer. The intense red comes from cochineal, an insect cultivated as a dye source for powerful patrons wealthy enough to afford such fine, colorful garments, whether to be worn in life or as a burial costume for eternity.

Textiles of the Andes

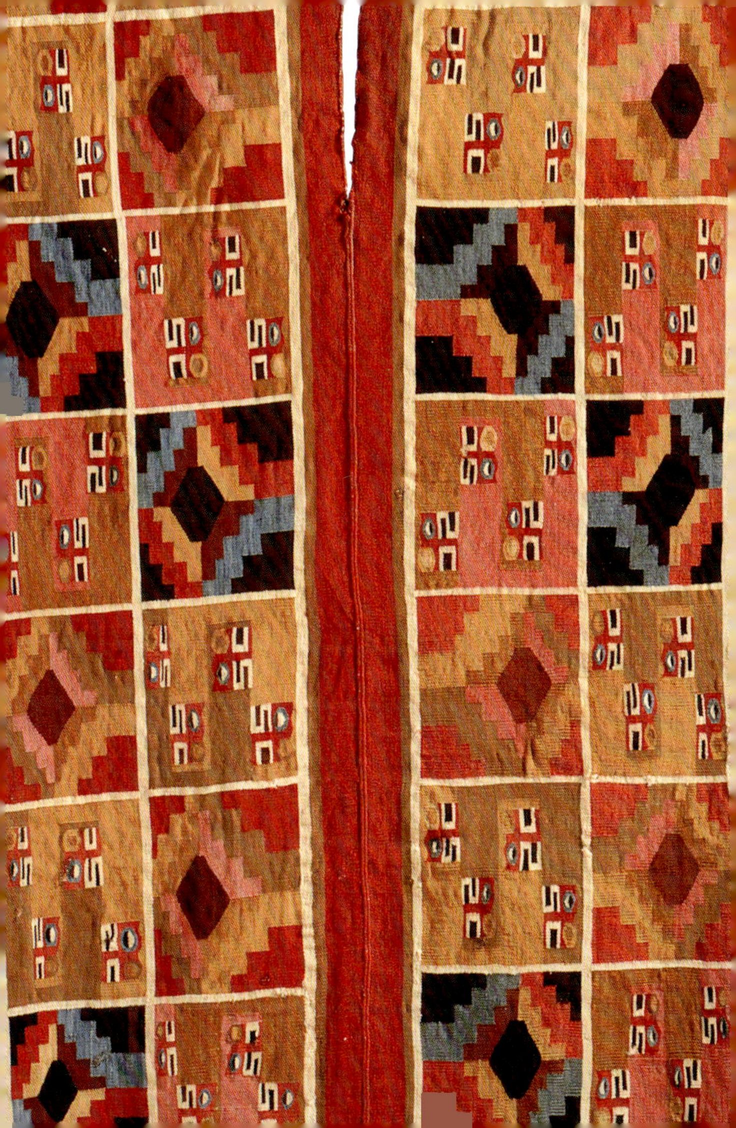

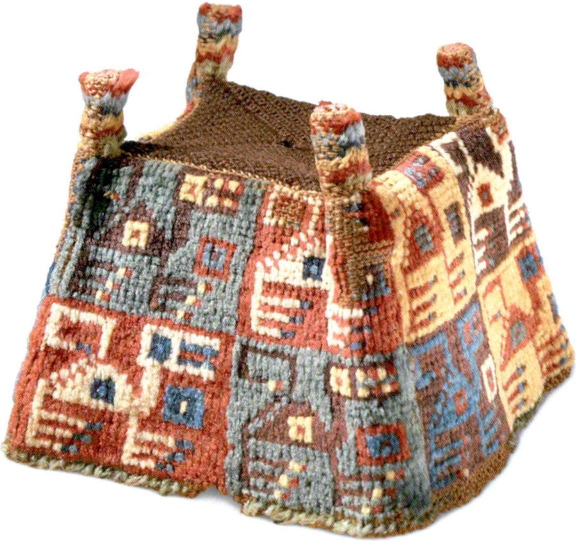

Peru, South Coast, Wari culture
Four-Cornered Hat, 600–800
Camelid fiber, knotting with cut pile; 3½ × 5 × 4¾ in.
Costume Council and Museum Associates Purchase, M.79.81.2

High-status Wari men wore small, brilliantly colored square hats like this. It is constructed of sections that were knotted separately then sewn together, and looped yarns were integrated within the knots. When the loops were cut, a velvety texture resulted, possibly in imitation of feathers or furred mammal pelts. Peaked appendages reminiscent of feline ears or bristling tassels evocative of bird plumage may have helped the wearer symbolically harness certain qualities of the animal world.

Textiles of the Andes

Graziella Laffi (Italy, 1923–2009, active Peru)
Necklace with Stylized Ancient Motifs, c. 1960–70
Silver; 10 7/8 × 6 3/4 in.
Gift of Giannina Laffi and Manolo Morales, M.2014.201.7a

The design of this striking necklace references Inka woven tunics and ceramics adorned with *tocapu*—complex geometric symbols denoting social status, rank, and ethnic affiliation. Graziella Laffi immigrated to Peru in 1947 to escape the ravages of World War II, traveling extensively throughout her adopted country. She was fascinated by Peru's ancient traditions, and her jewelry and hollowware designs combine Andean techniques and imagery with a modernist sensibility. For Laffi, pre-Hispanic metallurgy was "at the forefront in every aspect."

Modern Silver in Mexico and Peru

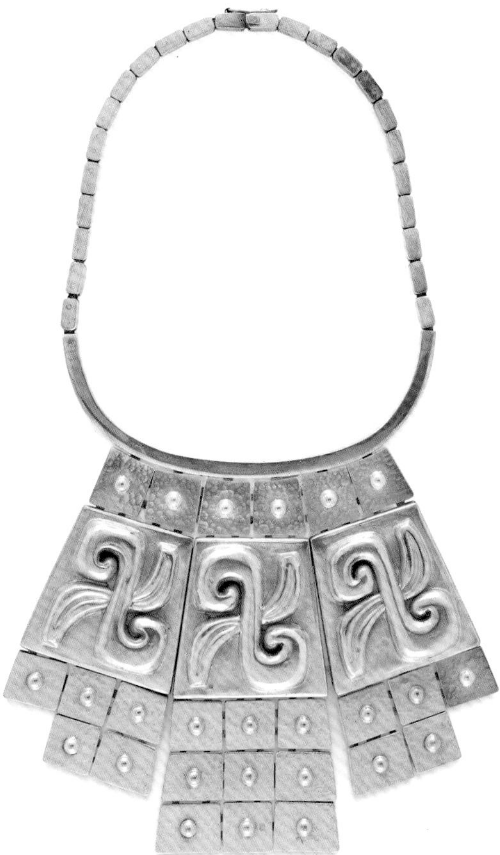

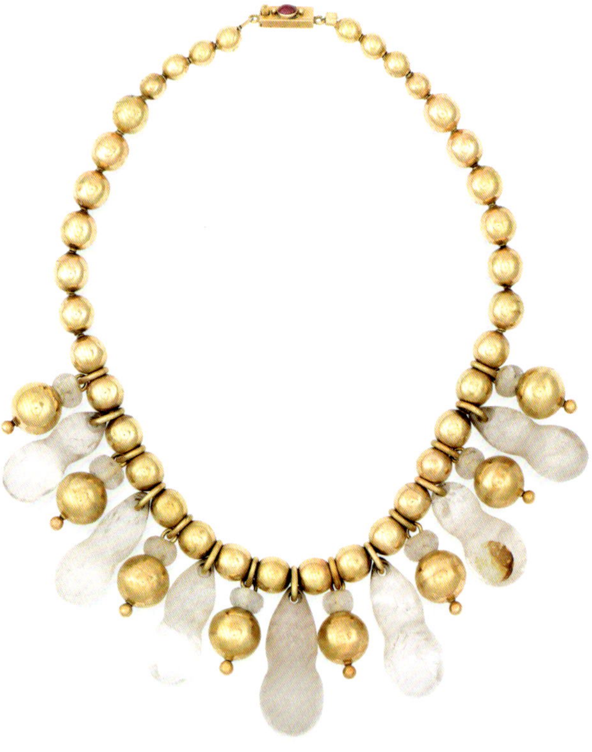

William Spratling (United States, 1900–1967, active Mexico)
Necklace (owned by Millard and Mary Baskerville Sheets), c. 1965
Gold, crystal, and ruby; 7¼ × 6¾ × ⅝ in.
Gift of Ronald A. Belkin, Long Beach, California, M.2018.68.62

The Southern California–based painter Millard Sheets purchased this striking necklace for his wife, Mary Baskerville Sheets, from the celebrated silver designer William Spratling. The two met in Taxco, Mexico, where Spratling operated a highly successful silver workshop. Silver designers in Mexico were fascinated with recently excavated Mesoamerican artifacts. The necklace's modern design draws inspiration from Mixtec jewelry and incorporates gold and rock crystal—materials highly prized in ancient times. This combination of elements was fashionable among Spratling aficionados.

Modern Silver in Mexico and Peru

Lisa Reihana (Aotearoa, b. 1964)
*Dancing Bride*, 2016
Inkjet print; 84⅞ × 57½ in.
Gift of Mark and Carolyn Blackburn, M.2017.117.1

*Dancing Bride* is a still image from Lisa Reihana's epic video *in Pursuit of Venus [infected]* (2015–17). The portrait depicts a Cook Islands bride from Mangaia wearing fringed tapa and a dramatic *kikau* headdress accented with small taxidermied birds. Captured in mid-performance, she embodies the grace and cultural richness of Polynesian dance traditions. Reihana's large-scale portraits invite close study of adornment, gesture, and identity while reflecting on Pacific histories and early encounters with Europeans.

Polynesia: "Our Sea of Islands"

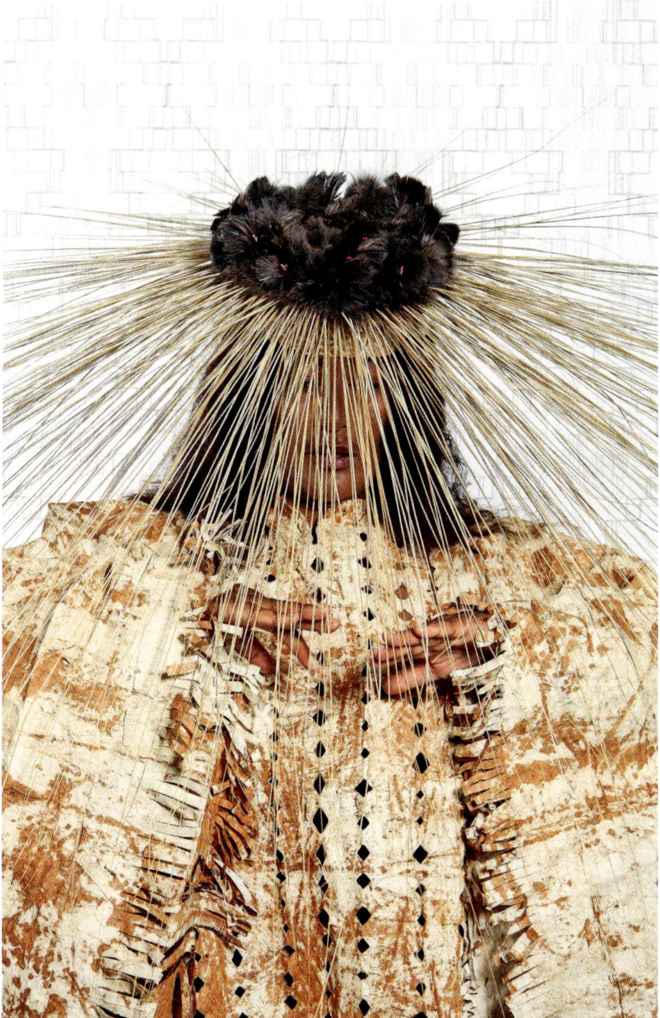

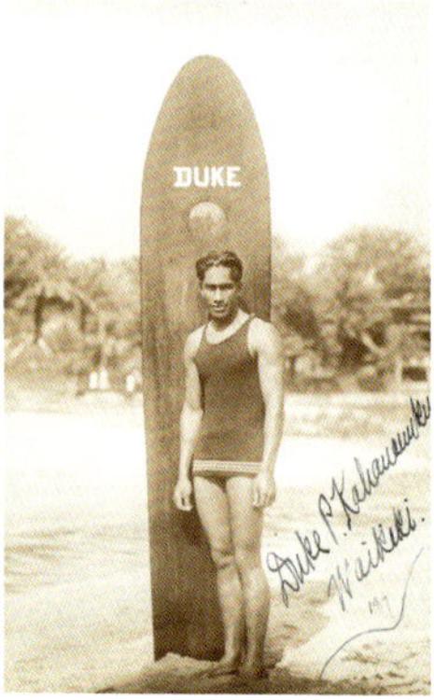
DUKE
Duke P. Kahanamoku
Waikiki.

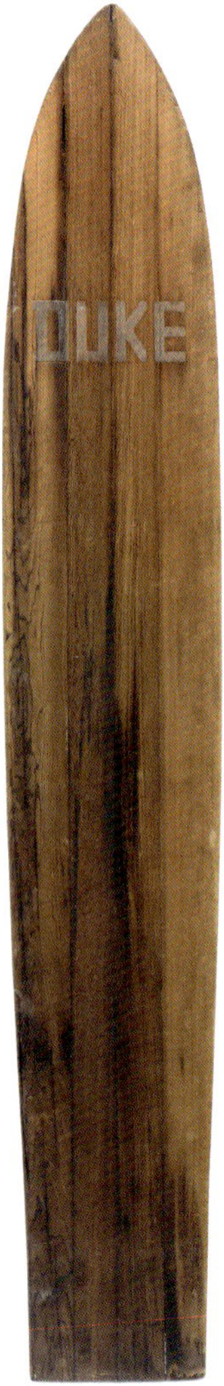
DUKE

Artist unrecorded
Duke Kahanamoku, c. 1917
Gelatin silver print; 7½ × 4¾ in.
Partial gift of Mark and Carolyn Blackburn and purchased with funds from LACMA's 50th Anniversary Gala and FIJI Water, M.2015.33.5

Samuel Alapa'i Kahanamoku (Hawai'i, 1902–1966) or David Pi'ikoi Kahanamoku (Hawai'i, 1895–1967)
Duke Kahanamoku's Surfboard, 1920s
Redwood; 133½ × 22 × 3 in.
Partial gift of Mark and Carolyn Blackburn and purchased with funds from LACMA's 50th Anniversary Gala and FIJI Water, M.2015.33.162

This redwood surfboard, carved in the 1920s for Duke Kahanamoku by one of his brothers, reflects the evolution of Hawaiian surfing from chiefly sport to global phenomenon. Early boards ranged from small *paipo* to large *olo* up to 24 feet and were originally fashioned from native woods such as koa, okinaulu, and wiliwili. Duke Kahanamoku, famed Olympian and ambassador of modern surfing, used mid-sized boards like this example, which measures over 11 feet.

Polynesia: "Our Sea of Islands"

Torres Strait Islands artist (Australia)
*Warup* (Hand Drum), c. 1850
Wood, fiber, shell, and cassowary feathers; 45 × 8¾ × 8 in.
Purchased with funds provided by the Eli and Edythe Broad Foundation with additional funding by Jane and Terry Semel, the David Bohnett Foundation, Camilla Chandler Frost, Gayle and Edward P. Roski, and The Ahmanson Foundation, M.2008.66.12

This hourglass-shaped *warup* drum, carved from a single imported wood log, features geometric and figurative motifs and a stylized whale or fish mouth at its open end. Richly adorned with shell, fiber, and cassowary feathers, it reflects the region's diverse cultural influences and maritime traditions. Drums of this type, no longer made today, played vital roles in ceremonies honoring mythical ancestors within a kinship-based society spanning the Torres Strait and New Guinea. The drum was in the collection of the Surrealist writer Tristan Tzara.

Navigating Pacific Asia

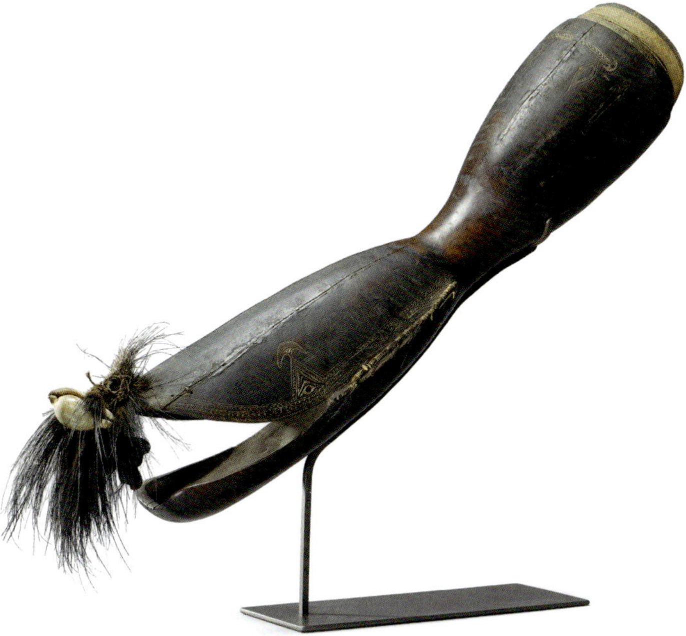

Eastern Java, Indonesia
Memorial Statue of a Deified Queen, 14th–15th century
Volcanic stone; 30 1/4 × 13 3/8 × 9 1/4 in.
Gift of Mr. Jerry Heymann, M.81.273

Ancestor worship in Eastern Java during the Majapahit empire (1293–1527) blended Hindu-Buddhist beliefs and connected royal ancestral lineage to veneration of the gods as a basis for the traditional authority of the monarchy. Memorial sculptures such as this indicate the subject's ultimate oneness with a supreme divinity. Used for both male and female deceased sovereigns, they were intended to represent the attainment of an abstracted absolute knowledge and deification.

Navigating Pacific Asia

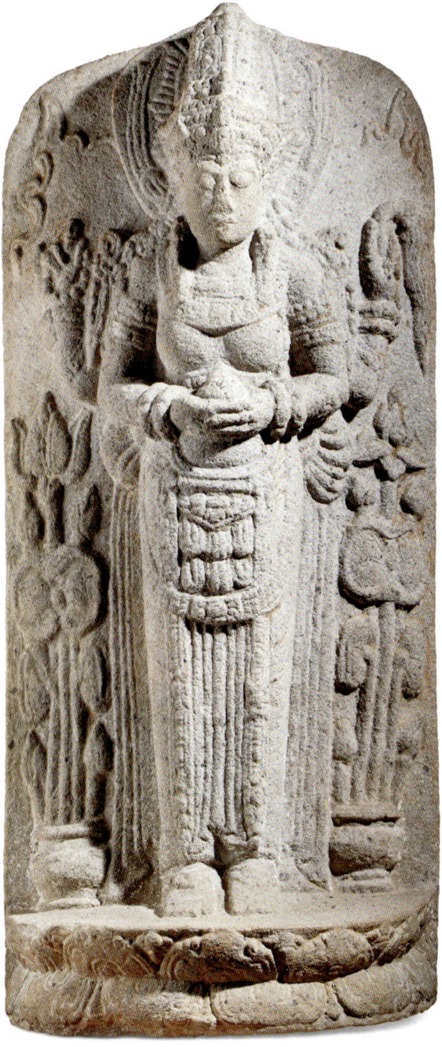

Left to right

Kenya (Japan, active 1825–89)
*Okame*, mid- to late 19th century
Stoneware with glaze and overglaze enamels; 1¾ × ⅞ × ⅞ in.
Raymond and Frances Bushell Collection, M.91.250.73

Suzuki Tōkoku (Japan, 1846–1913)
Gourd in String Bag, late 19th–early 20th century
Wood, metal, glass, and inlays; 2⅛ × 1 × 1 in.
Raymond and Frances Bushell Collection, AC1998.249.48

Tomotada (Japan, active before 1781)
Tiger and Cub, 18th century
Ivory, stain, ink (*sumi*), and inlays; 1⅝ × 1⅜ × 1⅛ in.
Raymond and Frances Bushell Collection, M.90.186.9

Ryūsa (Japan, active late 18th century)
Foreign Archer with Monkey, late 18th century
Wood with inlays; 4⅝ × 1⅝ × 1¼ in.
Raymond and Frances Bushell Collection, M.91.250.30

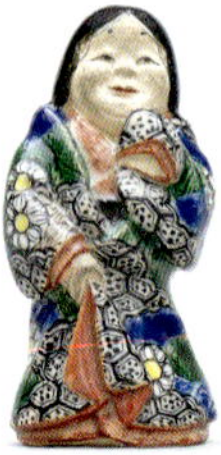

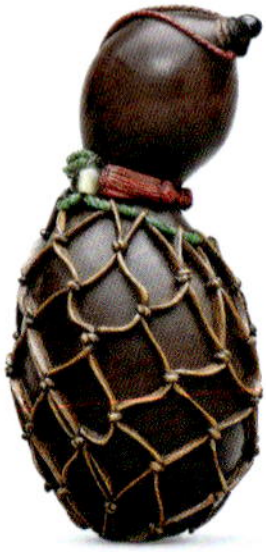

The Raymond and Frances Bushell Collection at LACMA encompasses nearly 900 netsuke. Originally produced as counterweights to secure small personal containers that hung from the obi (kimono sash), netsuke evolved into miniature works of art. Museum visitors are amazed at the creativity, workmanship, and enormous range of subjects portrayed in netsuke form. Animals and figures engaged in all manner of work and play are among the favorites. The collection includes carvings in ivory and wood as well as less common materials such as ceramic, lacquer, metal, and even glass.

Netsuke: Japanese Carvings, Foreign Connections

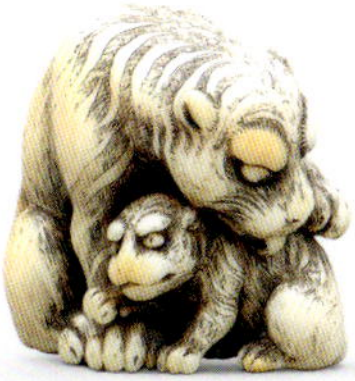

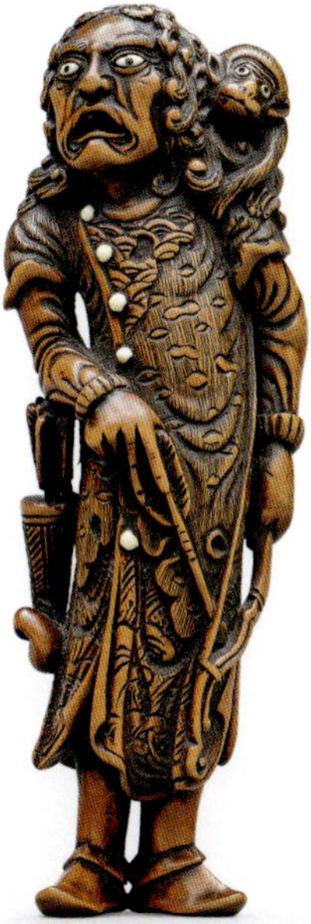

Hirado, Japan, Edo period
Sake Bottle with Chinese Landscape, second half of 18th century
Porcelain with underglaze colbalt blue and clear glaze; 5⅞ × 3⅞ in.
Gift of Allan and Maxine Kurtzman, AC1997.273.38

This vessel is among a small group of faceted bottles produced on Hirado, an island domain in Kyūshū known in the eighteenth and nineteenth centuries for its high-quality porcelain. Hirado decorators often drew landscape motifs from paintings and printed design manuals, as seen here in scenes painted by an artist employed by the workshop. Fabricated from several parts cast in molds, some of the seams are still visible. The green-tinged glaze is indicative of early Hirado ware.

Blue-and-White Porcelain of East Asia

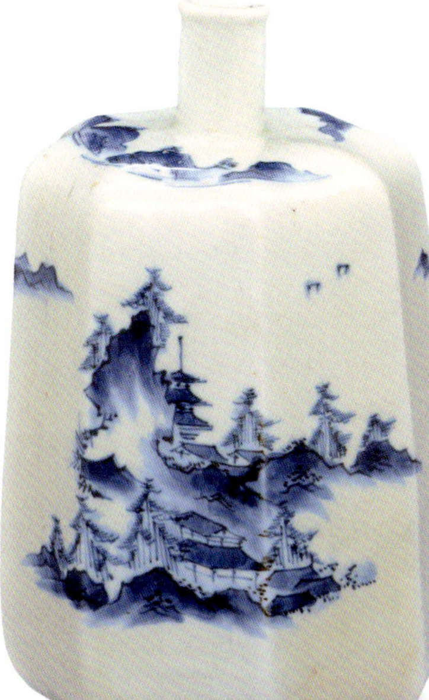

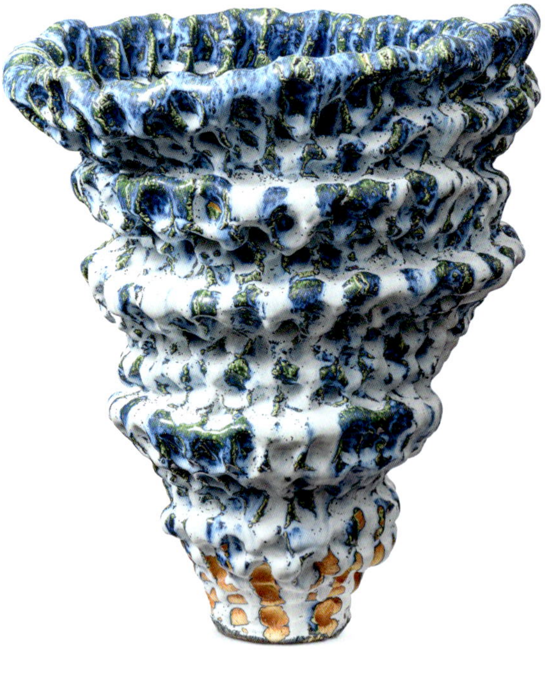

66 Pacific

Hoshino Satoru (Japan, b. 1945)
*Beginning Form / Spiral—Spring Snow '09*, 2009
Stoneware with glaze; 17 × 15¾ × 15½ in.
Gift of Gordon Brodfuehrer, M.2019.342.7

Hoshino Satoru, a member of the avant-garde ceramic group Sōdeisha from 1974 to 1980, forged both foundational and experimental ceramic practices. After a 1986 landslide destroyed his home-studio, he turned toward a raw, process-driven engagement with clay. *Beginning Form* embodies this shift: spiral coils, tactile finger impressions, and an organically emerging shape reveal the artist's direct dialogue with material. A layered glaze deepens this sensorial presence, evoking earthy matter melting and shifting like snow in spring.

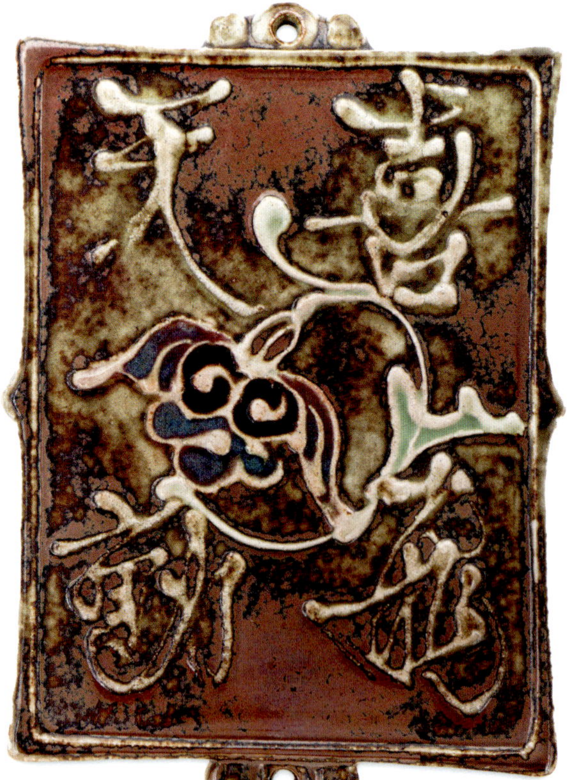

Kawai Kanjirō (Japan, 1890–1966)
*Toban* Ceramic Plaque with Flower and Characters *Kihi ten dō*, 1950s
Stoneware with slip (clay slurry) and glaze; 13⅛ × 9½ × 1 in.
Gift of David N. Barry III and Margaret C. Barry, M.2020.34.5

Although typically associated with the Mingei (folk art) movement, Kawai Kanjirō expanded its boundaries through innovative studio ceramics. He created both functional vessels and nonutilitarian works, often emphasizing sculptural form. Known for experimental glazes, including the striking copper-red seen here and his signature *gosu* blue, Kawai combined traditional techniques like slip-trailing with his motto, "Flying with joy, moving the heavens." His work balances craftsmanship, individual expression, and a celebration of materiality, redefining the possibilities of modern ceramics.

Ultramodern: Kyoto Ceramics

Kamisaka Sekka (Japan, 1866–1942)
Man's *Juban* (Under-Kimono) with Matsushima (Pine Islands), 1920–30
Silk, colors, and ink; center back length: 52⅜ in.; width (cuff to cuff): 49¾ in.
Gift of the 2010 Japanese Art Acquisitions Group, M.2010.43

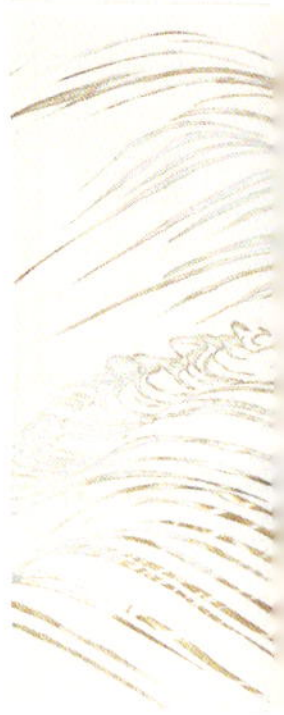

Kamisaka Sekka was the last master of a Japanese artistic tradition known as Rinpa (also referred to as Rimpa), which originated in the early seventeenth century. While it was not unusual for earlier Rinpa masters to paint directly onto a kimono, this hand-painted silk satin under-kimono featuring Matsushima (Pine Islands), with auspicious pine trees, moss-covered rocks surrounded by Rinpa-style gold and silver waves, and a hand-painted red seal, is a rare example of Sekka's oeuvre.

Japan: Living Landscapes, Flowing Waters

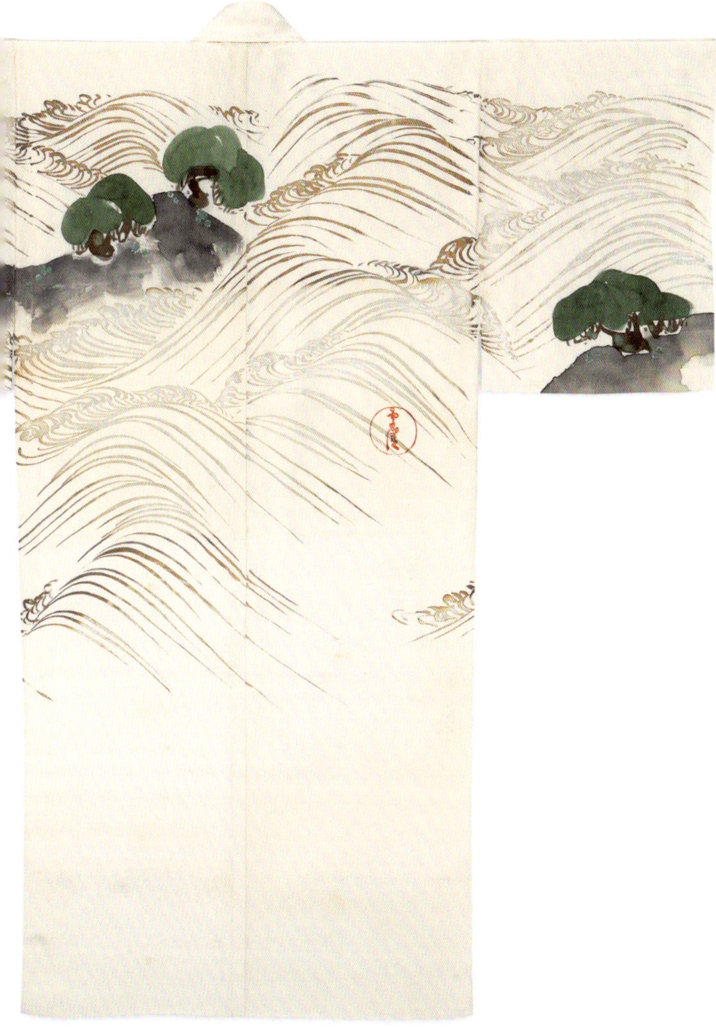

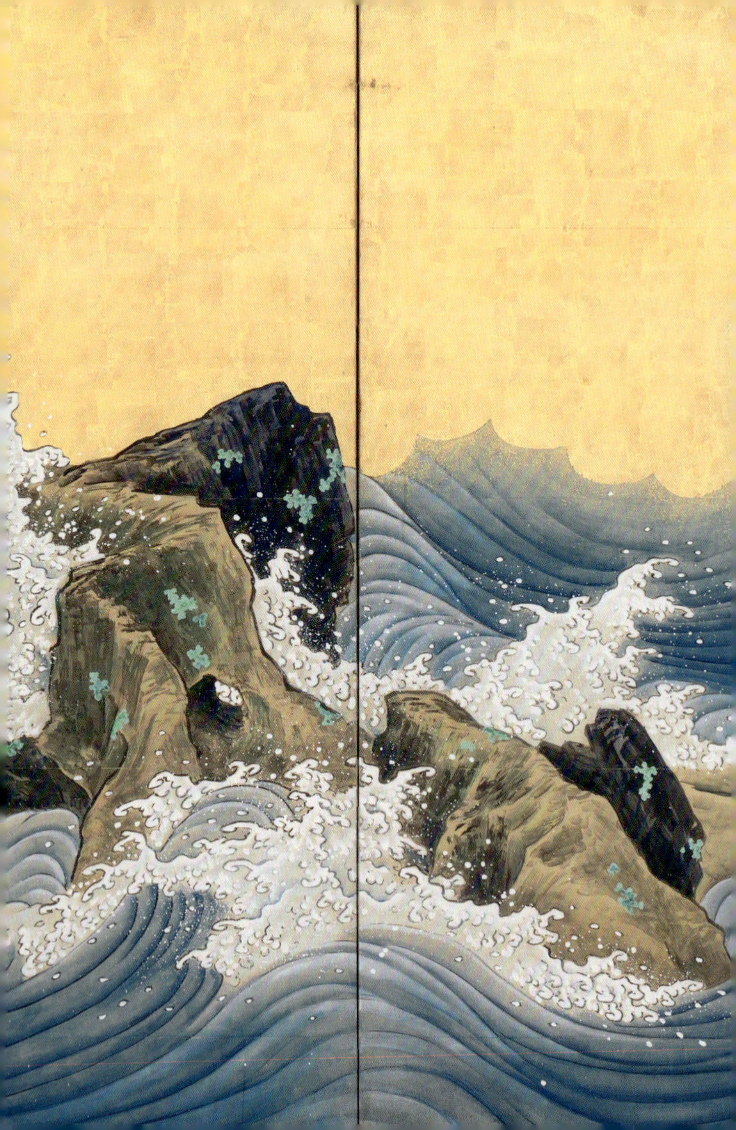

Yamaato Kakurei (Japan, active c. 1790–1820)
*Rocks amid Crashing Waves*, c. 1810 (detail of one of two screens)
Pair of eight-panel screens; gold leaf, mineral pigments, and ink on paper; each 64 7/8 × 191 1/4 in.
Gift of the 2017 Collectors Committee with additional funds provided by Laurie and Bill Benenson, M.2017.90.1–.2

Yamaato Kakurei, a leading disciple of famed Kyoto painter Maruyama Ōkyo (1733–1795), drew inspiration from his mentor's Kongōji temple sliding doors to create a pair of monumental screen paintings. Kakurei emphasizes the turbulent waters and rocks, immersing the viewer in the scene. Vibrant pigments and shimmering gold leaf heighten the drama. Simultaneously, the rare continuation of the painting across paper hinges unifies the panels, showcasing both technical innovation and dynamic visual composition in the Edo-period pictorial tradition.

Japan: Living Landscapes, Flowing Waters

Katsushika Hokusai (Japan, 1760–1849)
*The Great Wave off Kanagawa*, from the series *Thirty-Six Views of Mount Fuji*, c. 1830–31
Woodblock print; ink and colors on paper; 10¼ × 15 in.
Gift of the Frederick R. Weisman Company, M.81.91.2

*The Great Wave*, as it is popularly called, is among the most iconic works of Japanese art worldwide. Printed in the early 1830s as part of Hokusai's *Thirty-Six Views of Mount Fuji*, it depicts a towering wave threatening boats, with Mount Fuji looming in the distance. Celebrated for its bold composition and vibrant use of Prussian blue—a new pigment from the Netherlands—the print captures dramatic nature and the lives of ordinary people across Japan, all within view of this sacred mountain.

Japan: Living Landscapes, Flowing Waters

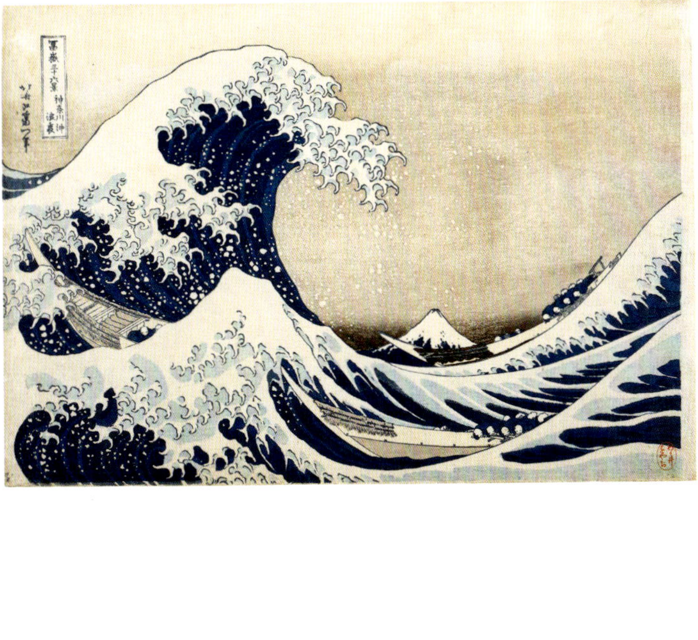
冨嶽三十六景 神奈川沖浪裏

June Wayne (United States, 1918–2011)
Printed by William Law III (United States, active 1960s–70s)
*White Tidal Wave II*, 1972
Lithograph; 41½ × 29½ in.
Gift of Dr. and Mrs. Milton Lane, M.81.166.6

Throughout the 1970s, June Wayne explored wave imagery, confronting the technical and aesthetic challenges of illustrating water in motion through the medium of lithography. To achieve towering verticality and elemental energy in this composition, she carved a straight edge along one side and left a portion of the paper untouched to form the body of the wave. During the printmaking process, extreme focus was required to prevent ink from marring this pristine white area.

L.A. Printmaking: June Wayne

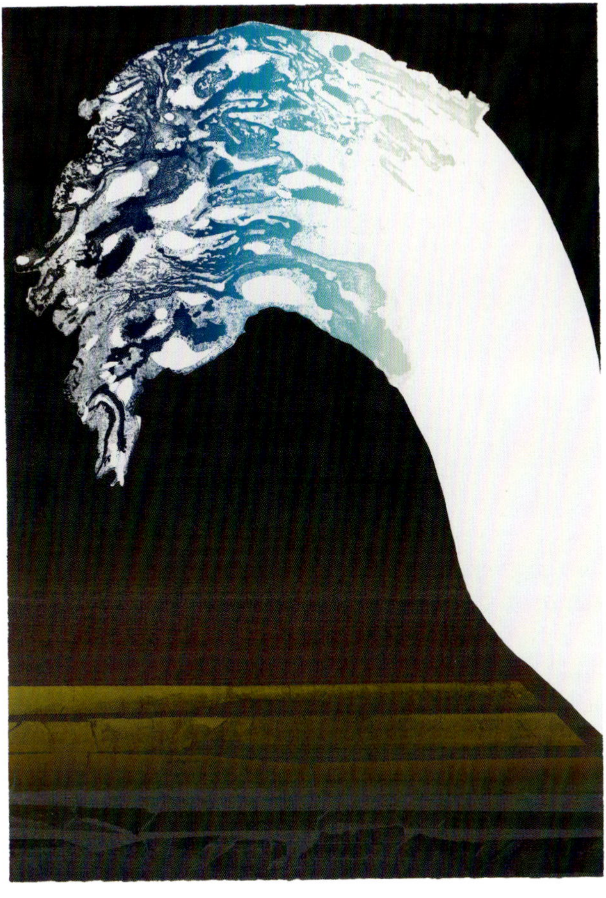

Ed Ruscha (United States, b. 1937)
*Parking Lots (May Company, 6067 Wilshire Blvd.) #25*, 1967, printed 1999
Gelatin silver print; 15 × 15 in.
Ralph M. Parsons Discretionary Fund, M.2001.27.25

This image originally appeared in Ed Ruscha's 1967 book *Thirtyfour Parking Lots*, a deadpan compilation of parking lots across Los Angeles and the San Fernando Valley. Shot from a helicopter on a Sunday morning, the empty lots become visual patterns. This example features the May Company department store on Wilshire Boulevard and Fairfax Avenue, adjacent to LACMA and now home to the Academy Museum of Motion Pictures.

Car Culture

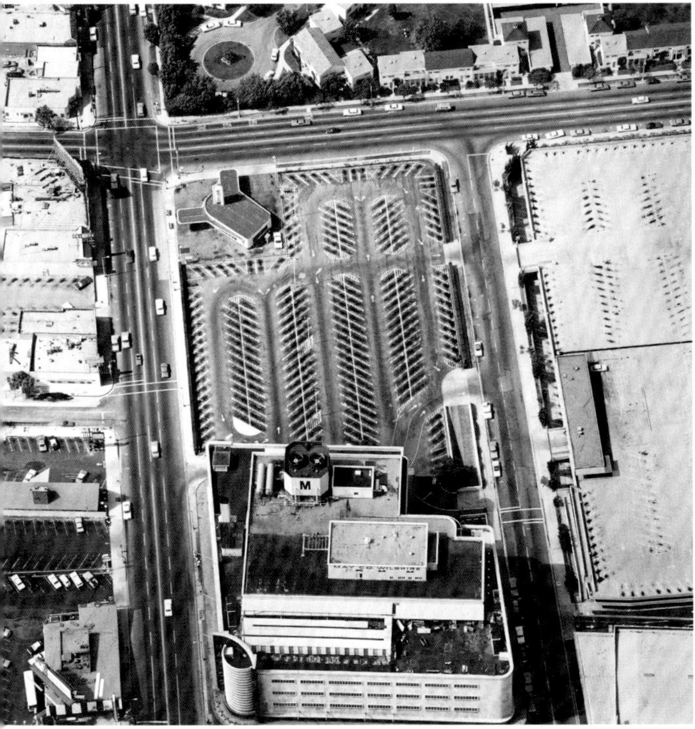
M
MAY CO. WILSHIRE

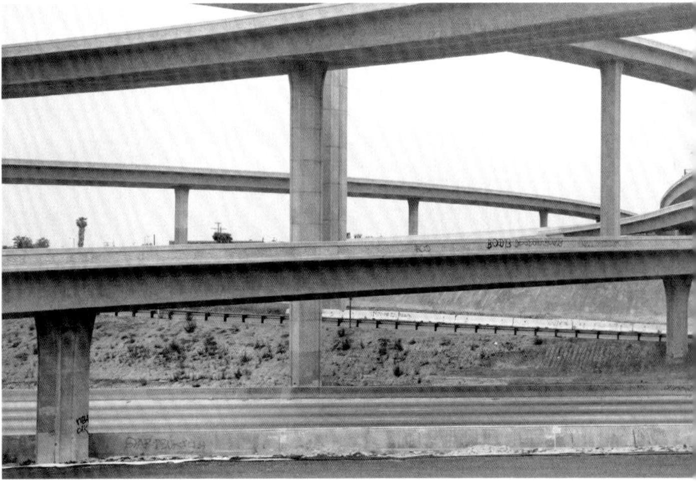

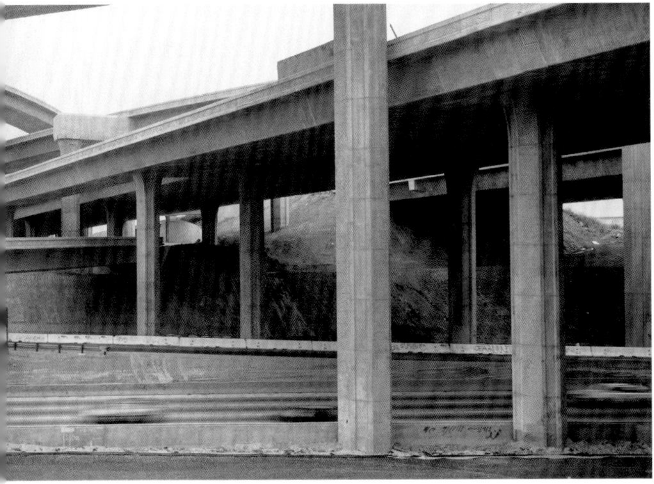

Catherine Opie moved to Los Angeles from Sandusky, Ohio, in 1988, and undertook multiple projects documenting herself and her new surroundings. She made her *Freeways* series early on weekend mornings to avoid the presence of people and cars in her panoramic compositions. She wanted to strip the freeways of their functionality and instead focus on their formal and architectural presence in the environment. Over time, her photographs have become documents of L.A.'s ever-changing urban infrastructure.

Car Culture

Catherine Opie (United States, b. 1961)
*105 Freeway, 1994*, 1994, printed 2024
Inkjet print (pigment based); 26¾ × 81¾ in.
Purchase funded by Andy Song, M.2024.132

Raymond Loewy (France, 1893–1986, active United States)
*Avanti*, designed 1961, manufactured 1963
Maufacturer: Studebaker Corporation
Fiberglass body; 55 × 71 × 194 in.
Purchased with funds provided by the 2014 Decorative Arts and Design Acquisitions Committee (DA$^2$) and partial gift of Michael, Susan, Jonathan, and David Rich, with conservation funded by Debbie and Mark Attanasio, Neil Lane, Viveca Paulin-Ferrell and Will Ferrell, Trina Turk, Suzanne Kayne, Alison and Sasha Palevsky, and Tina Gittelson through the 2022 Decorative Arts and Design Acquisitions Committee (DA$^2$) in memory of Peter Loughrey, and Marilyn B. and Calvin B. Gross, M.2014.78

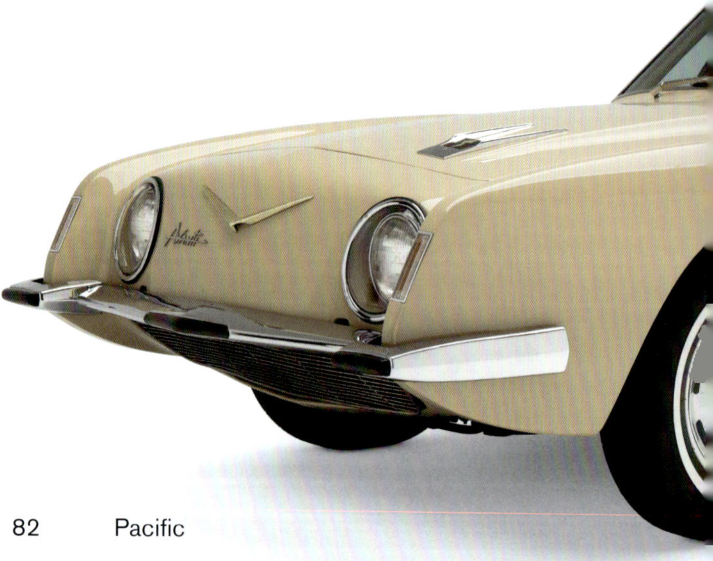

In 1961, Studebaker commissioned legendary industrial designer Raymond Loewy to create a sports car, which he insisted on designing at his California home rather than in the confines of company headquarters. The resulting *Avanti* was a revelation, setting several speed records, including an astonishing 196 mph at the Bonneville Salt Flats. Loewy customized this particular Avanti for himself, giving it a triple-color paint scheme, modifications that increased the car's top speed, and plaques noting its speed records.

Car Culture

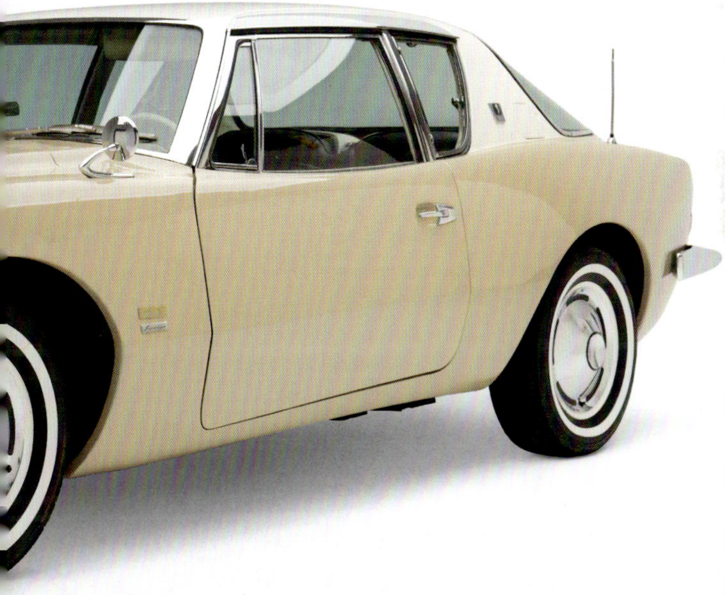

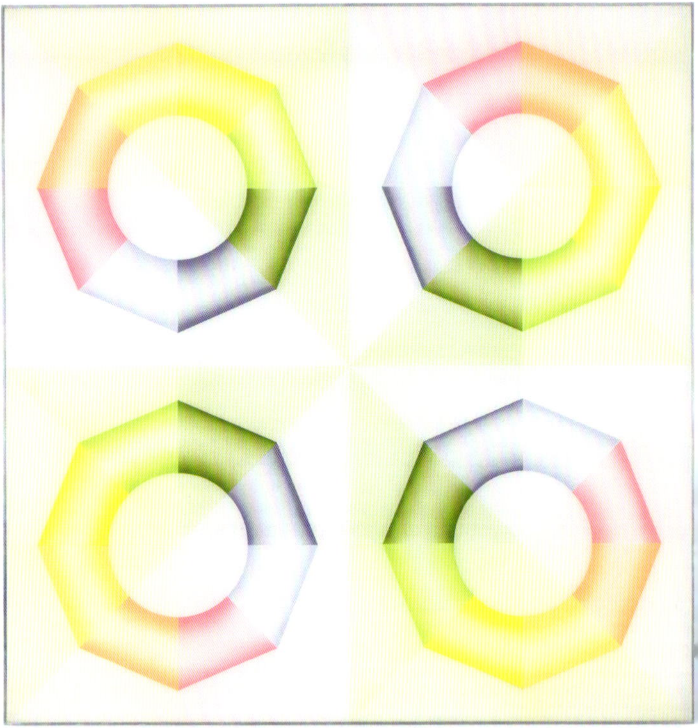

Judy Chicago (United States, b. 1939)
*Pasadena Lifesavers Yellow #4*, 1970
Sprayed acrylic lacquer on acrylic; 60 × 60 in.
Purchased with funds provided by the Ducommun and Gross Endowment and the Robert H. Halff Endowment, M.2020.158

Judy Chicago began her career in the early 1960s in Pasadena, where she challenged the male-dominated field of Minimalism with bold experiments using industrial materials and methods. Drawing on techniques she learned in auto-body school, Chicago refined her practice by spray-painting metal car hoods before shifting to acrylic surfaces—a transition that set the stage for her landmark *Pasadena Lifesavers* series. *Yellow #4*, one of fifteen works in the series, features a kaleidoscopic pattern of geometric shapes airbrushed onto sheets of acrylic.

Car Culture

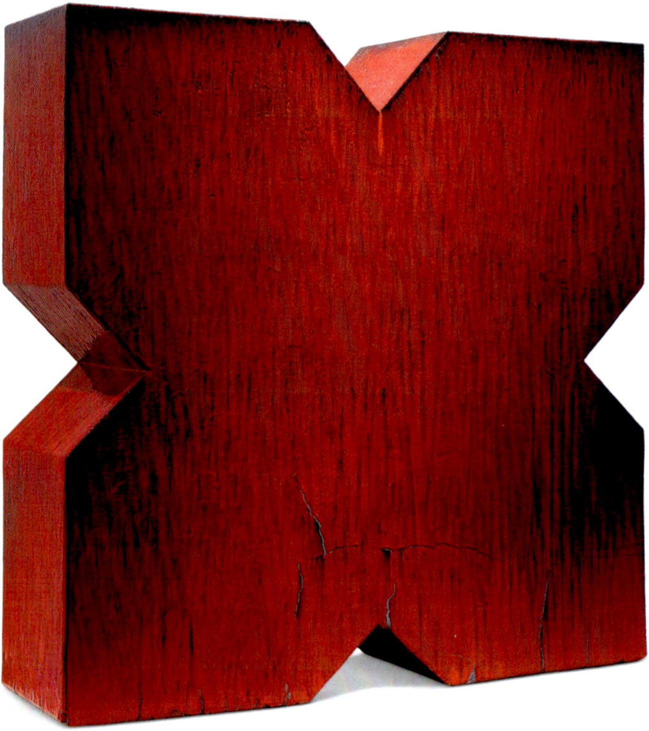

John Mason (United States, 1927–2019)
*Red X*, 1966
Stoneware; 58½ × 59½ × 17 in.
Gift of the Kleiner Foundation, M.73.38.11

John Mason was one of the first artists, along with his teacher and colleague Peter Voulkos, to use clay in creating sculptural forms rather than utilitarian ware, as had been the traditional focus of pottery. In *Red X*, Mason utilizes the geometry of the X's intersecting planes to produce an exaggerated sense of volume. His exuberantly colored ceramics demonstrate the pliability and suppleness of clay while retaining its monumental and solid presence.

Car Culture

Craig Kauffman (United States, 1932–2010)
*Untitled Wall Relief* (cast by the artist from irreparably damaged *Untitled Wall Relief*, 1967), 2008
Acrylic lacquer on vacuum-formed plastic; 53 × 77½ × 15 in.
Gift of The Kleiner Foundation, by exchange, M.2009.49

In the early 1960s, inspired by the plastic sculptures of early twentieth-century artists, Craig Kauffman began spray-painting sheet acrylic to achieve evenly covered surfaces; he then started vacuum-forming the plastic sheets into three-dimensional sculptures. Although these wall sculptures were produced commercially, Kauffman painted and finished them to achieve his desired level of visual perfection. Their vibrant colors were inspired by Jell-O and by soda he had seen bubbling in restaurant machines near his apartment.

The Stuff of Alchemy: Plastic in Art

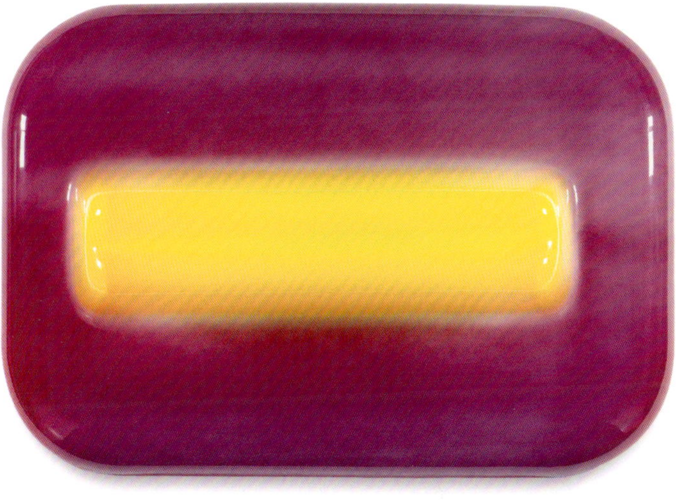

Helen Pashgian (United States, b. 1934)
*Untitled*, 1968–69
Cast polyester resin and acrylic insert; height: 8⅜ in.
Purchased with funds provided by The Hillcrest Foundation and the Modern and Contemporary Art Council Acquisitions Endowment, M.2010.88

Helen Pashgian is one of a group of Los Angeles–area artists who recognized that developments in local industries (for example, aerospace) and leisure cultures (surfboards, custom cars) could also be exploited by artists. They experiment with materials including fiberglass, polyester resin, plastics, and coated glass. This cast polyester resin dome epitomizes Pashgian's lifelong interest in how cutting-edge materials can capture and reflect light and color and respond to environmental changes.

The Stuff of Alchemy: Plastic in Art

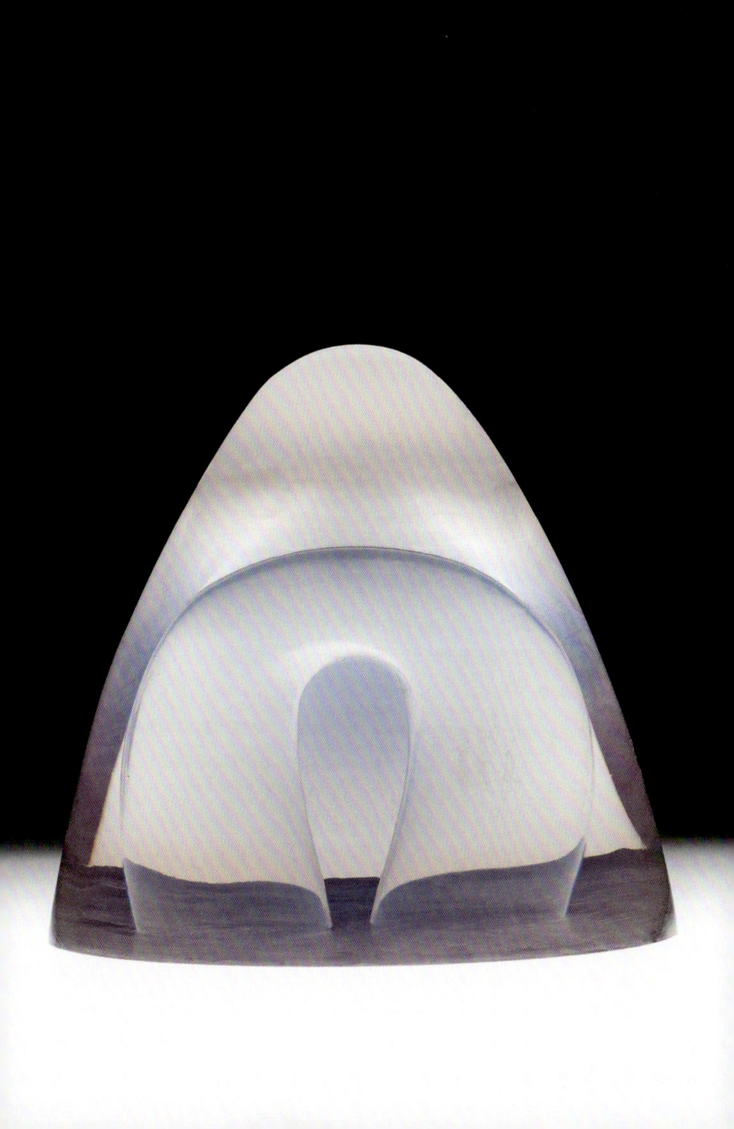

Issey Miyake (Japan, 1938–2022)
*Plastic Body*, Fall/Winter 1980–81
Fiber-reinforced molded plastic; length: 15 in.
Bernard Kester Costume and Textiles Acquisition Fund, M.2023.98.2

Robert Mapplethorpe (United States, 1946–1989)
*Lisa Lyon*, 1982
Gelatin silver print; 15⅛ × 15¼ in.
Gift of the Robert Mapplethorpe Foundation to the Los Angeles County Museum of Art and to the J. Paul Getty Trust, M.2016.152.706

In the early 1980s, fashion designer Issey Miyake challenged the traditional notion that clothing requires a human body to give it dimension and explored new materials beyond cloth. At first glance, *Plastic Body* appears to be a sculptural objet d'art of an idealized female upper body; however, it was constructed like a cuff bracelet to be worn and animated by a woman, as seen in Robert Mapplethorpe's notable 1982 photograph of bodybuilder Lisa Lyon.

The Stuff of Alchemy: Plastic in Art

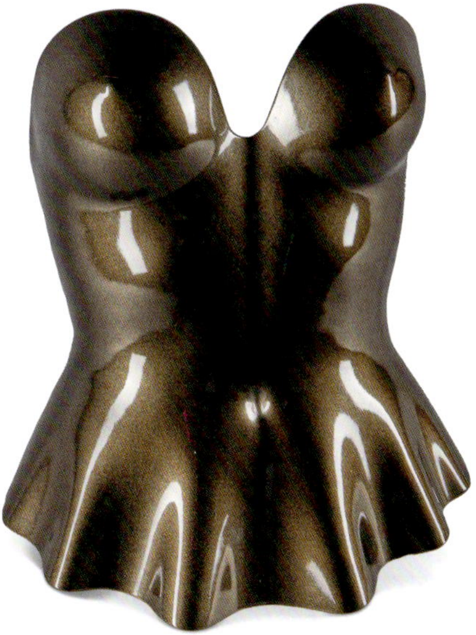

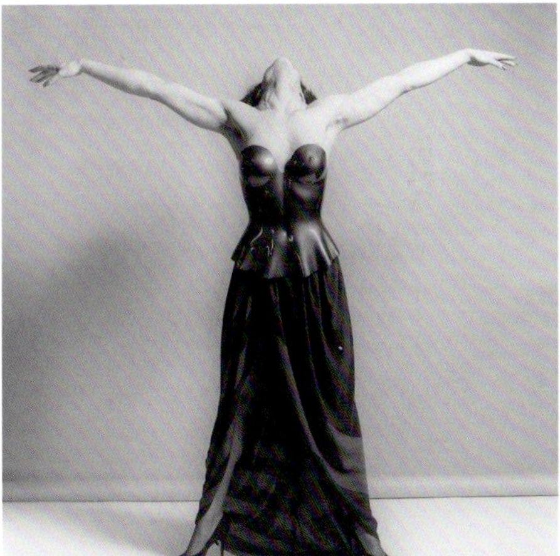

Roni Horn (United States, b. 1955)
*Untitled ("The sensation of satisfaction at having outstared a baby.")*, 2013
Solid cast glass; 36 × 36 × 36 in.
Gift of the 2014 Collectors Committee, with additional funds provided by Steve Tisch, M.2014.114

This work is a solid glass form. Its rough sides evidence the process of casting, while the top surface has been fire-polished to reveal, within its interior, a seemingly endless depth. Horn explores mutable and fleeting experiences through photographic series and the use of amorphous materials such as water. Here, she captures the nuanced and ever-changing interaction between glass, pigment, and light. The title derives from Hollis Frampton's book *Circles of Confusion*, which addresses critical discourses on photography, video, and film.

In This Light

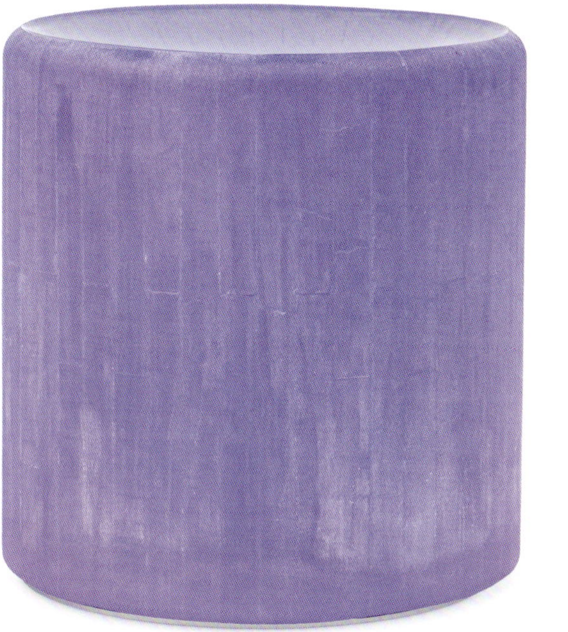

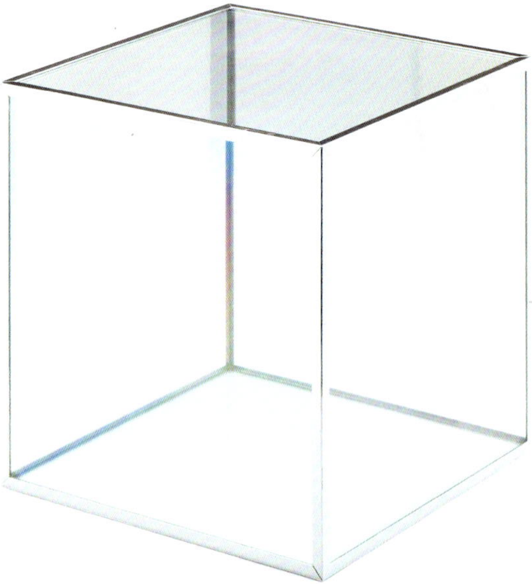

Larry Bell (United States, b. 1939)
*Cube*, 1966
Vacuum-coated glass; 12⅛ × 12⅛ × 12⅛ in.
Gift of the Frederick R. Weisman Company, M.82.112.2

For Larry Bell, surface is paramount, and it was the surface properties of glass—simultaneously hard, transparent, and reflective—that attracted him to the material. He began vacuum-coating glass in 1962, a process that deposits a thin film on the surface. This coating modifies how the glass absorbs, reflects, and transmits light, allowing Bell to create infinite variations in the color, transparency, and reflectivity of his glass works. Vacuum-coated sculptures like *Cube* form the core of Bell's practice, and over the years he has added paper and polyester film to his repertoire of materials.

In This Light

Ruth Asawa (United States, 1926–2013)
*Untitled (S.027, Hanging, Six-and-a-Half Open Hyperbolic Shapes That Penetrate Each Other)*, 1954
Iron, copper, and brass wire; 99 × 22½ × 22½ in.
Gift of an anonymous donor and the 2018 Collectors Committee with additional funds from The Buddy Taub Foundation, Dennis A. Roach and Jill Roach, Directors, M.2018.77

Ruth Asawa's looped wire hangings redefine the notion of sculpture as solid form. After being incarcerated because of her Japanese heritage during World War II, she studied art at the avant-garde Black Mountain College in North Carolina. On a trip to Toluca, Mexico, in the 1950s, she observed artisans forming baskets of looped wire. Asawa recognized the material's sculptural potential and began a lifelong journey of transforming a functional technique and modest industrial materials into poetic works of art.

In This Light

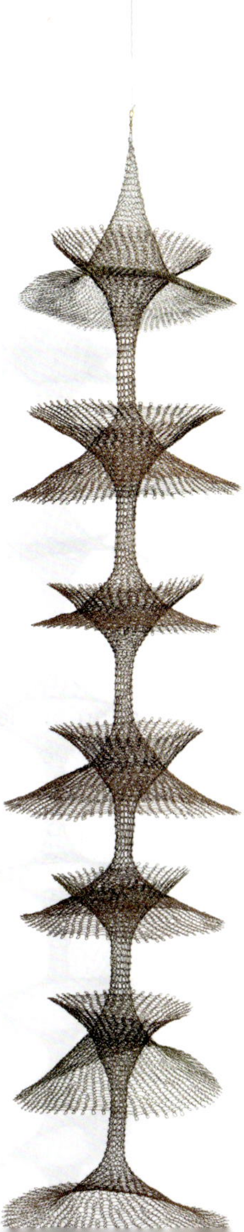

Dora De Larios (United States, 1933–2018)
*Earth Goddess*, 2009
Stoneware with glazed porcelain, aluminum, and wood; 96 × 40 × 26 in.
Gift of Dora De Larios, M.2022.200a–b

This monumental figure embodies the earth through boldly sculpted features and delicate animal forms, capturing nature's power and fragility. De Larios explored goddess imagery for decades, infusing her work with symbolism from her Mexican heritage as well as her broader fascination with global spiritual practices and the multicultural artistic community of her native Los Angeles. The subject was also personal, reflecting her strength as a Mexican American woman in a field dominated by white men.

Earth and Water

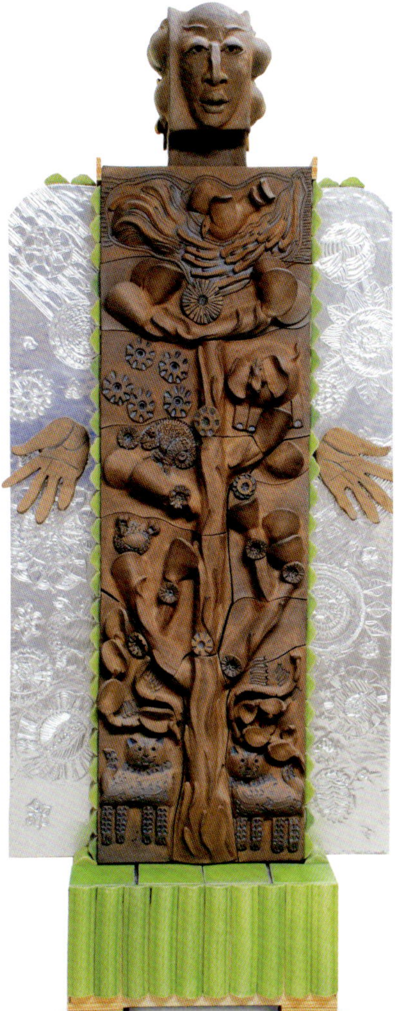

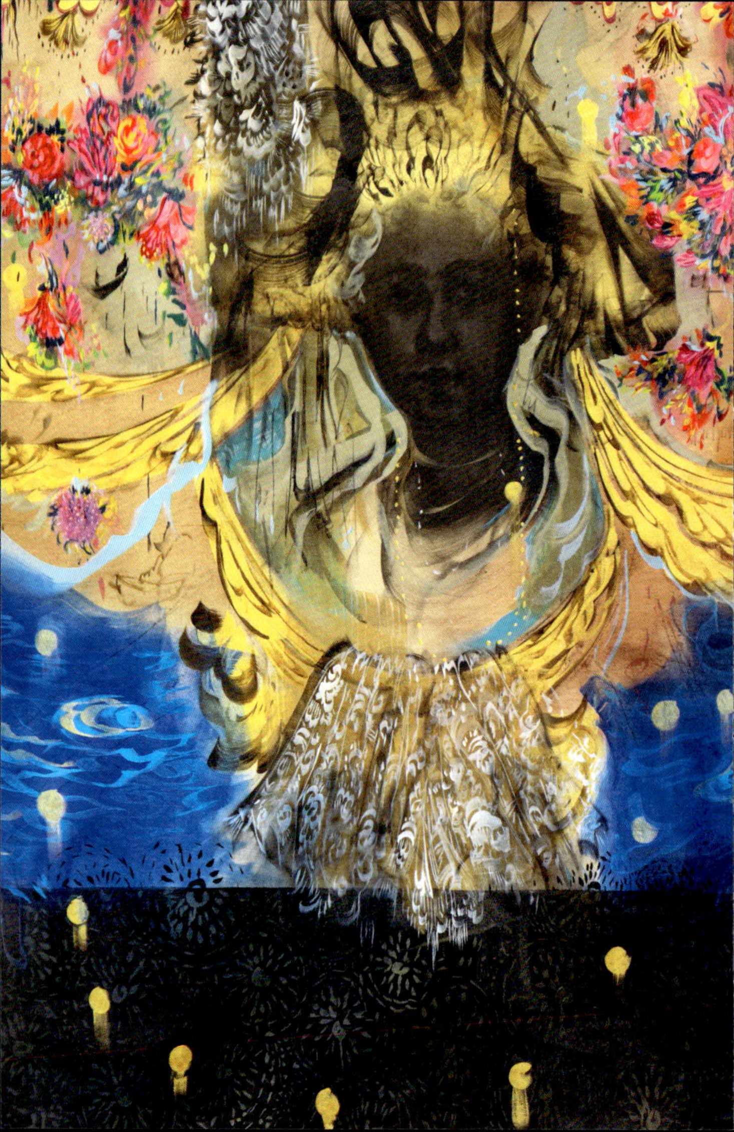

Scherezade García (Dominican Republic, b. 1966, active United States)
*Harvest of the Sea*, 2023 (detail)
Acrylic, pigment, charcoal, and ink on linen; 82½ × 162 in.
Purchased with funds provided by Contemporary@LACMA, 2023, M.2023.187

In this grand composition, the deep cobalt of the ocean links three ethereal yet resilient female figures. Each holding onto a flotation ring symbolizing the precariousness of modern migration, the women embody the multiple cultures of the Americas, Europe, and Africa that have shaped Latin America in the postcolonial period. Scherezade García is herself an islander, born in the Dominican Republic and now living in New York. For her, water is a "liquid highway that carries our history, memories, DNA."

Pueblo of Acoma maker (United States)
Water Jar, c. 1870–80
Acoma clay and pigment paints; height: 8¾ in.; diameter: 10½ in.
Gift of Camilla Chandler Frost, M.2008.113.6

Using local clay, water, and fire, a maker from the Pueblo of Acoma handcrafted a jar that encapsulates a microcosm: a body of earthen clay, covered with symbols of the sky and land (clouds, rainbows, and fields), and made to contain water. Designed to balance on the top of the head, water jars with bulbous bodies and tapering necks were critical to survival in the high desert climate of New Mexico. Today, Pueblo pottery continues to connect communities to their ancestors.

Earth and Water

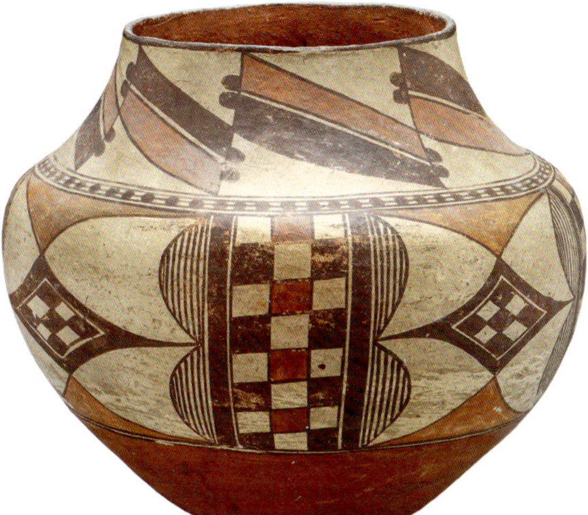

Lucie Rie (Austria, 1902–1995, active England)
Vase, 1979
Glazed porcelain; height: 7¼ × 4 × 4 in.
Gift of Howard and Gwen Laurie Smits, M.87.1.132

Hans Coper (Germany, 1920–1981, active England)
Vase, c. 1969
Glazed stoneware; 11½ × 8¼ × 3½ in.
Gift of Howard and Gwen Laurie Smits, M.87.1.27

These two vessels demonstrate the longstanding dynamic of creative exchange between Lucie Rie and Hans Coper, two of the twentieth century's most influential studio potters. Both refugees of Nazi Germany, Coper became an assistant in Rie's London studio in 1946, and they maintained close ties for the remainder of their lives. Rie's vase exemplifies her elegant, thin-walled forms, enhanced with fine white sgraffito decoration. Similarly reductionist, Coper's spade-shaped vase is a totem of geometric shapes, its form and matte abraded surface evoking ancient Cycladic sculptures.

Earth and Water

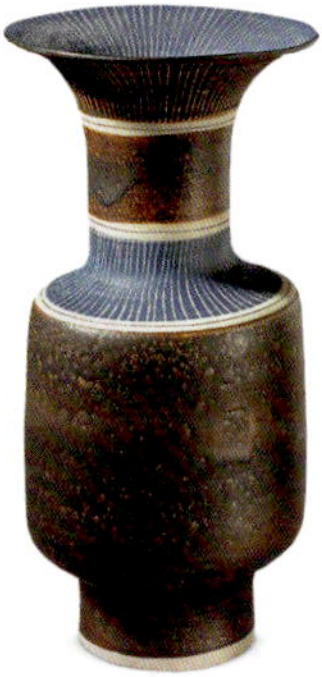

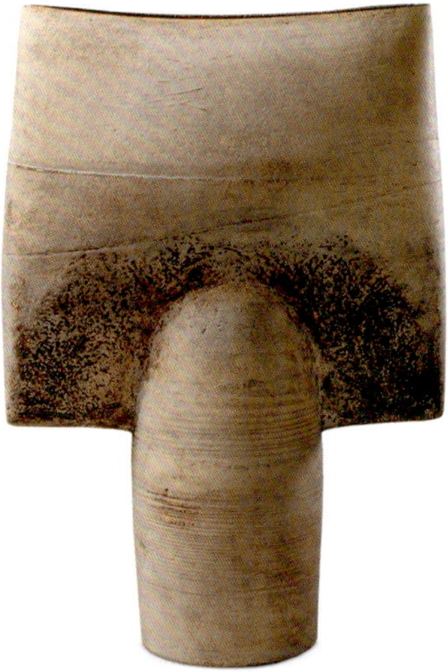

Granville Redmond (American, 1871–1935)
*California Poppy Field*, c. 1926
Oil on canvas; 40 1/4 × 60 1/4 in.
Gift of Raymond Griffith, 40.7

Among the most prominent artists working in Los Angeles at the turn of the twentieth century, Granville Redmond developed a reputation for his paintings of golden poppies—California's state flower. In this exceptionally large example, he worked on a rough-hewn canvas to add texture to the scene. He skillfully contrasted the warm orange hues of the foreground flowers with the cool blues of the distant mountains, capturing a peak springtime bloom when wildflowers carpet Southern California's landscape.

Earth and Water

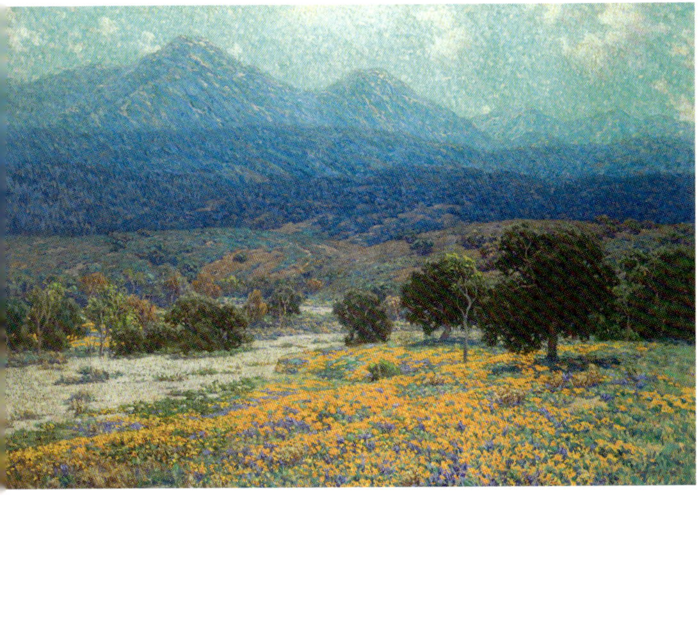

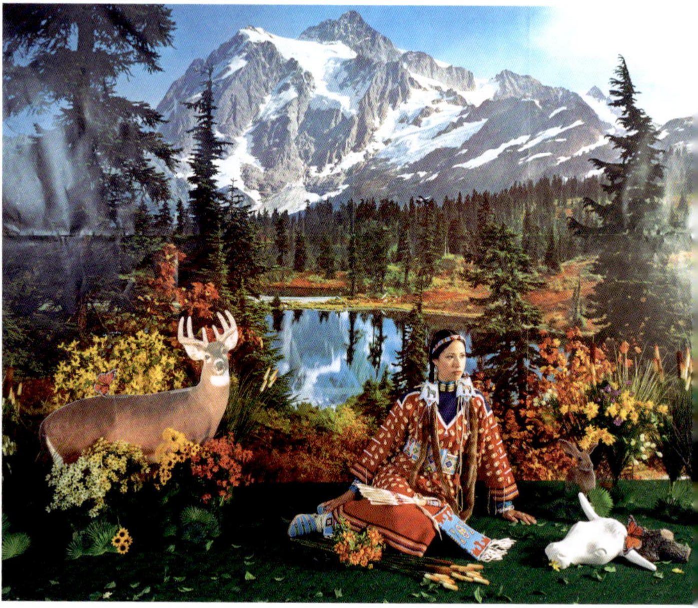

Wendy Red Star (United States, b. 1981)
*Fall*, 2006
Inkjet print (pigment based); 31½ × 35⅝ in.
Gift of Loren G. Lipson, M.D., M.2016.289.3

Aware of photography's legacy in depicting Native people as exotic others, Wendy Red Star (Apsáalooke/Crow) reclaims the camera as a tool of self-representation. In her *Four Seasons* series, she appears in a traditional elk-tooth dress amid a blatantly staged environment. Humor is key to her work. Using playful, kitschy elements, she challenges stereotypes of Indigenous people as "primitive" or "closer to nature" and encourages viewers to rethink their assumptions about contemporary Native American identity.

Picturing the American West

Richard Prince (Panama Canal Zone, b. 1949, active United States)
*Untitled (cowboy)*, 2016
Dye coupler print; 59½ × 89¾ in.
Anonymous gift, M.2017.254.3

Since the mid-1970s, Richard Prince has used advertisements to challenge notions of authorship and expose commercial mythmaking. For this 2015–16 series, he returned to Marlboro cigarette campaigns of the 1980s and '90s, scanning magazine spreads at high resolution and digitally

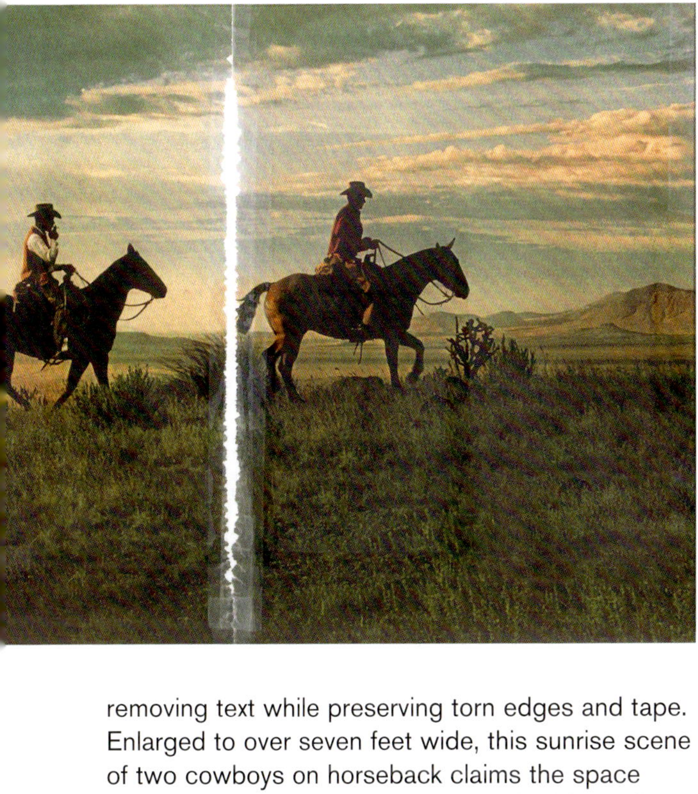

removing text while preserving torn edges and tape. Enlarged to over seven feet wide, this sunrise scene of two cowboys on horseback claims the space of traditional landscape painting and critiques its staging of masculinity and Manifest Destiny.

Laura Gilpin (United States, 1891–1979)
*The Rio Grande Yields Its Surplus to the Sea*, 1947
Gelatin silver print; 9⅝ × 13⅝ in.
The Marjorie and Leonard Vernon Collection, gift of the Annenberg Foundation, acquired from Carol Vernon and Robert Turbin, M.2008.40.934

Laura Gilpin was a fiercely independent artist whose documentation of the American Southwest landscape reflects her desire for clarity, spirituality, and permanence amidst the incursions of modern migration. During her sixty-year career, Gilpin worked serially and is perhaps best known for her books. This photograph is the final image in her 244-page 1949 publication *The Rio Grande: River of Destiny; An Interpretation of the River, the Land, and the People*, which includes not only her exquisite photographs but also her passionate writing about the region.

Picturing the American West

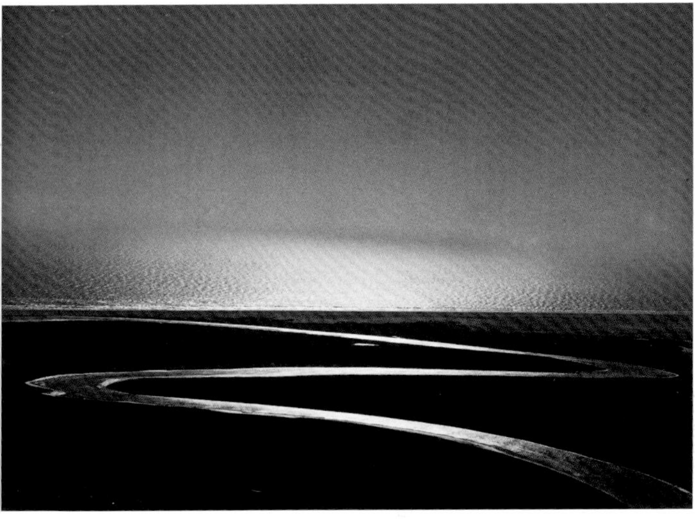

Kimsooja (Korea, b. 1957, active New York and Seoul)
*A Needle Woman, Patan (Nepal), Havana (Cuba), Rio de Janeiro (Brazil), N'Djamena (Chad), Sana'a (Yemen), Jerusalem (Israel)*, 2005
Six-channel video installation, silent (10 min. 40 sec.)
Purchased with funds provided by AMOREPACIFIC Corporation, M.2011.64.1–.4

In these poetic videos, Kimsooja inserts herself into the fabric of urban life, a "needle" piercing through the motion and tension of the surrounding world. The artist stands amid the crowds of cities across Asia, Africa, and the Americas—each marked by unrest at the time. "By doing nothing but being a presence," Kimsooja explains, "while creating [a] void of my identity, I wish to reveal the human condition in existential, geo-cultural, and sociopolitical dimensions."

Kimsooja: *A Needle Woman*

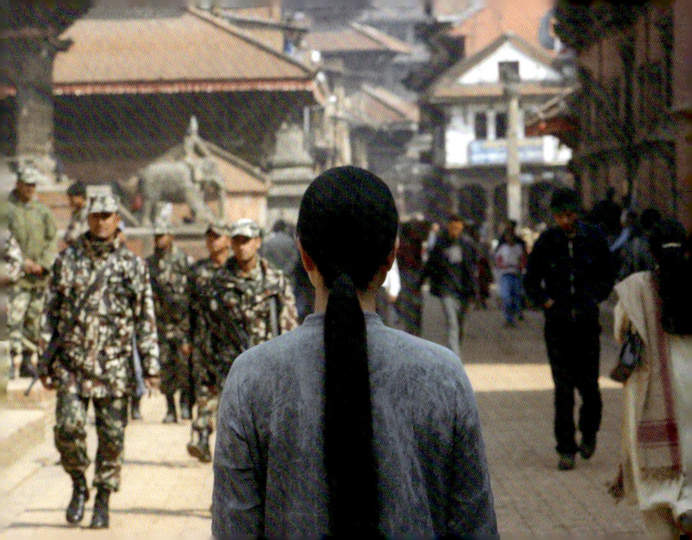

Shizu Saldamando (United States, b. 1978)
*Mario at Elysian Park*, 2023
Colored pencil and collage on paper; 39½ × 32¼ in.
Purchased with funds provided by Karen R. Constantine, M.2025.122

Shizu Saldamando's primary subject is her community of friends, in this case, fellow artist Mario Ybarra Jr. She drew his portrait in delicate strokes of colored pencil, adding bits of green sumi paper for the blades of grass peeking from beneath his feet. Identified in the title, the setting—Elysian Park, near Dodger Stadium in Los Angeles—is meaningful as a gathering place for Mexican Americans decades after the displacement of local communities to make way for the ballpark.

rafa esparza: *...we are the mountain*

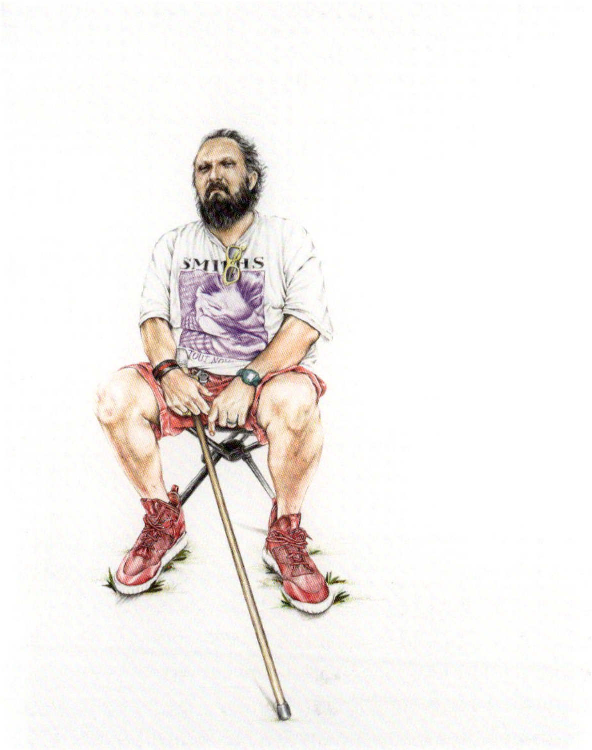

rafa esparza (United States, b. 1981)
*...we are the mountain*, 2019
Acrylic on adobe panel (local dirt, horse dung, hay, Hoosic River water, chain-link fence, plywood); 92 × 180 × 1¾ in.
Purchased with funds provided by AHAN: Studio Forum, 2020 Art Here and Now purchase, and the Vincent Price Art Museum Foundation, with funds provided by Kevan and Norma Newton, M.2020.215a–d

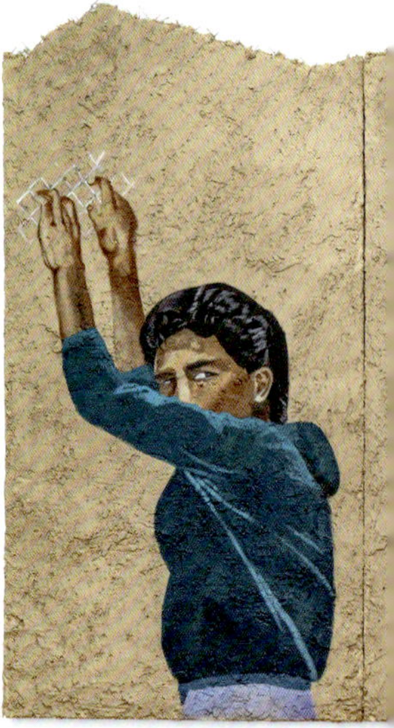

Multidisciplinary artist rafa esparza works primarily in performance, installation, and painting. He uses adobe to create objects of brown earth, a skill he learned from his father, which in time helped rebuild a relationship strained when esparza came out as queer.

This powerful wall sculpture references the movement of individuals across the United States–Mexico border. The figure's eyes peer surreptitiously at the viewer, hands curved into a painted patch of chain link; it is unclear whether the figure is coming or going over the fence.

rafa esparza: *...we are the mountain*

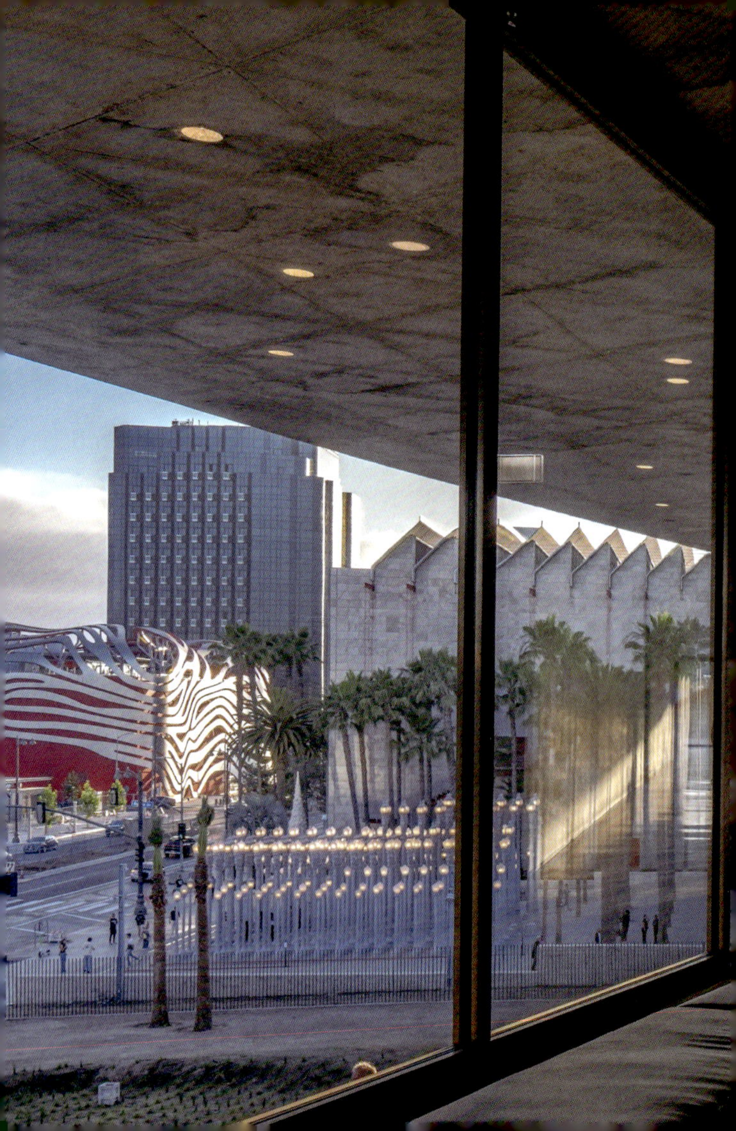

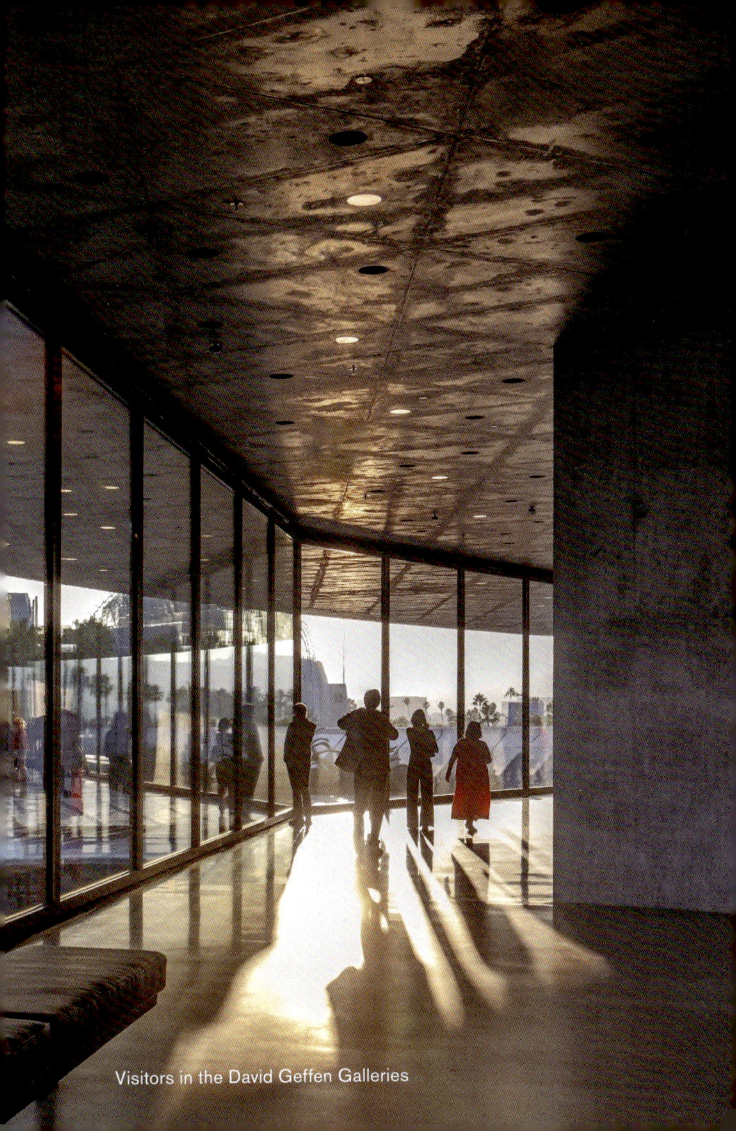

Visitors in the David Geffen Galleries

# Indian Ocean

1. Images of the Divine in South Asia
2. Do Ho Suh: *Jagyeong Hall, Gyeongbok Palace*
3. Founding a Collection: A Gift of Korean Art
4. Venerable Fragments: Korean Ceramic Shards
5. Ceramic Vessels of Neolithic China
6. Ritual Vessels and Jades of Bronze Age China
7. Henri Cartier-Bresson: China in Transition
8. An Imperial Robe of China
9. Luxury Arts of the Great Mughals
10. The Evolution of Abstract Painting in Modern Korea
11. Persianate Arts: The Ardabil Carpet and Manuscript Painting
12. Han Youngsoo: Korea in Transition
13. From Kashmir to Cashmere
14. China's Influence in East Asia and Beyond
15. Pan-Asian Buddhist Art
16. The Global Appeal of Blue-and-White Ceramics
17. Indonesian Batiks and Cultural Exchange
18. Andreas Gursky: Oceans
19. The Enduring Influence of Mathura
20. Gandhara and Rome: Crossroads of the Classical World

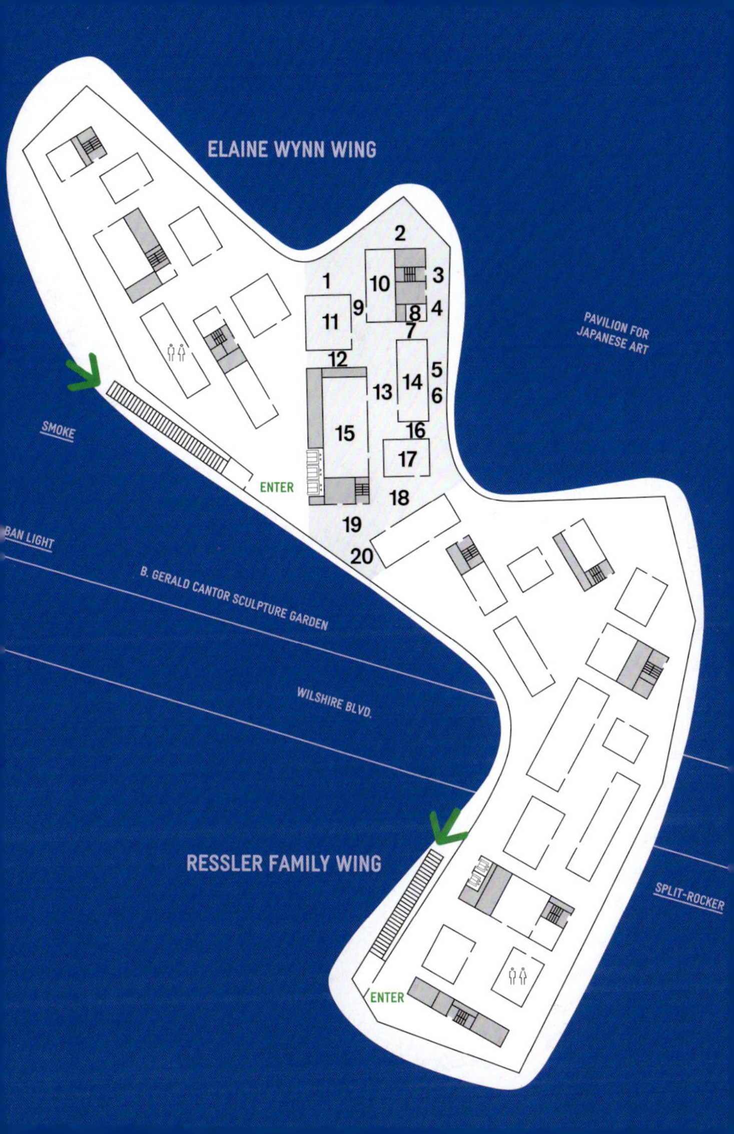

ELAINE WYNN WING
PAVILION FOR JAPANESE ART
SMOKE
ENTER
BAN LIGHT
B. GERALD CANTOR SCULPTURE GARDEN
WILSHIRE BLVD.
RESSLER FAMILY WING
SPLIT-ROCKER
ENTER
1
2
3
4
5
6
7
8
9
10
11
12
13
14
15
16
17
18
19
20

# Indian Ocean

For three thousand years, the Indian Ocean functioned as humanity's longest continuous maritime exchange network, powered by a geographic feature that set it apart from every other ocean in the world: predictable seasonal wind reversal. Each summer, from June through September, monsoon winds carried vessels northeast from East Africa and Arabia toward South and Southeast Asia. Each winter, from November through February, the winds reversed, providing return passage home. This annual rhythm meant that merchants, artisans, religious teachers, and materials could circulate continuously among three major regions: South and Southeast Asia, East Africa, and the Persian Gulf.

The Indian Ocean's wind calendar created sustained multidirectional trade where no single power dominated. Round-trip voyages took as much as two years, which meant merchants often resided for extended periods in foreign ports. Tamil merchants in Southeast Asian kingdoms, Arab traders in East African Swahili cities, Persian craftspeople at South Asian courts, and Chinese porcelain exporters throughout the basin all participated in exchanges where multiple cultural traditions coexisted. Port cities became cosmopolitan artistic centers where workshop systems integrated techniques from distant regions.

Geographic variation in resource distributions directly affected artistic production. Southeast Asian volcanic stone enabled massive temple construction at Borobudur and Angkor Wat. South Asian cotton cultivation supported textile industries employing hundreds of thousands in specialized dyeing workshops. East African coral limestone shaped Swahili architectural traditions in regions where timber was scarce. Arabian frankincense and myrrh monopolies generated wealth that funded architectural patronage for centuries.

Artworks exhibited in the Indian Ocean galleries span the full chronological range of the collection, from some of the oldest works to some of the newest. Sculptures from South and Southeast Asia—one of LACMA's strengths—are considered in a variety of contexts, including religious practice, historical significance, and stylistic development. Textiles are also prominently featured from Indonesian batiks and Kashmir shawls to the grand Ardabil Carpet.

Gandhara region, Pakistan
*The Aristocratic Women*, 2nd century
Schist; 23⅛ × 13¾ × 6 in.
Purchased with funds provided by Mrs. Harry Lenart, Robert and Mary Looker, Robert F. Maguire III, and The Hillcrest Foundation through the 1998 Collectors Committee, Stephen Markel in memory of Catherine W. Markel, the Southern Asian Art Council, and S. Sanford and Charlene S. Kornblum, AC1999.3.1

Ancient Gandhara was a region in present-day Pakistan and Afghanistan at the east-west juncture of the fabled Silk Road between Rome and China. The syncretic art of Gandhara merged Roman stylistic forms with Indian subject matter. These naturalistic figures wear Classical garments and coiffures of second-century Rome, but the subject may depict an incident from one of the Buddha's past lives in which he resolved a dispute between two women over a necklace of scented threads.

Gandhara and Rome: Crossroads of the Classical World

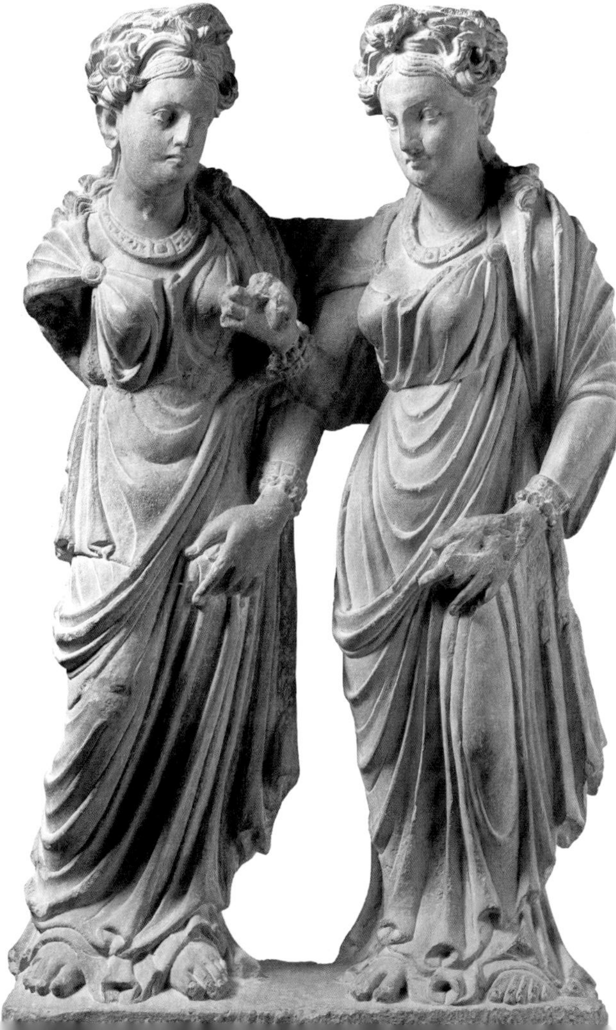

Gandhara region, Pakistan
*Atlas*, 2nd–3rd century
Schist; 15⅜ × 12 × 5¼ in.
The Phil Berg Collection, M.71.73.136

Stone or stucco images of Atlas often adorned the bases of Buddhist stupas (funerary monuments) in ancient Gandhara (an important nexus of the Silk Road in present-day Pakistan and Afghanistan). They were conceptually based on Classical Western architectural Atlantes figures but portrayed as winged representations of the Greek titan Atlas, who was condemned by Zeus to support the celestial spheres on his shoulders for eternity. The depictions of Atlas symbolized the strength and stability of sacred monuments.

Gandhara and Rome: Crossroads of the Classical World

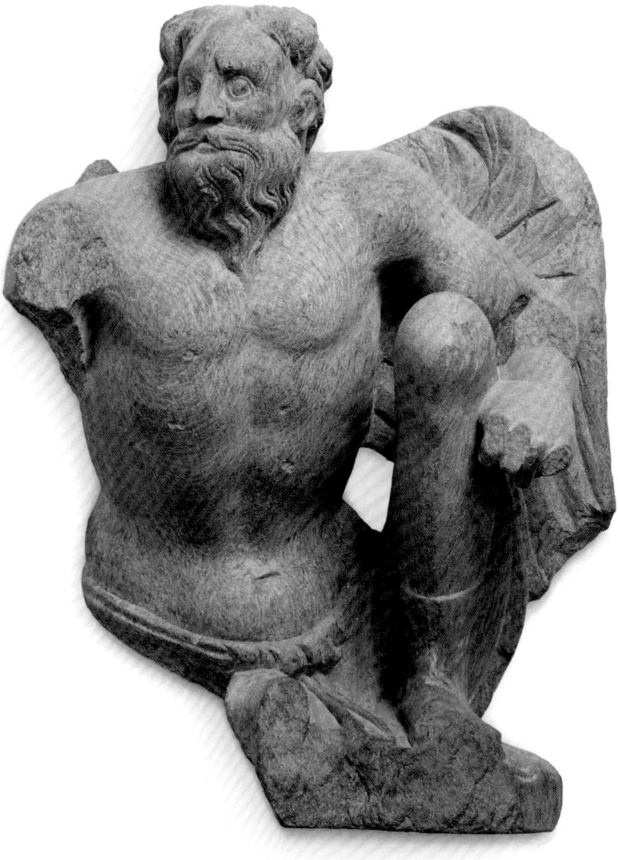

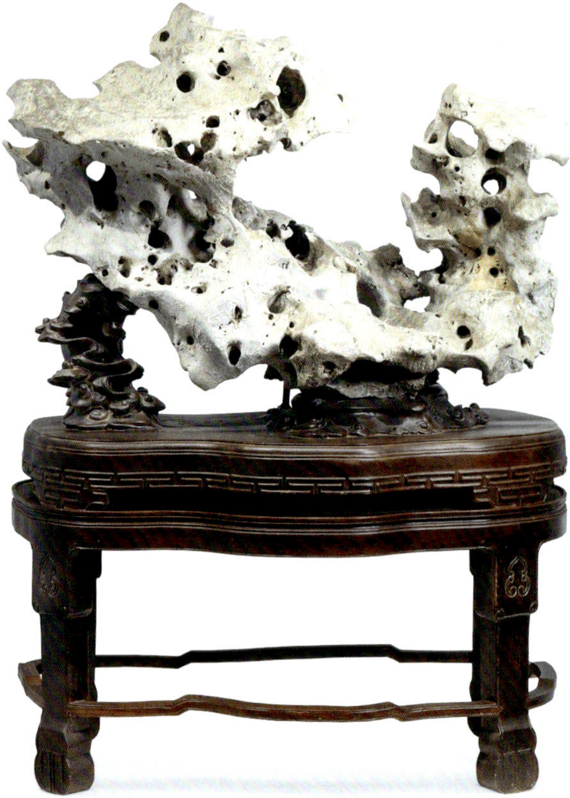

Lake Tai, Jiangsu Province, China
*Guai shi* (Strange Stone)
Taihu stone (limestone); 25¼ × 37 in.
Gift of the 2017 Collectors Committee, M.2017.73a–b

While in ancient China strange stones (*guai shi*) conveyed considerable social status through their otherworldly beauty, they were also seen as made of the purest energies left over from the creation of the world. The Chinese saw in strange stones the fundamental structures and processes of the universe. Such stones also symbolized the human virtues of strength and endurance. This particular stone was dredged from the depths of Lake Tai in Jiangsu Province.

Ritual Vessels and Jades of Bronze Age China

China, Neolithic period, Majiayao culture, Banshan type
Jar, 2700–2400 BCE
Painted and burnished earthenware; 16⅝ × 16⅝ × 15¾ in.
Purchased with funds provided by Ann Ziff, M.2021.259.41

Chinese Neolithic earthenware vessels of this type present the earliest evidence in East Asia of both kiln-fired ceramics and brush painting. The body of the vessel, boldly painted with geometric designs, was made by the coiling method, before the invention of the potter's wheel. It was in the prehistoric period of the Yangshao (5000–2400 BCE) and other Neolithic cultures that the foundations of Chinese civilization were established.

Ceramic Vessels of Neolithic China

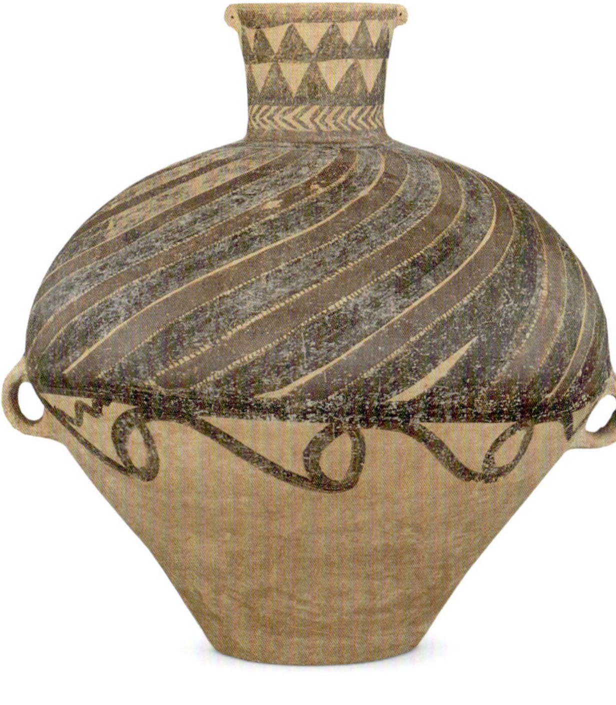

China, Late Shang dynasty, middle or late Anyang phase
Shallow Ritual *Ding* (Food Cauldron) with Legs in the Form of Dragons, c. 1200–1050 BCE
Cast bronze; 7⅜ × 6¼ × 5¾ in.
Inscribed with a clan sign: two arrows in an enclosure
Gift of Mr. and Mrs. Eric Lidow, AC1998.251.7

In China's Early Bronze Age, *ding* cauldrons were used for cooking food, often during rituals performed for gods and deified ancestors. Many such bronze vessels bear some of the earliest known examples of Chinese writing, dating to the twelfth and eleventh centuries BCE. The pictographic inscription cast into the interior of this vessel is interpreted as a clan sign. Over time, these pictographs evolved into longer inscriptions that documented royal favor, military conquests, and treaties between rival states.

Ritual Vessels and Jades of Bronze Age China

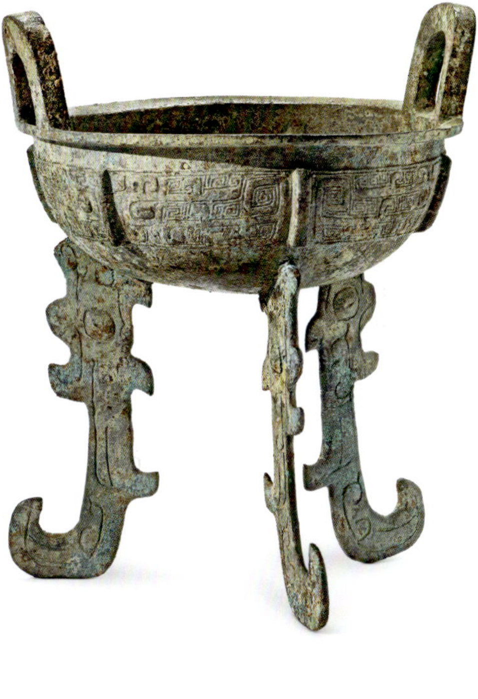

China, Qing dynasty, Kangxi reign
*Chaopao* (Man's Formal Court Robe),
18th century (detail)
Silk, brocaded and embroidered; 53⅝ × 84 in.
Gift of the 2017 Collectors Committee with additional funds provided by an anonymous donor, Sue Tsao, and Louise and Brad Edgerton, Edgerton Foundation, M.2017.175

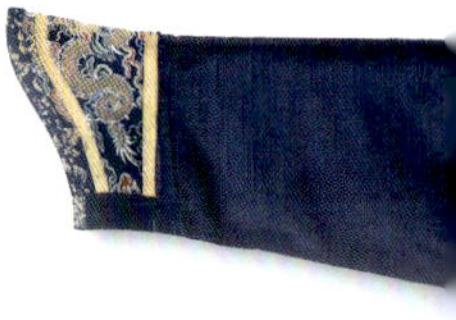

In 1644, the Manchu army swept into Beijing to claim the Dragon Throne from the Han Chinese Ming dynasty. To celebrate their cultural and national identity, the Manchu reconfigured the formal court robe into this rare *chaopao*. Structurally, it retains vestiges of Manchu nomadic garments, such as the overlapping front closure with loop-and-button fasteners and the long tapered tripartite sleeves finished with "horse hoof" cuffs (*ma ti xiu*) that recall the riding coats of Manchu equestrians. Decoratively, strategically placed woven dragons maintain traditional iconographies of Chinese imperial authority and good fortune.

An Imperial Robe of China

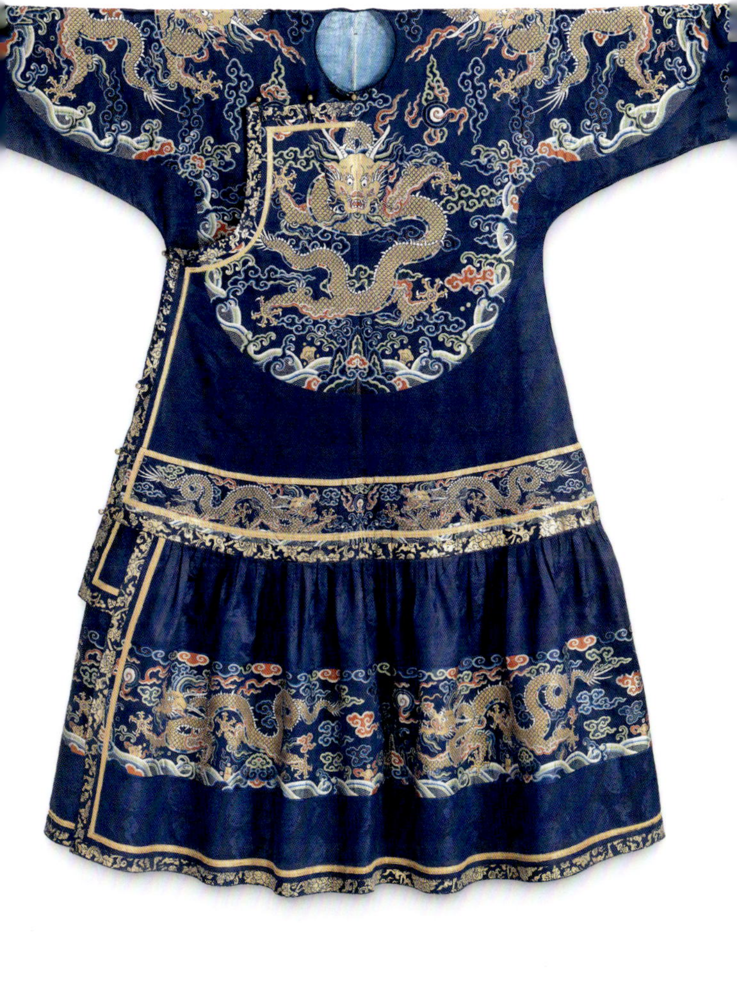

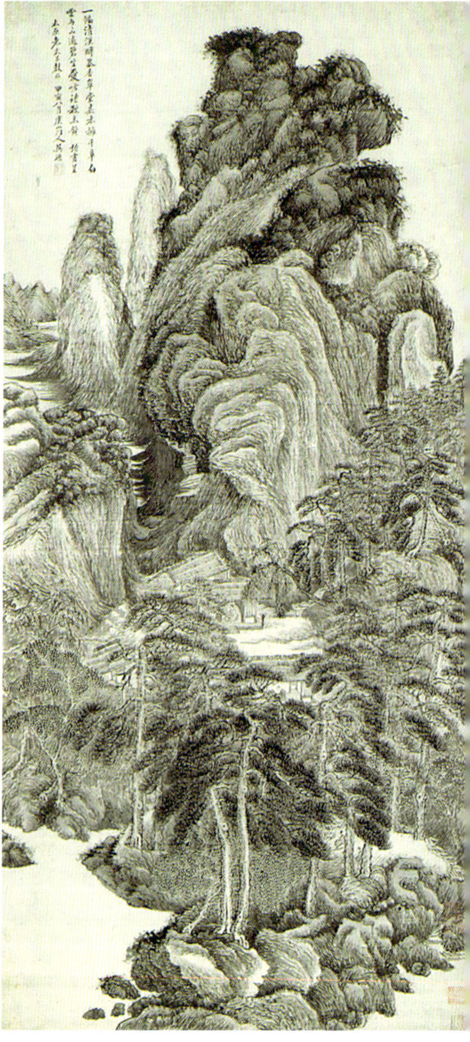

Wu Li (China, 1632–1718)
*Reciting Poetry before the Yellowing of Autumn*, 1674
Hanging scroll; ink on paper; 104 1/2 × 32 in.
Los Angeles County Fund, 56.18

Wu Li's fluid brushwork presents a landscape coursing with energy. The painting embodies a central concept of Daoist cosmology, namely that everything is infused with a primordial energy called *qi*. Daoists see mountains not as solid objects but as concentrations of these flowing energies. Once owned by the great twentieth-century painter Zhang Daqian, the work is dedicated to Wu Li's teacher, Wang Shimin, shown seated in a thatched hut at the center of the composition.

Traditionally attributed to Yue Fei
(China, 1103–1142)
*Memorial on Going into Battle*
*(Chushi biao)*
*by Zhuge Liang (181–234)*, 19th
century (detail)
Handscroll; rubbing, ink on paper;
21¾ × 884¾ in.
Gift of Mei-Lee Ney, M.91.189

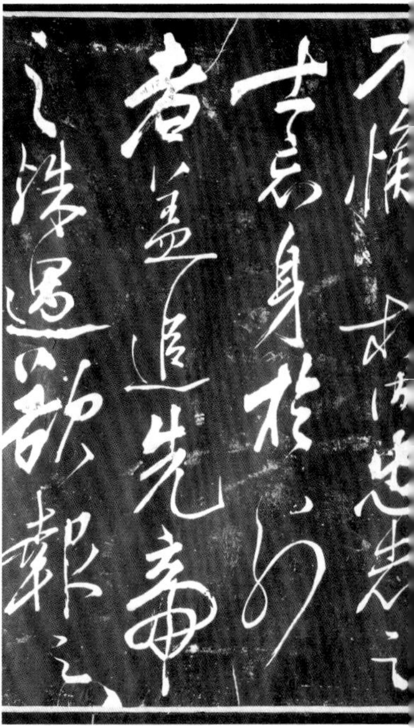

Yue Fei was a general famous for his attempts to restore Song-dynasty rule over northern China, which had been invaded by foreign Jurchen armies. At the age of thirty-nine, he was put to death after being falsely charged with treason by an official who proposed compromising with the Jurchen by

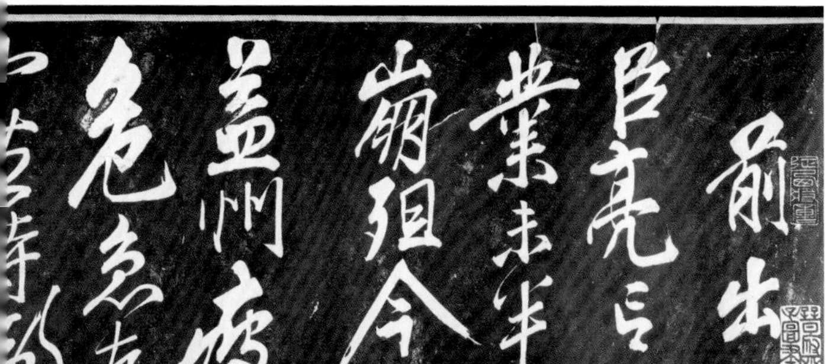


exchanging cash for peace. This dynamic calligraphy, long attributed to Yue Fei, transcribes a memorial on rulership by the ancient strategist Zhuge Liang.

Han Youngsoo (Korea, 1933–1999)
*Sogong-dong, Seoul, Korea*, 1956–63, printed 2019
Toned gelatin silver print; 18 × 12 in.
Gift of Robin-Hwajin Yoon Kim, M.2019.232.6

During Seoul's rapid postwar transformation into a modern metropolis in the 1950s and '60s, Han Youngsoo portrayed everyday Koreans as they were, and not as a victimized people. Here, a young boy examines a box of American comic books, curious despite the fact that he likely cannot read English. With an impeccable eye for social detail and a prevailing optimism that defined his unique photographic style, Han captured the era when Western cultural influences had begun to permeate daily life.

Han Youngsoo: Korea in Transition

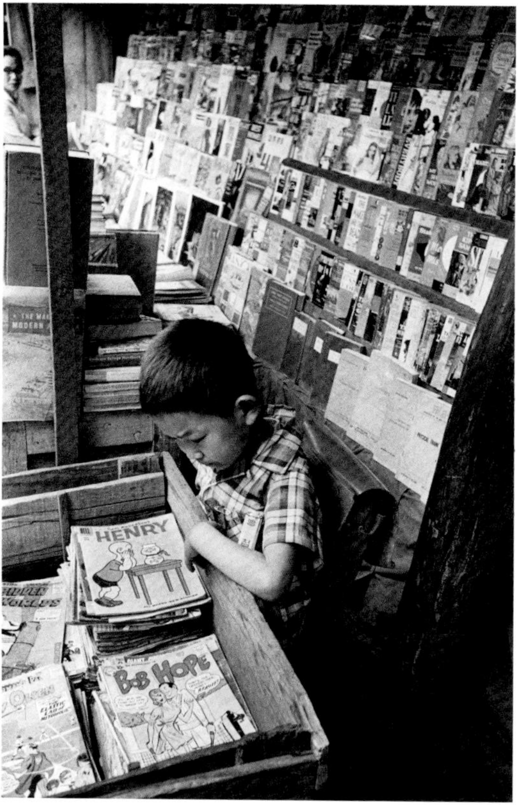
HENRY
BOB HOPE

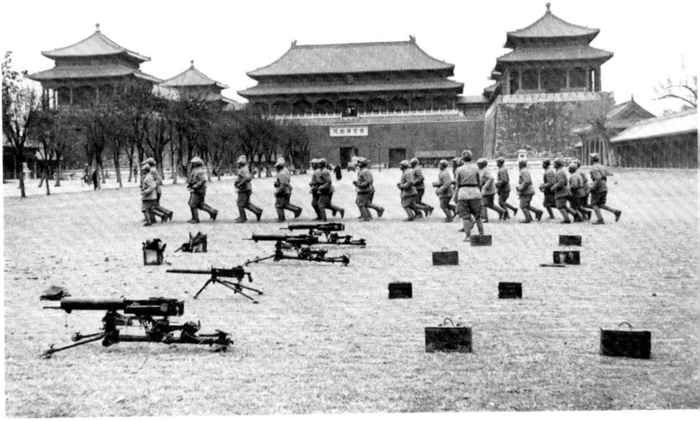

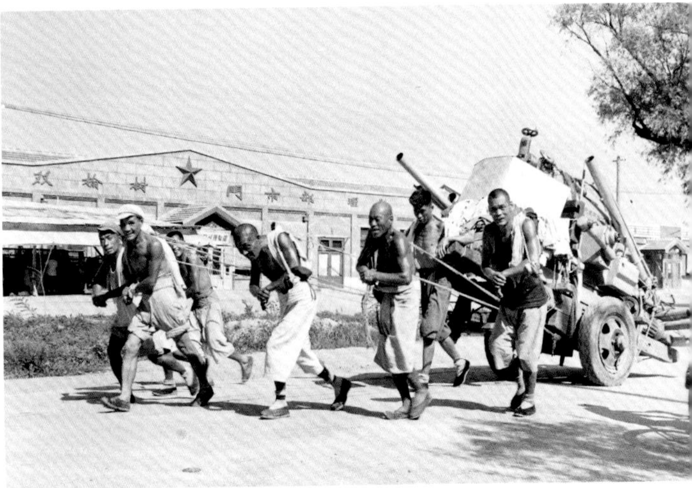

Henri Cartier-Bresson (France, 1908–2004)

*In one of the courtyards of the Imperial Palace, Beijing*, 1948
Gelatin silver print; 6½ × 10 in.
Gift of Dennis and Pamela Beck, M.2009.174.4

*Beijing*, 1958
Gelatin silver print; 7¾ × 11¾ in.
Gift of Dennis and Pamela Beck, M.2006.144.20

Between December 1948 and September 1949, Henri Cartier-Bresson made more than nine hundred photographs in China for *Life* magazine documenting the retreat of Nationalist forces and the establishment of communism. The militarization of Beijing is seen here as soldiers drill in a courtyard of the Imperial Palace.

In 1958, Cartier-Bresson spent four months in China documenting cultural events, propaganda campaigns, and ordinary people at the onset of the Great Leap Forward. Here, he captured workers pulling a new lathe through the streets of Beijing with the five-pointed communist star visible above them. This composition exemplifies Cartier-Bresson's notion of "the decisive moment"—when the precise organization of forms and the significance of an event come together in a fraction of a second.

Henri Cartier-Bresson: China in Transition

Korea, Goryeo dynasty
Flower-Shaped Dish with Peony Spray Design, 12th century
Stoneware with celadon glaze; decorative pattern in relief; diameter: 7 in.
Gift of Nasli M. Heeramaneck, M.73.48.117

This elegant Goryeo dish exemplifies the iconic green glaze of celadon ceramics. The forms and decorations of Goryeo celadons gained recognition within East Asia as an exquisite ceramic unique to Korea. Motifs from nature like this luxurious peony branch were commonly used as decorative patterns. These peonies, rendered in a relief technique, were achieved by pressing damp clay into pre-carved molds and onto the dish's surface before the glaze was applied and fired.

Venerable Fragments: Korean Ceramic Shards

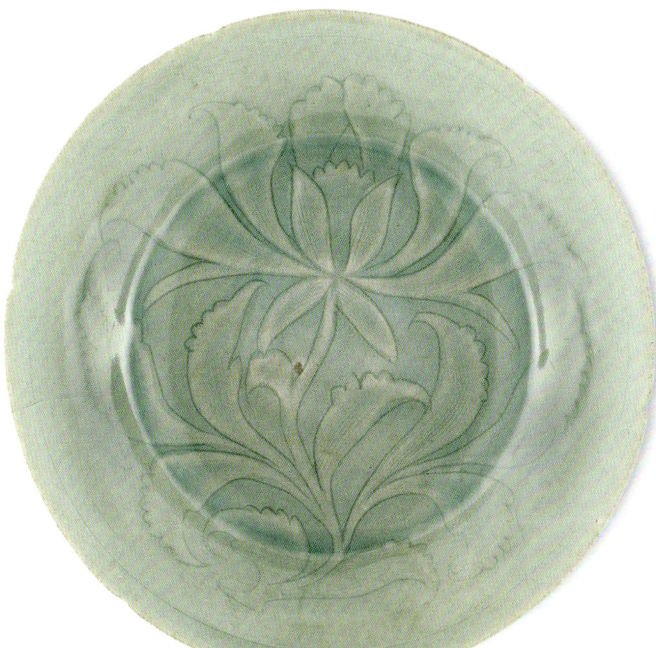

Korea, Joseon dynasty
Bottle with Arabesque Scroll Design, 15th–early 16th century
Stoneware with underglaze iron and pale green glaze; 10⅝ × 6 in.
Gift of Park Chung Hee, Former President of the Republic of Korea, 66.3.19

Buncheong ceramics represent a significant aesthetic shift in Korean ceramics. They emerged under the Joseon dynasty with the adaptation of techniques from earlier Goryeo-period blue-green celadons into a more experimental and rustic style. The unevenness of this bottle's clay body was deliberately exposed. Drenched in white slip, the vessel's deep brown designs were created with iron-oxide pigment. Buncheong bottles served diverse purposes, from high-status ritual containers to common household items.

Founding a Collection: A Gift of Korean Art

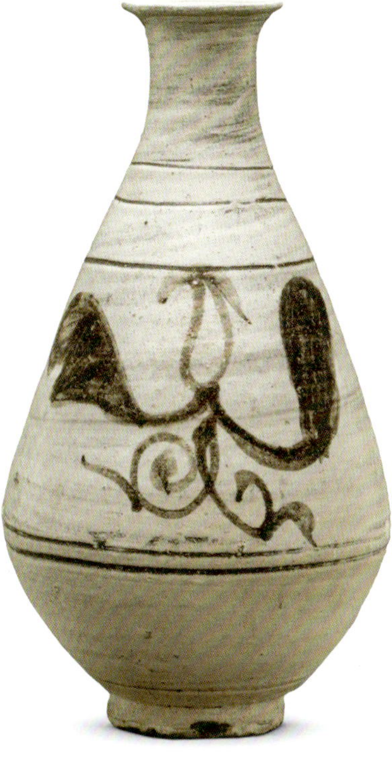

Artists of the Dohwaseo (Royal Bureau of Painting) (Korea, Joseon dynasty)
Screen depicting Banquets for Dowager Queen Sinjeong
in Gyeongbokgung, 1868 (detail)
Ink, color, and gold on silk; closed: 70 1/2 × 18 1/2 × 4 3/4 in.;
open: 70 1/2 × 148 × 1/2 in.
Museum Funds, M.2000.15.35a–h

An eight-panel screen records the elaborate, multi-day celebration of Dowager Queen Sinjeong's sixtieth birthday in 1868. The first two panels, starting from the right, depict the formal Great Court Ceremony, where an empty throne symbolizes the king's presence. Subsequent panels show informal celebrations in the inner quarters with a final night-time banquet illuminated by candles and lamps. The exquisite details of the procession and dance performances exemplify documentary painting in the Joseon period.

The Evolution of Abstract Painting in Modern Korea

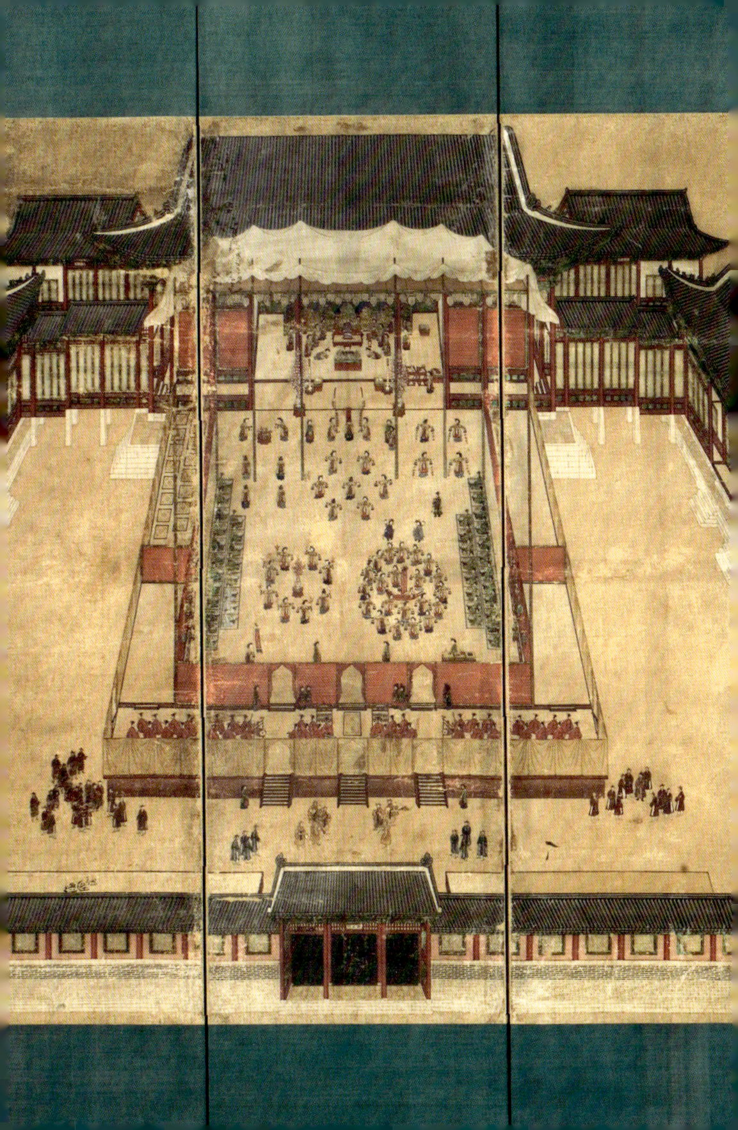

Do Ho Suh (Korea, b. 1962, active United Kingdom)
*Jagyeong Hall, Gyeongbok Palace*, 2026 (partial rendering)
Polyester fabric on stainless steel and aluminum frame with ceramic coating
Commissioned from Do Ho Suh by the Los Angeles County Museum of Art with funding provided by Shinsegae, Korea Foundation, and CJ Entertainment

Do Ho Suh's installation is a meticulous, actual-size contemporary re-creation of a section of Jagyeong Hall in Gyeongbok Palace, the primary Joseon royal palace in Seoul. The chosen section replicates the Cheongyeon Pavilion residence of Joseon Dowager Queen Sinjeong (1809–1890), one of the few original Joseon tiled-roof wood structures within the palace complex to have survived the widespread destruction caused by the Korean War (1950–53). The artist's translucent fabric gives the building an elusive, ghost-like presence.

Do Ho Suh: *Jagyeong Hall, Gyeongbok Palace*

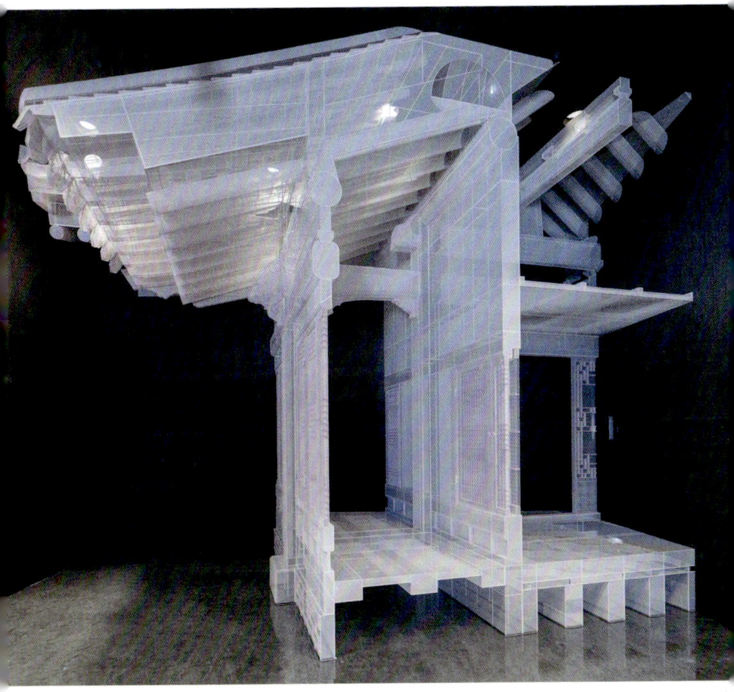

Mathura, Uttar Pradesh, India
Head of Buddha Shakyamuni, c. 150–200
Sandstone; 14¼ × 12½ × 13½ in.
From the Nasli and Alice Heeramaneck Collection, Museum Associates Purchase, M.69.13.9

The historical Buddha Shakyamuni (thought to have lived 563–483 BCE) was born as Prince Siddhartha Gautama in present-day Nepal. But he renounced his royal life and traveled for more than four decades throughout northern India teaching and establishing a monastic order. Here, the Buddha is portrayed with symbolic features. His now-damaged cranial protuberance represents his enlightened insight. His elongated earlobes, distended from wearing heavy gold earrings as a prince, symbolize his abandonment of the mundane world.

The Enduring Influence of Mathura

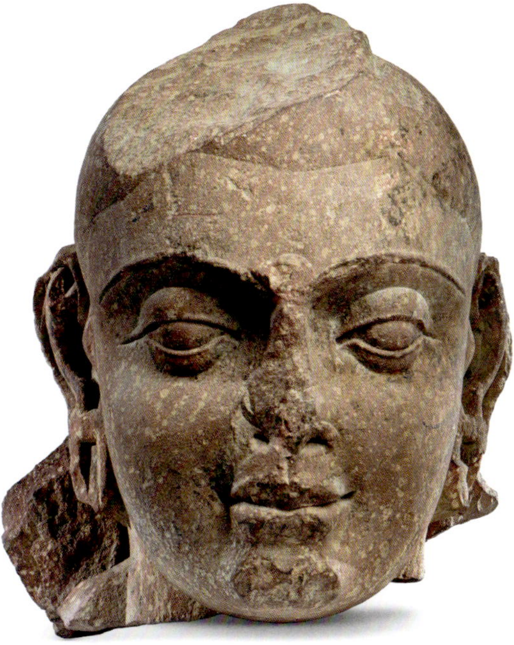

Mathura, Uttar Pradesh, India
*Shivalinga*, late 4th century
Sandstone; 12 × 5½ × 8½ in.
Gift of Harry and Yvonne Lenart, M.2010.131

The Shivalinga (literally, the "sign" of Shiva) is the quintessential symbol of the Hindu god Shiva. In its core conception as an aniconic column, the Shivalinga symbolizes the deity's transcendental nature and primordial potency. The Shivalinga was later anthropomorphized by the addition of Shiva's head or multiple heads to provide lay worshippers with a physical form that was more accessible than his abstract philosophical nature and thought to help his devotees establish a personal spiritual bond.

The Enduring Influence of Mathura

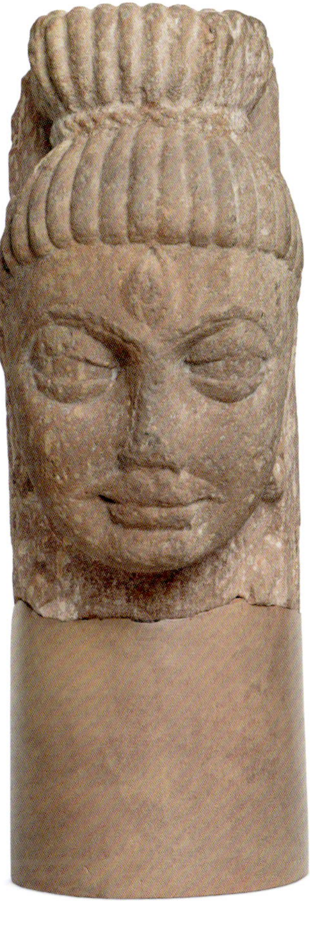

Manjunath Kamath (India, b. 1972)
*Vikatonarva*, 2024 (detail)
Colored terracotta; 138 × 45 × 45 in.
Gift of Kelvin and Hana Davis through the 2024 Collectors Committee, M.2024.101

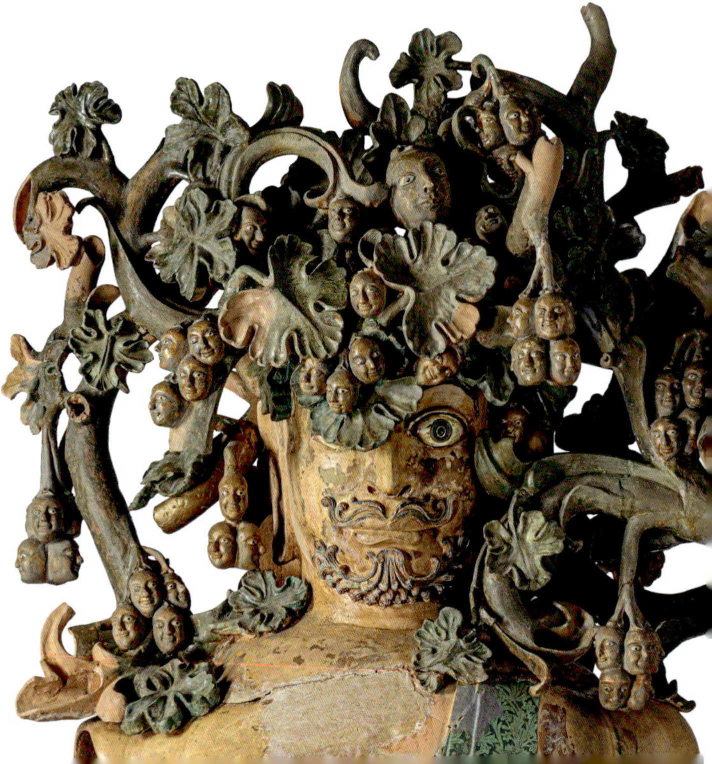

Manjunath Kamath merges global iconography into imaginative terracotta sculptures. Growing up in Mangalore, India, he absorbed art history through temples and churches filled with multi-armed gods and monumental terracotta forms. Terracotta, Latin for "baked earth," is the most common sculptural material around the world, found in cultures from Greece to Iran, China to the Americas. In *Vikatonarva*, Kamath treats history as a field of fragments, selecting and transforming different references—a mudra-like hand, a Vishnu-like chest—into forms that feel familiar yet untraceable, inviting viewers into open-ended interpretations.

Images of the Divine in South Asia

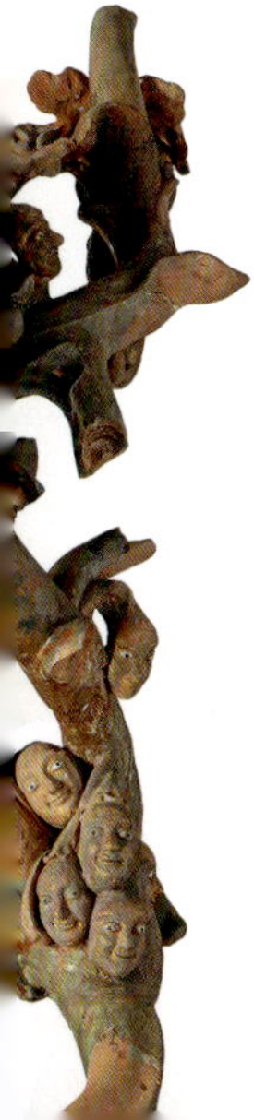

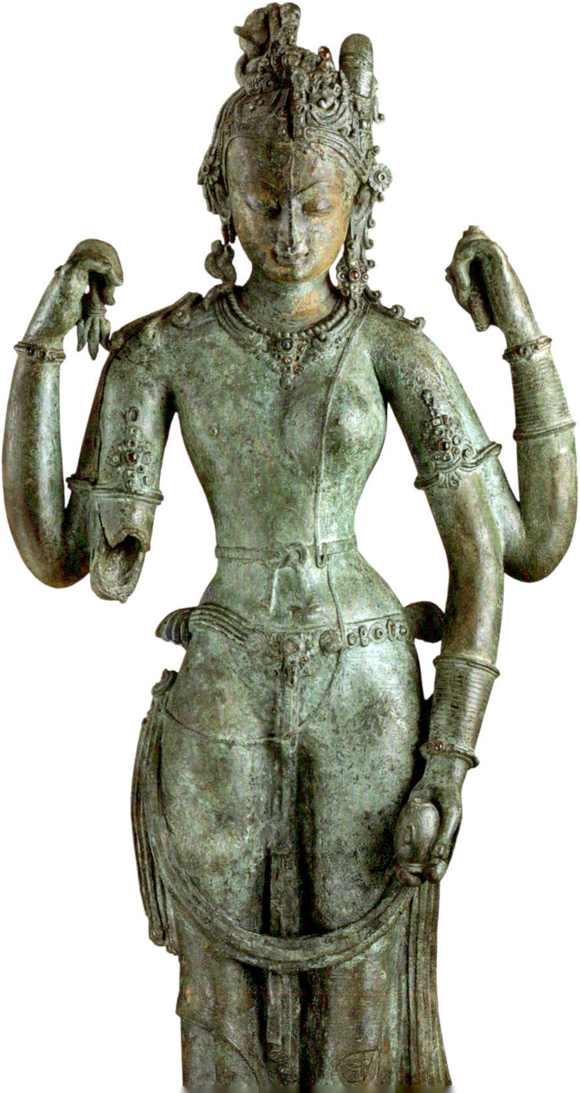

Nepal
*Androgynous Form of Shiva and Parvati*, c. 1000 (detail)
Unalloyed copper inlaid with garnets and an emerald; paint;
33 × 14½ × 5 in.
From the Nasli and Alice Heeramaneck Collection, Museum Associates Purchase, M.82.6.1

Ardhanarishvara, the Lord Who Is Half Woman, represents the combined form of Shiva and his consort Parvati. This androgynous image was devised by theologians to manifest the nonduality of the divine principle uniting masculinity and femininity. The proper right side of the figure is the male Shiva, while the proper left side is the female Parvati. Physical characteristics and subtle differences in physique differentiate the two halves, but the harmonious balance symbolizes their cosmic unity.

Images of the Divine in South Asia

Tamil Nadu, India
*Shiva as the Lord of Dance*, c. 950–1000
Copper alloy; 30 × 22½ × 7 in.
Anonymous gift, M.75.1

Shiva, one of Hinduism's principal deities, is embodied here as Nataraja, Lord of the Dance. The aureole ringed by flame represents the universe and its ultimate destruction by fire. His outer hands hold a drum representing the primordial sound at the creation of the universe and the flame of its destruction. His inner hands make the gesture of reassurance and point to his foot, which is overcoming the demon of ignorance.

Images of the Divine in South Asia

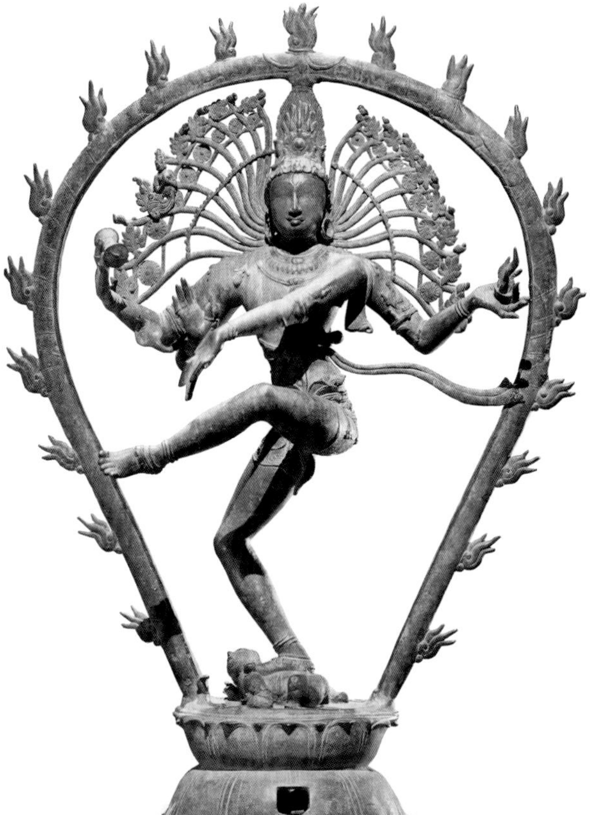

Tamil Nadu, India
*Ganesha, Lord of Obstacles*, 12th century
Granulite; 32 × 21 × 11½ in.
Gift of Mr. and Mrs. Paul E. Manheim, M.74.122.2

According to legend, Ganesha's mother Parvati created him from her own body to guard her while her husband Shiva was away. When Shiva returned, Ganesha refused him entry. Unaware that Ganesha was his son, Shiva cut off the boy's head and sent it flying. Parvati was inconsolable, so Shiva searched the universe for the head. Unable to find it, he took the head of a baby elephant that had sinned and with it restored Ganesha to life.

Images of the Divine in South Asia

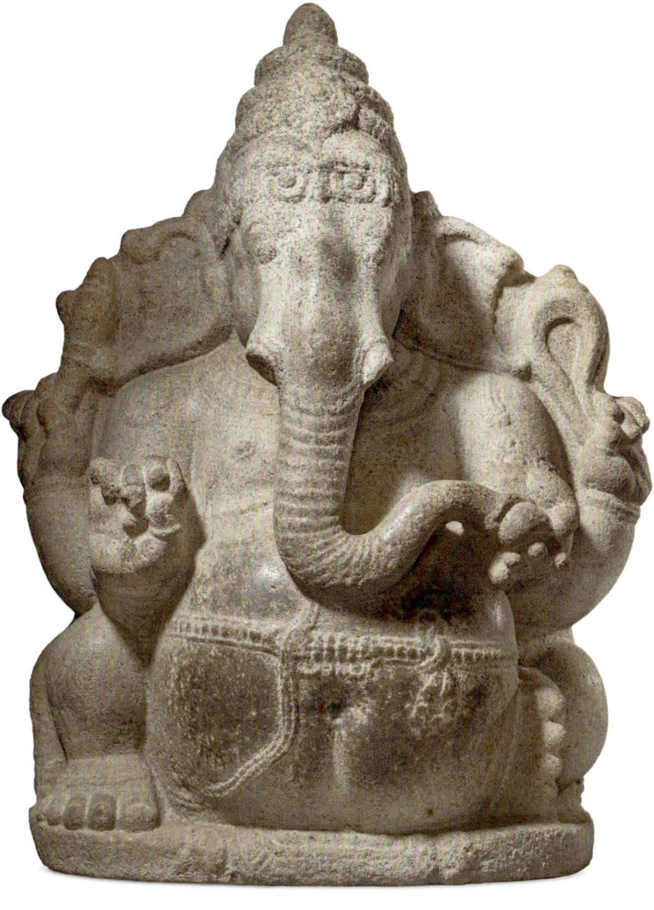

Karnataka or Tamil Nadu, India
Probably Jina Mahavira, c. 850–900
Copper alloy; 8⅞ × 7⅝ × 3¼ in.
From the Nasli and Alice Heeramaneck Collection, Museum Associates Purchase, M.82.6.2

Jina Mahavira (c. 599–527 BCE) was born a prince in Bihar in eastern India. He became the 24th Jain savior (or Jina). Conceived as an ideal yogi, the Jina is seated in the meditation posture with his hands in his lap. His shorn hair and distended earlobes symbolize his renunciation of his princely life when he wore long locks and heavy gold ear ornaments. He is depicted nude as per the strictures of the Digambara ("sky-clad") Jain order.

Images of the Divine in South Asia

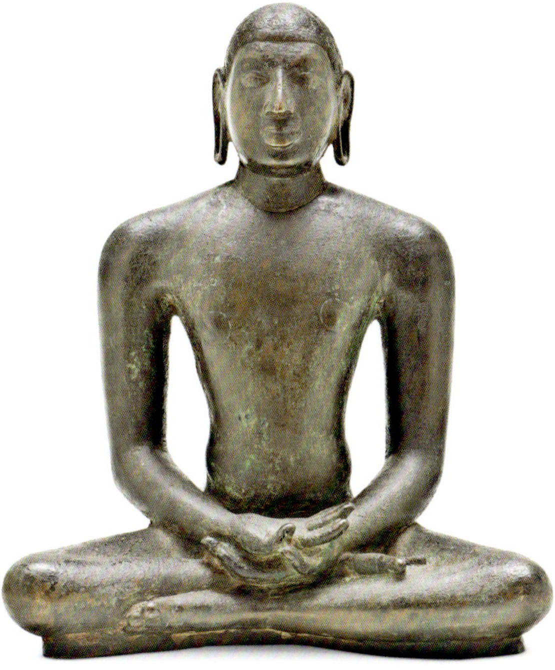

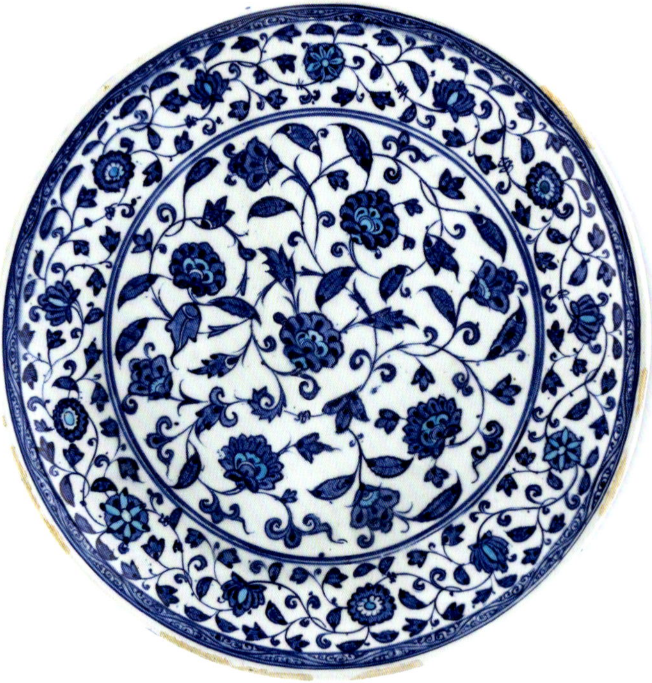

Iznik (Turkey)
Plate, c. 1530–35
Fritware, underglaze-painted; diameter: 12⅜ in.
Gift of the 2024 Collectors Committee, M.2024.134

The development of porcelain decorated in underglaze blue in fourteenth-century China had an enormous impact in Islamic lands, both as an imported elite tableware and as a source of emulation. Perhaps the greatest of the Islamic wares influenced by Chinese porcelain are those from Iznik, in western Turkey, such as this beautiful plate. The dynamic floral scrolls are inspired by related designs in Chinese porcelain, while the plate's shape is indebted to porcelain prototypes.

The Global Appeal of Blue-and-White Ceramics

Lahore, Mughal empire, Pakistan
Ewer, c. 1675–1700
Brass with inlaid resin ground; 14 × 10 1/2 × 6 3/4 in.
Purchased with funds provided by Harry and Yvonne Lenart and Camilla Chandler Frost through the 1995 Collectors Committee, AC1995.52.1

Water ewers and basins were used by Muslims during the Mughal era (1526–1858) principally for washing hands during ceremonial and mundane ablutions. Fashioned in Lahore, the northern capital of the Mughal empire, this ewer epitomizes the fine brassware created in the Panjab, the border region shared today by Pakistan and India. The ewer's cast floral decoration, featuring rose shrubs in the central panels, was once highlighted by a dark resin ground (now mostly lost).

Luxury Arts of the Great Mughals

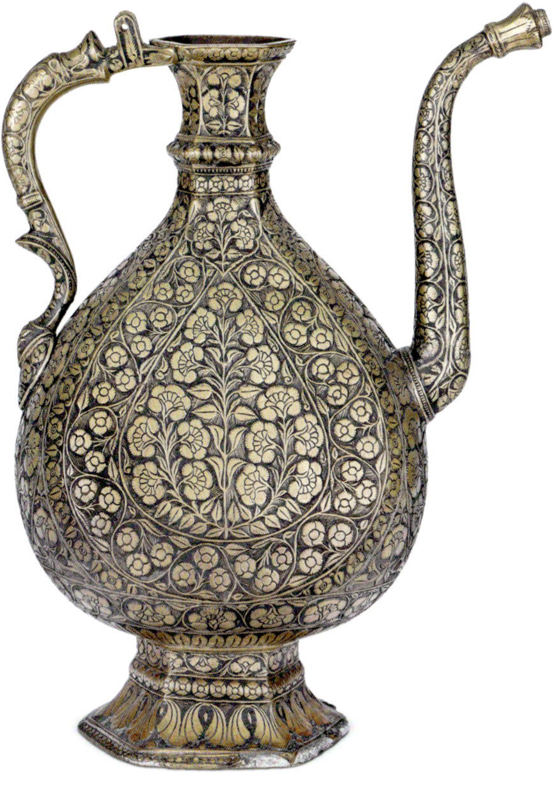

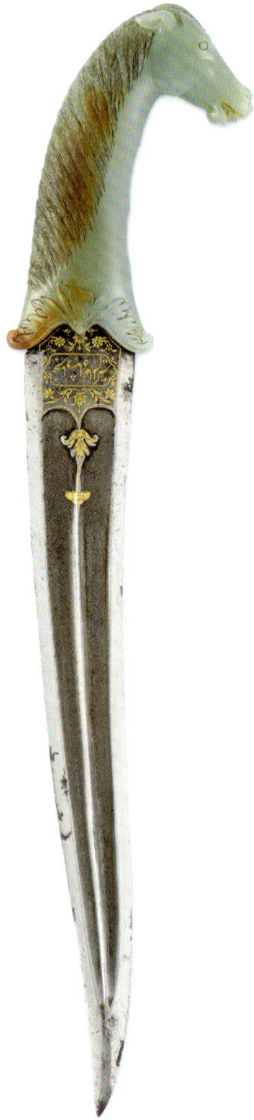

Mughal empire, India
Dagger of Emperor Aurangzeb (r. 1658–1707), dated 1660–61
Nephrite jade hilt; steel blade inlaid with gold; 13¾ × 2 in.
From the Nasli and Alice Heeramaneck Collection, Museum Associates Purchase, M.76.2.7a

This dagger once belonged to the Mughal emperor Aurangzeb and is dated to 1660–61 by a gold inscription on the blade. The dagger's exquisite nephrite jade hilt in the form of an Arabian stallion is rendered naturalistically and imbued with a martial spirit appropriate to Aurangzeb, who spent much of his rule on military campaigns. The imperial charger is ready for battle: his ears are laid back, his nostrils flare, and his lips snarl!

Luxury Arts of the Great Mughals

Haji Ehsan (Java, active early to mid-20th century)
*Sarung* (Woman's Hip Wrapper), c. 1930–40 (detail)
Cotton, wax resist dyed (batik); 35 × 41½ in.
Inger McCabe Elliott Collection, M.91.184.498

On this *sarung*, wax-resist-dyed depictions of natural and mechanized modes of transportation by both sea (fish and steam boats) and air (birds and airplanes) combine notions of technological progress and tradition in early twentieth-century Java. These images not only reference movement off of the land but also symbolize Dutch colonization and its influence in Indonesia. Batik of this sort was worn in the archipelago by those who felt themselves part of Java's hybrid culture.

Indonesian Batiks and Cultural Exchange

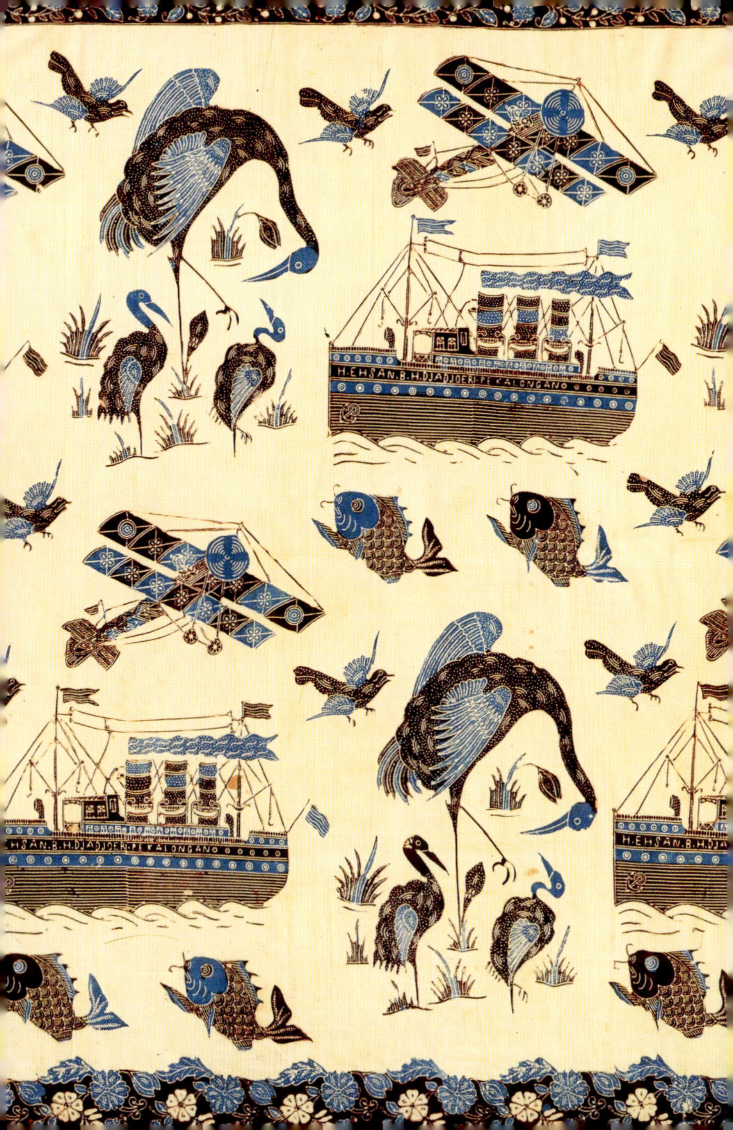
H.EHSAN.B.H.DJADJOERI-PEKALONGANO

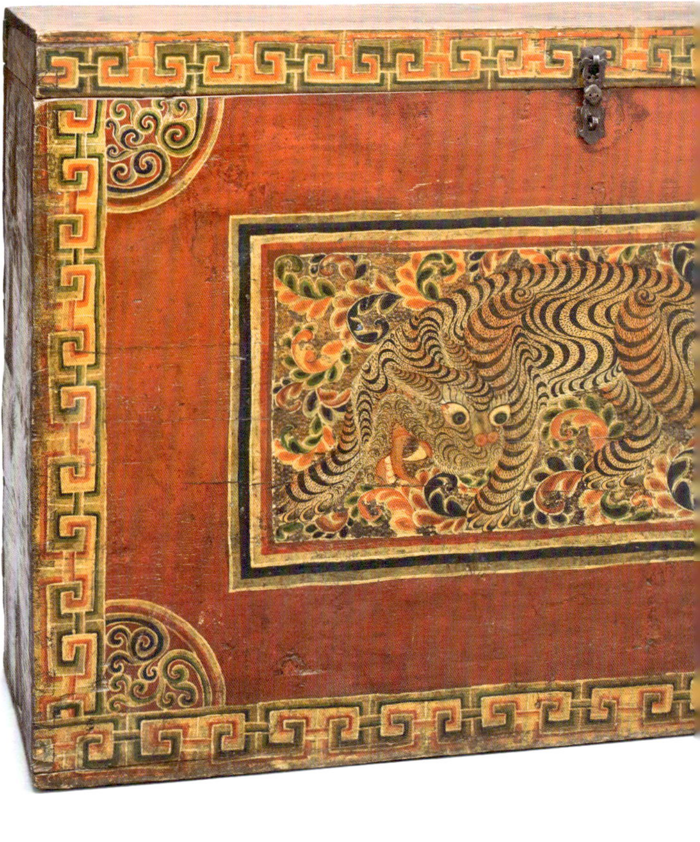

Kham region, Eastern Tibet
Trunk with Tiger, 19th–early 20th century (detail)
Wood with mineral pigments; brass fittings; 36 × 54 × 20 in.
Gift of the 2010 Collectors Committee, M.2010.82.1

Tigers and other animals are typically represented in Tibetan Buddhist canonical painting and sculpture as subsidiary elements of the larger composition. In contrast, Tibetan furniture designers would selectively enlarge an animal as the primary subject. This snarling tiger is poised in a field of vibrant flowers. Bold stripes form a rhythmic pattern that enlivens the animal with a dynamic vitality and sense of movement, perfectly suited to express its wild nature and widely believed mystical power.

Pan-Asian Buddhist Art

Japan, Heian period
*Kannon, Bodhisattva of Compassion*, 12th century
Wood; 85 × 32½ × 36 in.
Mr. and Mrs. Allan C. Balch Fund, M.62.6a–c

In twelfth-century Japan, sculptors carved Buddhist deities from single wood blocks, as in this Kannon (Skt. Avalokiteshvara), revered for boundless compassion. The bodhisattva's gentle, impassive expression reflects late Heian aesthetics, while the left hand forms the *raigō-in* welcoming gesture. Although Kannon could appear in male or female form, Japanese depictions became increasingly feminized after the eighth century. The separately carved crown and lotus pedestal, symbolizing purity, are attached to the figure with metal joiners and wood pegs.

Pan-Asian Buddhist Art

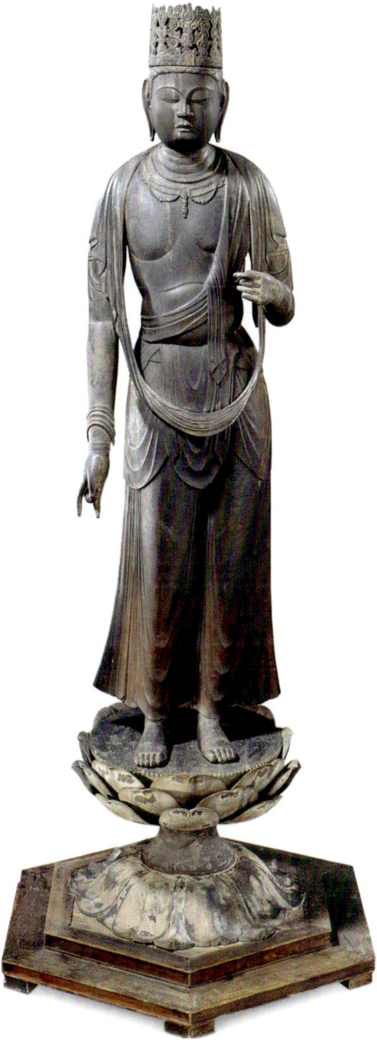

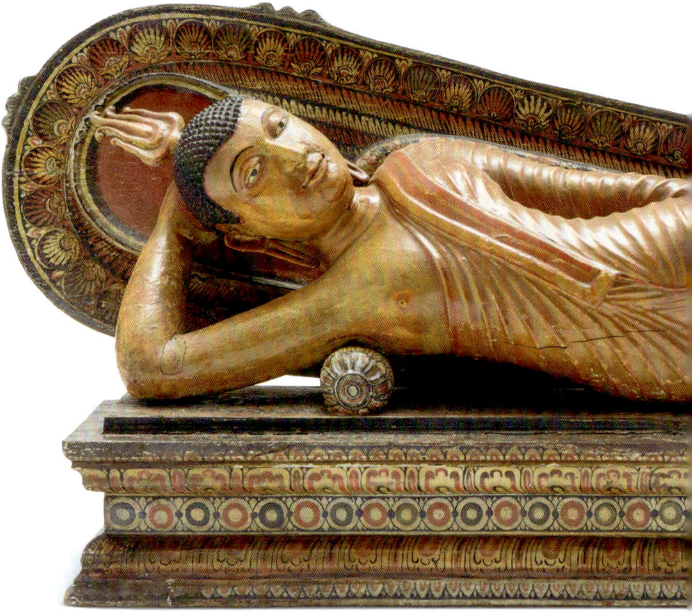

The historical Buddha Shakyamuni, whose life dates are traditionally given as 563–483 BCE, died in Kushinagara, India. Before his final enlightenment, he presented his last discourse to his disciples from his deathbed. Here, the Buddha's open eyes and raised head supported by his right hand indicate

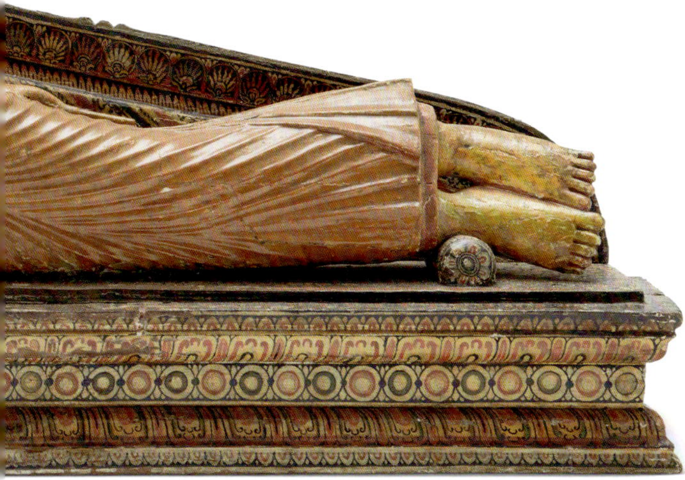

that he is alive and still cognitive, rather than being shown with eyes closed and near death as he is depicted in some differing regional Buddhist art traditions.

Pan-Asian Buddhist Art

Sri Lanka
*Buddha Shakyamuni Reclining*, 18th century
Wood with paint; 14½ × 37¾ × 6⅝ in.
Purchased with funds provided by Anna Bing Arnold, M.80.189

China, Ming dynasty
*Seated Avalokiteshvara (Guanyin), Bodhisattva of Compassion,*
c. 1550–1644
Cast brass with gilding, lacquer, and pigments; 32¼ × 22½ × 15 in.
Gift of Dr. and Mrs. Charles L. Pincus, M.76.146

The most popular of the many bodhisattvas worshipped in East Asia is Avalokiteshvara (Ch. Guanyin), Bodhisattva of Compassion. An entire section of the seminal *Lotus Sutra* is devoted to Avalokiteshvara, where thirty-three manifestations of the bodhisattva are described. Avalokiteshvara is savior, and in Buddhist art this bodhisattva can often be identified by the presence of a seated image of Amitabha, Buddha of the Western Paradise, in the figure's crown.

Pan-Asian Buddhist Art

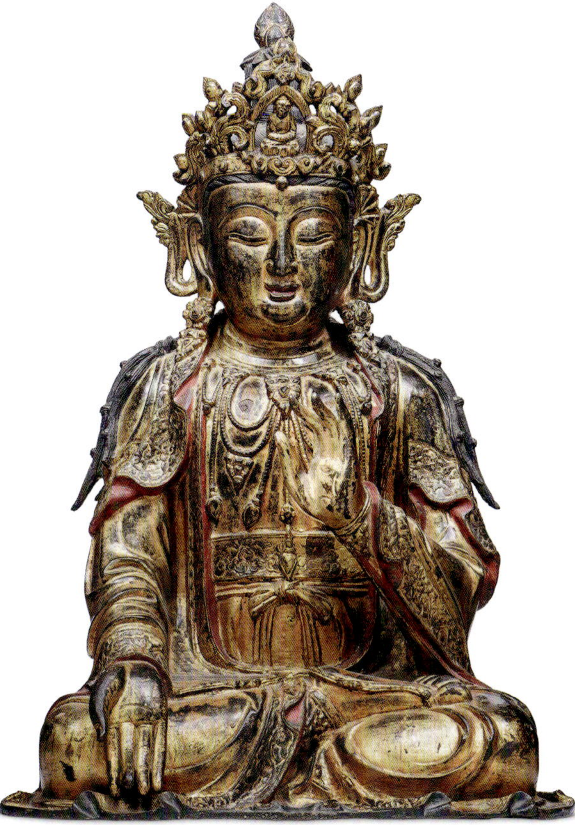

Hiroshi Sugimoto (Japan, b. 1948)
*Sea of Buddha 049 (Triptych)*, 1995 (detail)
Gelatin silver print; 94 × 121¼ in.
Gift of the 2025 Collectors Committee, M.2025.131

*Sea of Buddha* is a photographic series depicting the 1,001 statues of the thousand-armed Kannon, Bodhisattva of Compassion, at Kyoto's Sanjūsangendō. This triptych highlights the monumental seated Kannon sculpted by Tankei (1173–1256). After seven years of negotiation, Sugimoto used delicate sunrise light to evoke the way the statues might have originally been experienced. The work transforms the historic sculptures into luminous symbols of compassion, transcendence, and time, blending technical precision and conceptual depth to convey both spiritual and philosophical infinity.

Pan-Asian Buddhist Art

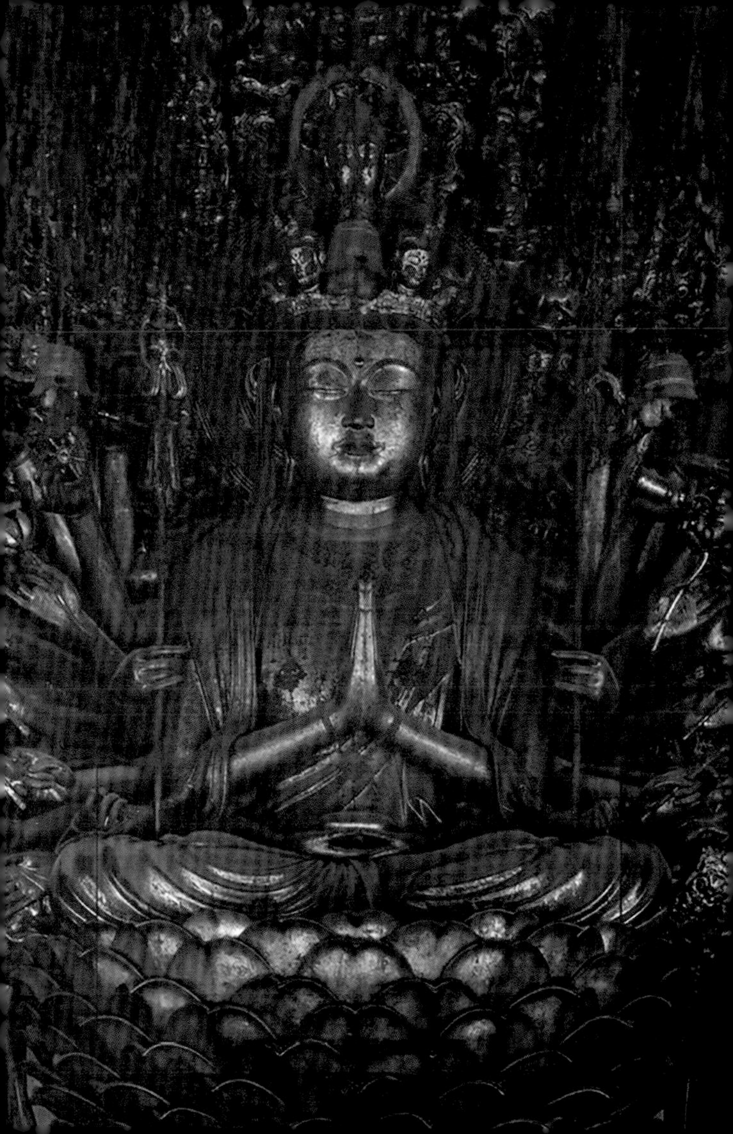

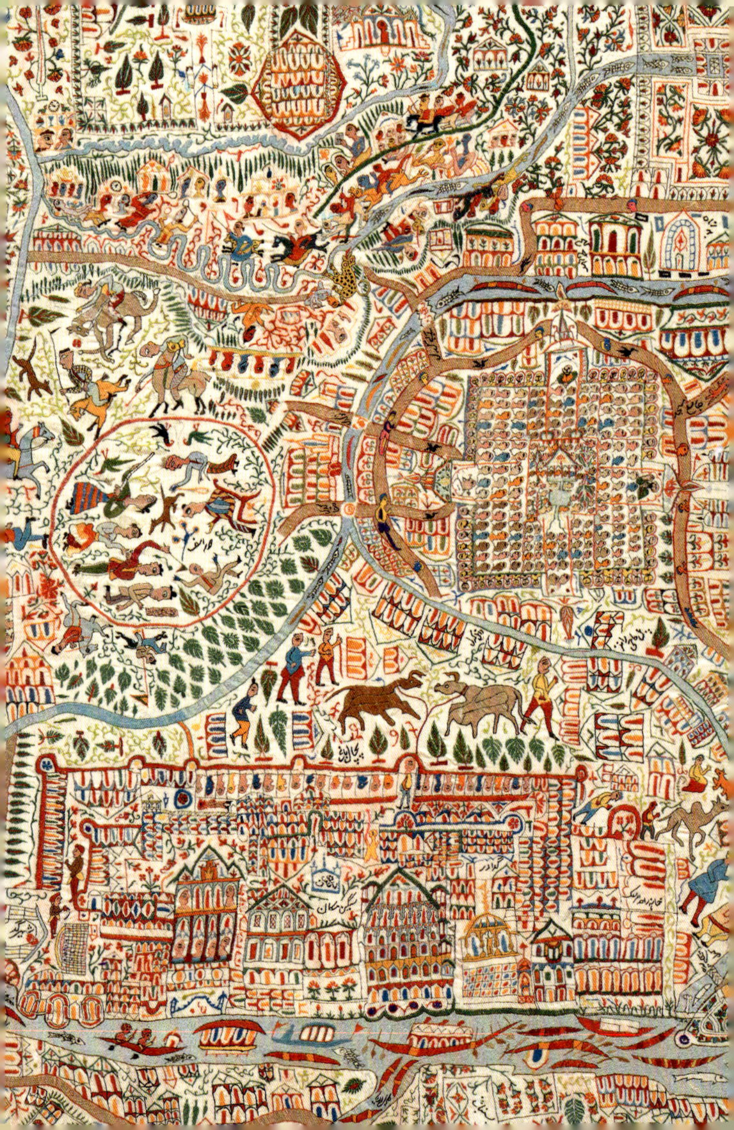

Kashmir region, Jammu and Kashmir, India
Map Shawl, second half of 19th century (detail)
Goat hair (pashm), embroidered; 76½ × 76 in.
Gift of Vickie C. Elson, M.2024.214

Map shawls, the rarest type of Kashmiri shawl, feature dense embroidered illustrations of the city of Srinagar. This example depicts life in the city under the Mughals. The Jhelum River anchors the composition, dotted with bridges and winding around the central mosque and the palace. Buildings and gardens, all labeled in Kashmiri script, teem with the activities of daily life—athletes, bathers, soldiers, religious congregants, and animals populate the scene. The map shawl is entirely embroidered on both sides using fine slanted stitches that mimic traditional twill-tapestry weave, the only known example created in this labor-intensive technique.

From Kashmir to Cashmere

Attributed to Muzaffar-'Ali (Iran, active c. 1530–50)
Nushirvan Receives an Embassy from the Khaqan, from a Manuscript of the *Shahnama* (Book of Kings), c. 1530–35
Ink, watercolor, and gold on paper; 18⅝ × 12¾ in.
Gift of the 1989 Collectors Committee, M.89.55

The *Shahnama* (Book of Kings), completed by Firdawsi around 1010, is Iran's national epic and a cornerstone of Persian literature. This folio comes from the now-dispersed copy of the *Shahnama* made for Shah Tahmasp (r. 1524–76) in Tabriz, celebrated as one of the most magnificent Persian manuscripts ever produced. Attributed by contemporary scholarship to Muzaffar-'Ali, it reflects royal patronage and artistic collaboration, with rich colors, poised figures, and a gilded landscape evoking an idealized royal court.

Persianate Arts: The Ardabil Carpet and Manuscript Painting

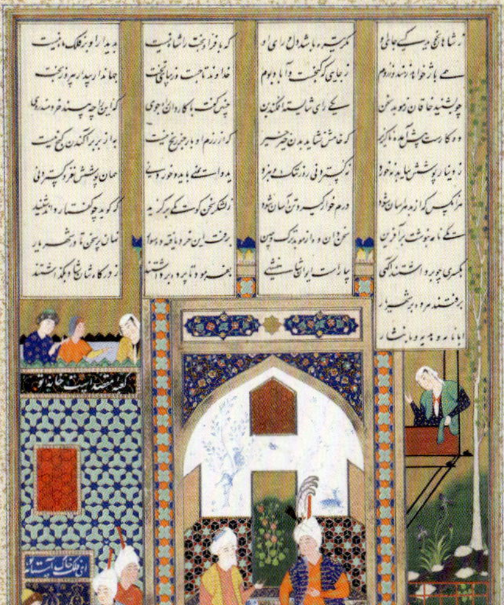

Maqsud Kashani (Iran, active 16th century)
Ardabil Carpet, AH 946/1539–40 CE (detail)
Iran, attributed to Tabriz
Wool knotted pile on silk; 283 × 157½ in.
Gift of J. Paul Getty, 53.50.2

One of the finest preserved Iranian carpets, the Ardabil Carpet was commissioned as one of a matched pair for the ancestral shrine of the Safavid dynasty at Ardabil in northwestern Iran. It is an exceptional work of art not only on account of its design, which uniquely includes depictions of lamps projecting from the top and bottom of central medallions, but also because it is signed and dated in a small panel at one end.

Persianate Arts: The Ardabil Carpet and Manuscript Painting

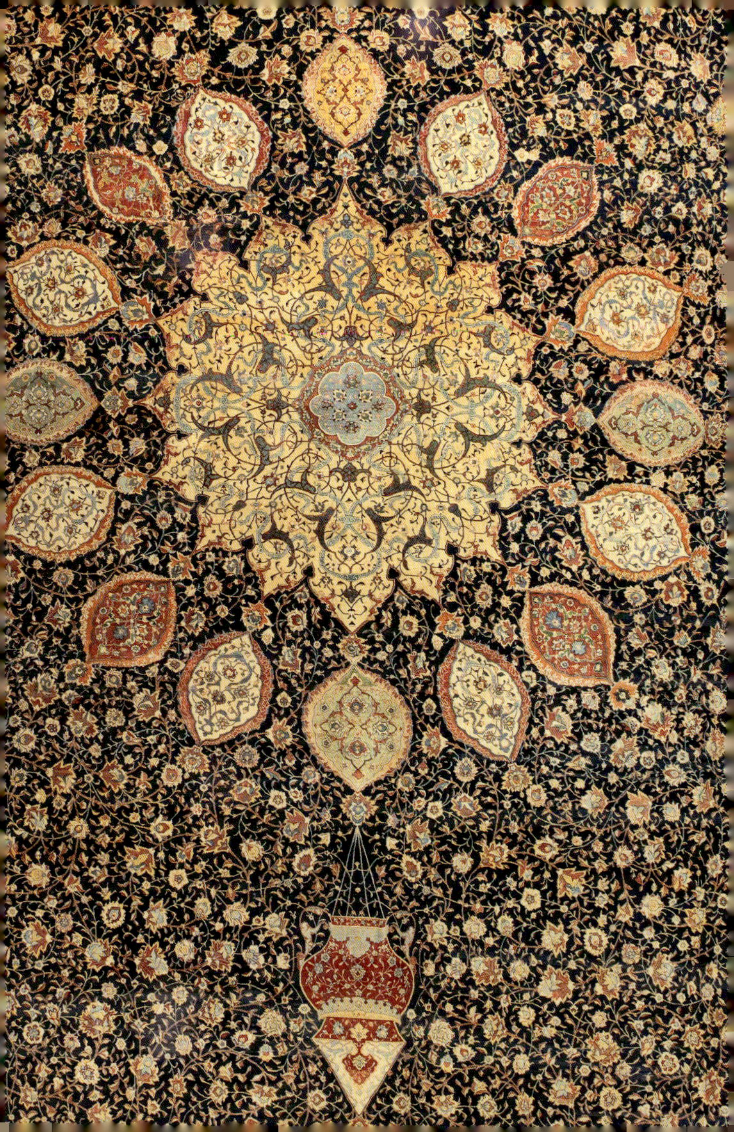

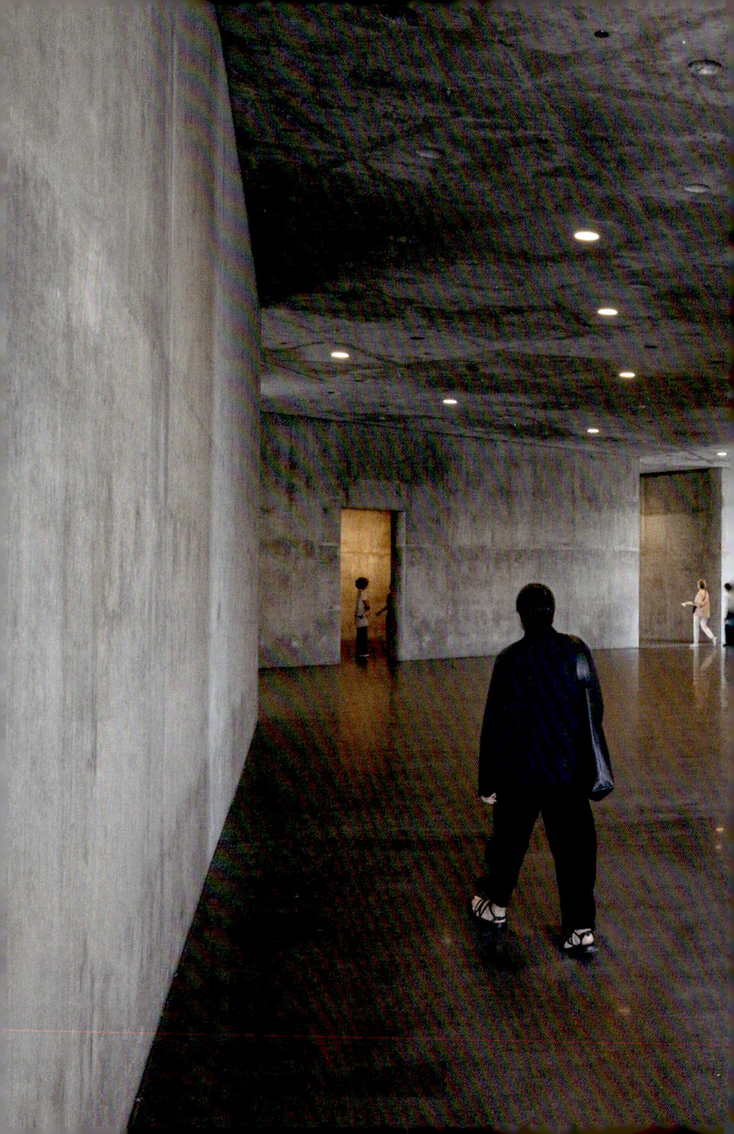

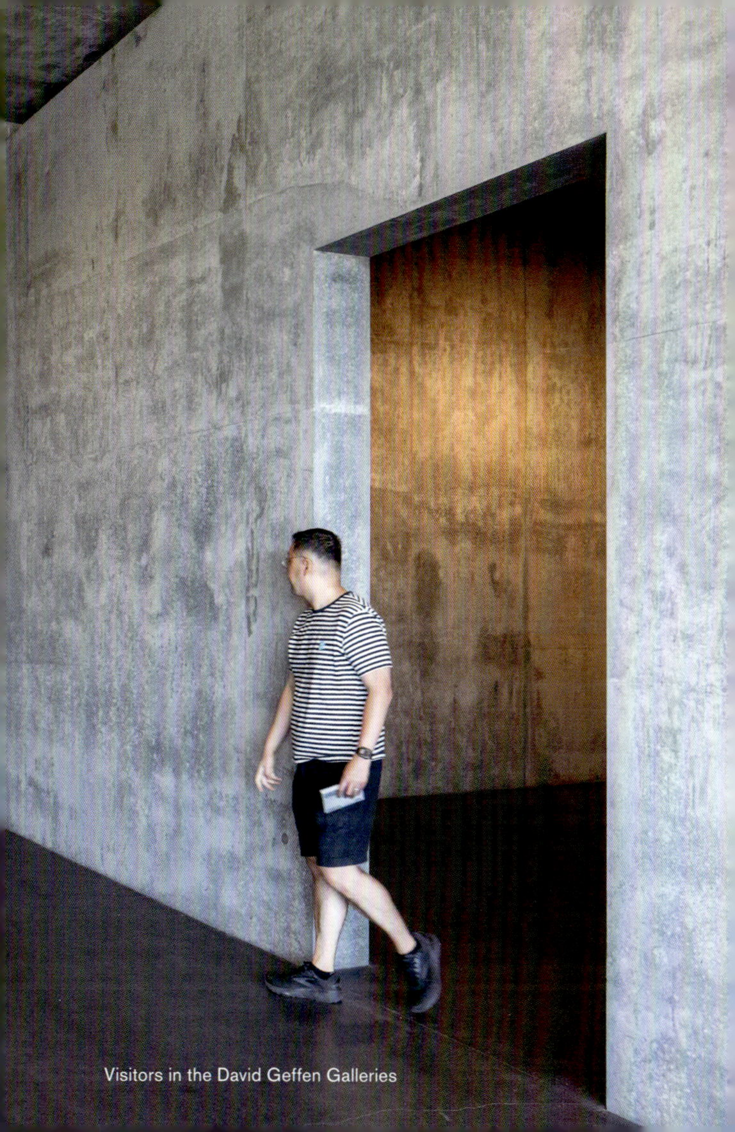

Visitors in the David Geffen Galleries

# Mediterranean Sea

1. Mediterranean Crossings
2. Luxury Arts of the Ottoman Empire
3. Islamic Art and Late Antiquity
4. Art of the Word, Word as Art
5. Model Lives in Baroque Italy
6. Classical Revivals in Europe and America
7. Print Culture: After Raphael
8. Drawn to Devotion: Piety in Practice
9. Picturing the Divine in Spanish America
10. The Iberian World: From Spain to Spanish America
11. The Ancient Mediterranean: Gods and Goddesses
12. The Ancient Mediterranean: Merging Beliefs
13. Juan Patricio Morlete Ruiz: Seascapes and Copies
14. Life and Afterlife: Imagery of Early Egypt
15. Shaping Dutch Identity:
    The Mr. and Mrs. Edward Carter Collection
16. Assyrian Reliefs

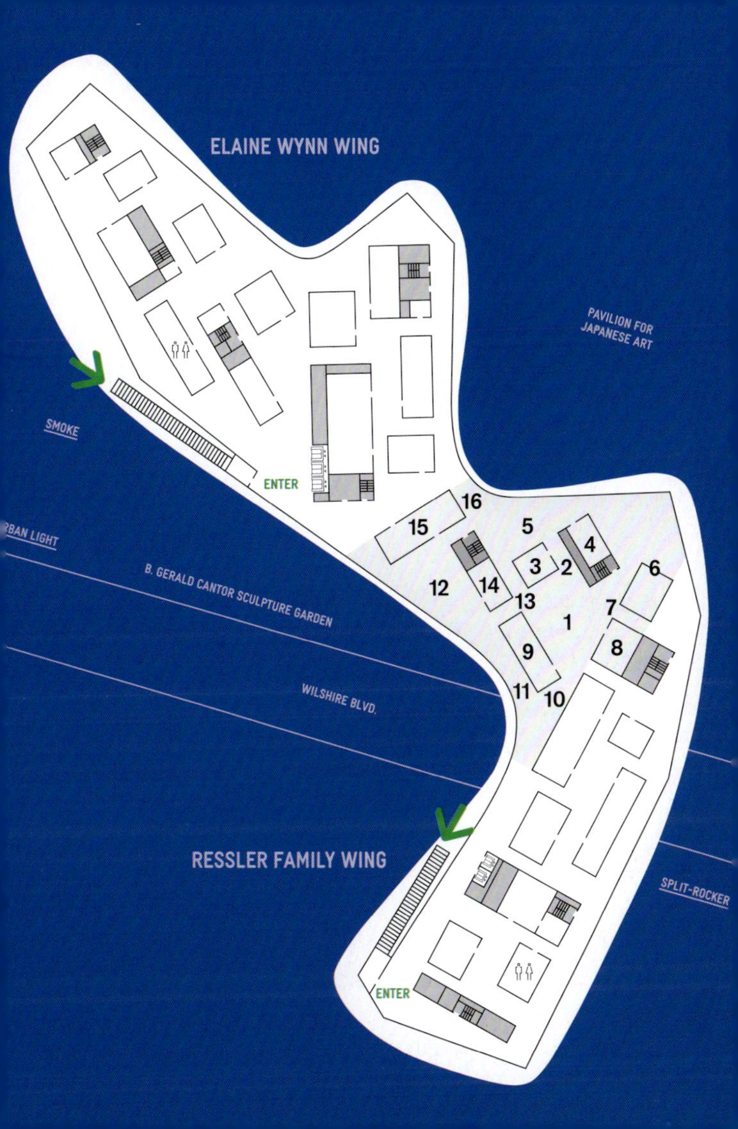

ELAINE WYNN WING
PAVILION FOR JAPANESE ART
SMOKE
ENTER
16
15
5
4
3
2
6
12
14
13
7
1
8
9
11
10
RBAN LIGHT
B. GERALD CANTOR SCULPTURE GARDEN
WILSHIRE BLVD.
RESSLER FAMILY WING
SPLIT-ROCKER
ENTER

# Mediterranean Sea

The Mediterranean serves as a transportation network between regions, an enclosed sea where three continents—Europe, North Africa, and Western Asia—have met across thousands of years of documented artistic production. Unlike oceans requiring sophisticated navigation technologies for transoceanic crossing, the Mediterranean's 2.5 million square kilometers enabled Bronze Age sailors to traverse many routes within days to weeks, creating the region's defining characteristic of concentrated connectivity.

For millennia, trade routes spanning the Mediterranean connected resource-rich areas in patterns informed by reciprocal needs, while overland routes linked coastal regions to inland communities. Port cities functioned as cosmopolitan economic and artistic hubs featuring diverse populations, multilingual merchant communities, and multiple workshop traditions. Alexandria under Ptolemaic, Roman, and Islamic control remained a Mediterranean trade center for a thousand years. Constantinople's control of Black Sea access sustained its importance through Byzantine and Ottoman administrations. Venice,

Marseille, Cairo, and contested islands such as Sicily and Cyprus served as exchange points between competing powers.

Artistic production in the Mediterranean responded to both resource abundance and scarcity. Clay deposits along Greek, Egyptian, and Anatolian coasts supported ceramic production centers—Greek black-figure and red-figure techniques, Egyptian faience, and Islamic lusterware. Scarcities drove innovation: Italian maiolica developed as a less expensive porcelain substitute; Islamic artisans perfected tin-glaze techniques compensating for limited access to precious metals; Roman concrete emerged from Campanian volcanic ash.

The artworks on display in the Mediterranean galleries offer a consideration of the region's cultural interconnectedness expressed through shared materials, techniques, and stylistic practices. They feature paintings, drawings, sculpture, and decorative arts from the Islamic world and Europe; highlights of the arts of the Spanish Americas; Egyptian, Greek, and Roman antiquities; large-scale sculpture from the United States; an elaborate reception room from Damascus, Syria, and much more.

Nimrud (Iraq), Palace of Ashurnasirpal II
Eagle-Headed Supernatural Being, 9th century BCE
Alabaster; 99¼ × 71½ × 6 in.
Purchased with funds provided by Anna Bing Arnold, 66.4.4

The interior walls of King Ashurnasirpal II's palace (r. 883–859 BCE) at Nimrud were decorated with an extensive sequence of alabaster slabs that were carved in place and originally painted. This panel depicts an eagle-headed, winged supernatural being holding a bucket and a cone standing before a stylized "sacred tree," possibly connected with some purifying or protective ritual. A cuneiform inscription runs across the center of all the panels, enumerating the king's accomplishments.

Assyrian Reliefs

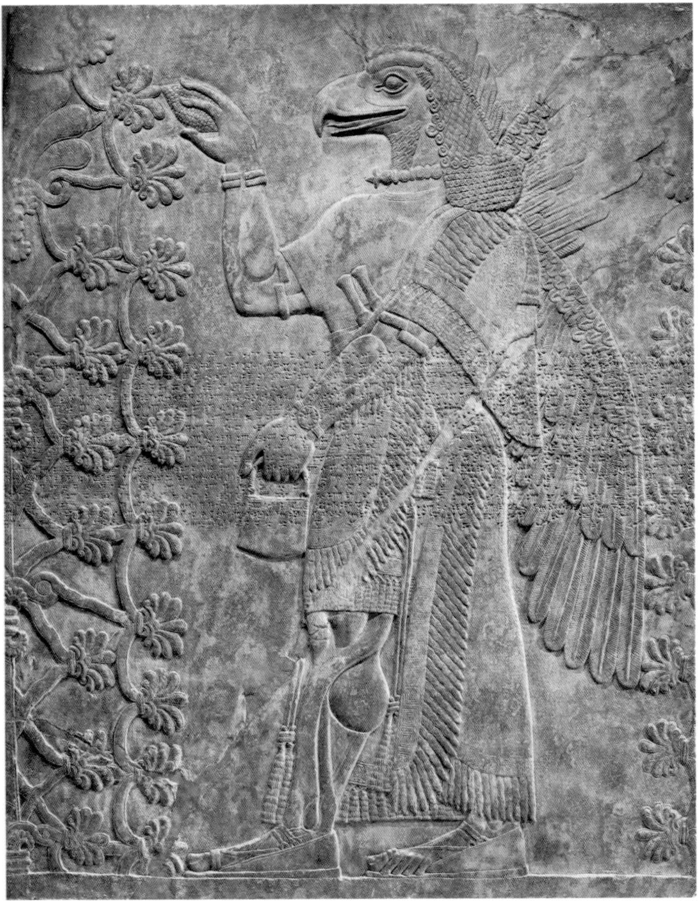

Damascus (Syria)
Interior from a Courtyard Home, AH 1180/1766–67 CE (detail)
Wood (poplar) with gesso relief, tin and brass leaf, glazed and painted plaster with stonepaste inlays, and multicolored stones; 240 × 180 × 144 in. Conservation of the room was organized in partnership with the King Abdulaziz Center for World Culture; additional conservation support was provided by the Friends of Heritage Preservation, M.2014.33

Once a prized space in an eighteenth-century home in Damascus that was demolished in 1978, this largely complete interior served as a winter reception room that opened onto a courtyard. The well-preserved polychrome wood paneling is remarkable for the vivacity of its palette. The room's cornices incorporate detailed depictions of platters of fruit, nuts, and perhaps baklava, which must have stimulated the appetites of visitors awaiting similar refreshments.

Mediterranean Crossings

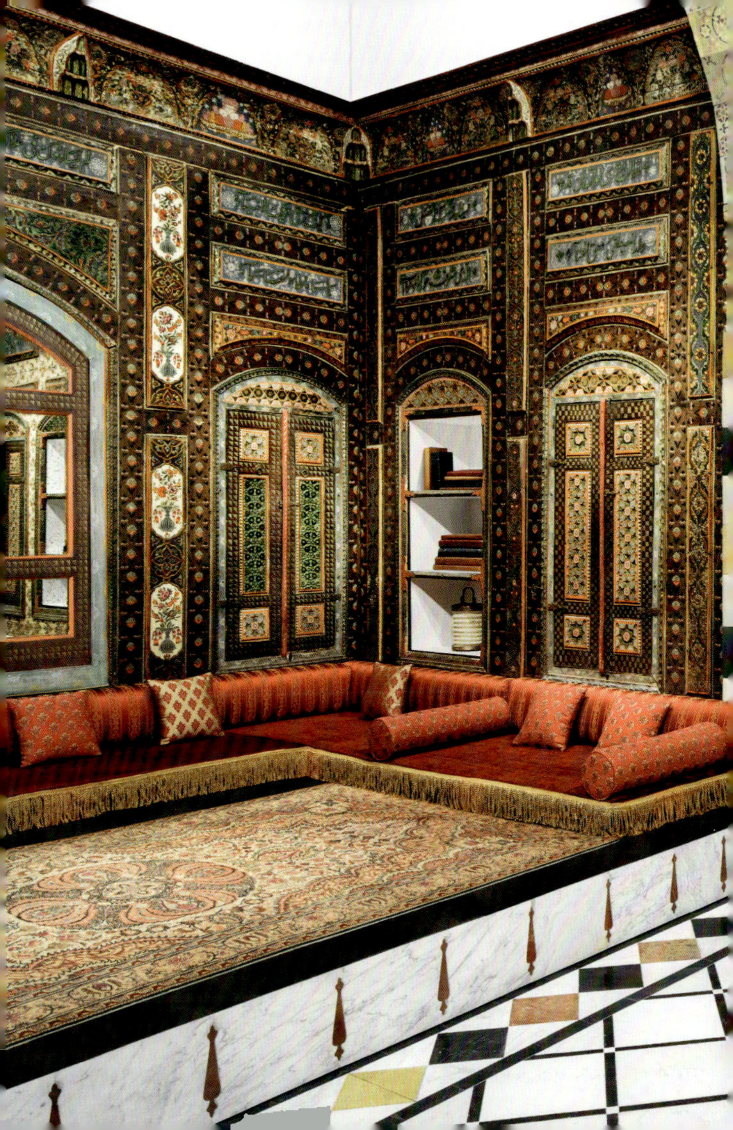

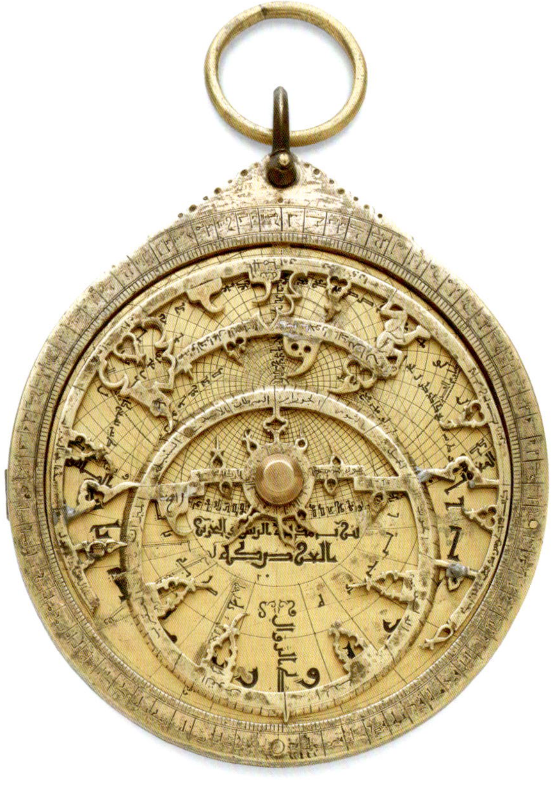

Muhammad ibn ‘Abd al-‘Aziz al Khama’iri (Spain, active 13th century)
Astrolabe, AH 624/1226–27 CE
Gilded copper alloy; 8⅜ × 5½ × 1⅛ in.
Gift of Carolyn Merchant, M.2003.116a–k

The astrolabe is an astronomical device that Muslims inherited from the Hellenistic world, refined and passed on to medieval Europe. It was designed to measure the altitude of the stars, sun, or moon and to establish different astronomical and topographic associations without resorting to calculations or formulas. It was particularly valuable in a religious context, to find the direction of prayer (qibla) and Muslim times of prayer, which are astronomically determined.

Mediterranean Crossings

Paolo Caliari Veronese (Venice, 1528–1588)
*Allegory of Navigation with an Astrolabe*, 1555–60
Oil on canvas; 80 × 44⅜ in.
Gift of The Ahmanson Foundation, M.74.99.1

A bearded and muscular figure leans against a classical column clutching an astrolabe, a device that plots the position of the stars. This and the neighboring picture in the galleries (of a clothed figure with a cross-staff) are allegorical representations of navigation, critical for Venetians whose commercial and military success was tied to the sea. Veronese, one of the most prolific artists of sixteenth-century Venice, likely painted these pictures for a library in the city.

Mediterranean Crossings

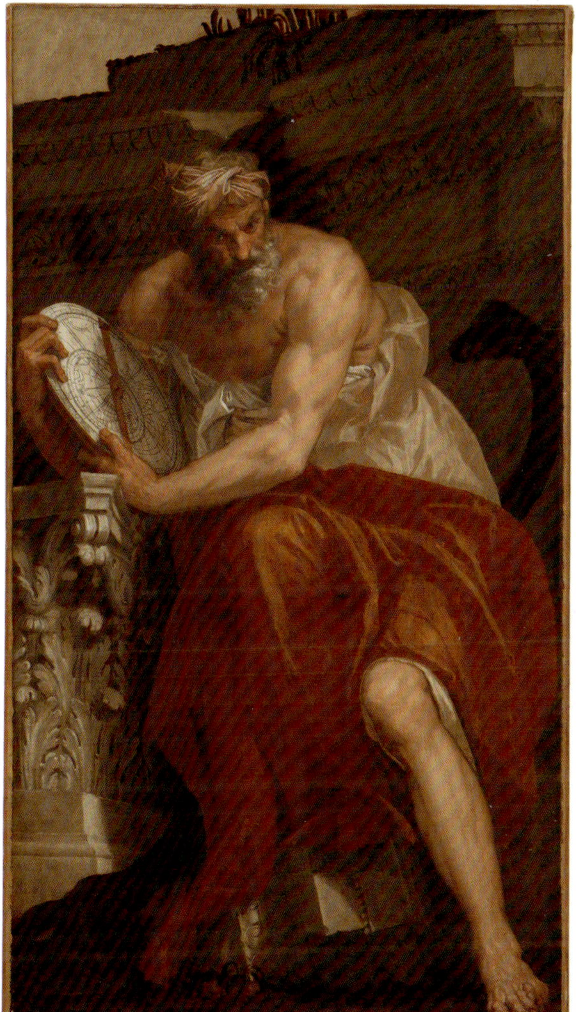

Toledo (Spain)
Panel from a Ceiling, mid-14th to mid-15th century;
*muquarnas* element, 2015 (detail)
Wood (pine), with colored pigments and silver; 79 × 52 × 30½ in.
Gift of The Faculty Club, University of California, Santa Barbara, Inc., in honor of the museum's 50th anniversary, M.2014.179.1

Between the late thirteenth and sixteenth centuries, the wealthy elite throughout the Iberian Peninsula, North Africa, and parts of the Americas colonized by Spain decorated their palaces and religious buildings with luxurious polychrome wood ceilings known in Spanish as *artesonados*. The ceilings were composed of a series of panels like this one and often featured heraldic emblems, like the rampant lion and three-towered castle associated with the kingdoms of Castile and León seen here.

The *muqarnas* element was fabricated by Taujel, S.L., a Spanish company specializing in restoration and construction of historic woodwork; it is based on historical methods of construction.

Mediterranean Crossings

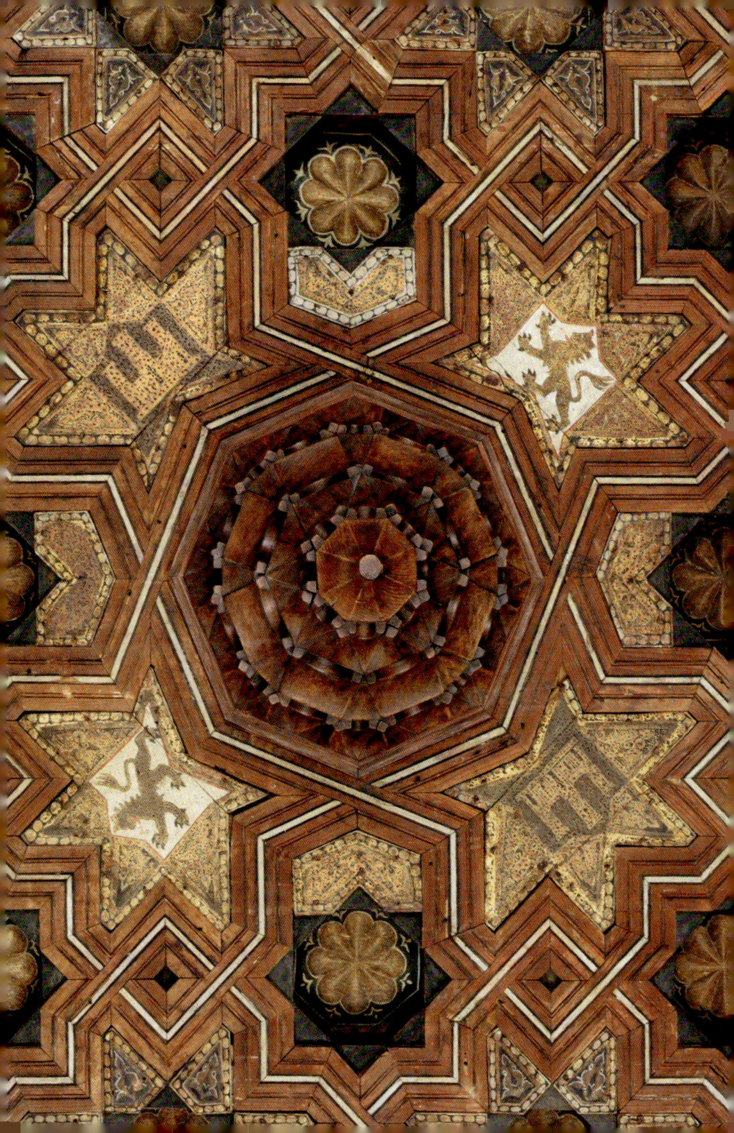

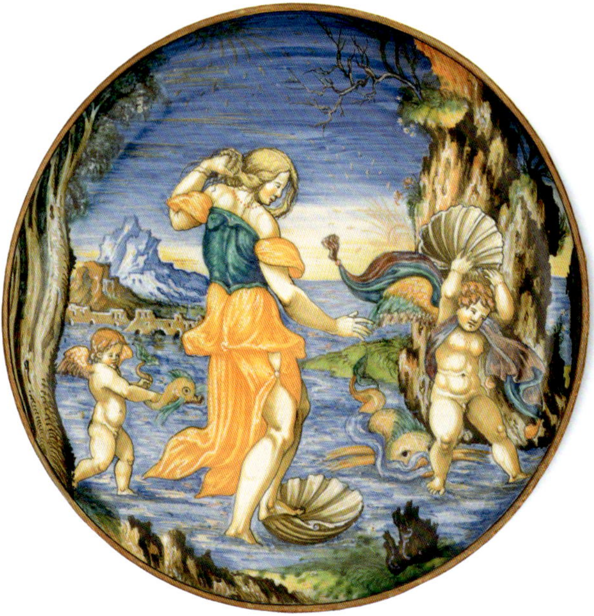

Francesco Xanto Avelli da Rovigo (Urbino, active 1530–42)
Footed Charger with the Birth of Venus, 1533
Glazed earthenware and metallic oxide pigments (maiolica); diameter: 11⅞ in.
William Randolph Hearst Collection, 50.9.17

In the fifteenth to early sixteenth century, Urbino became a center for producing maiolica, a type of earthenware ceramic covered with tin-opacified glaze and painted with bright colors. Xanto, one of Urbino's most distinctive and prolific maiolica painters, illustrated this narrative (*istoriato*) plate depicting the birth of Venus, the goddess of love. Painted tableware entertained an educated elite, who would have recognized and discussed the mythological scenes while dining in the Italian countryside.

Mediterranean Crossings

Albrecht Dürer (Nuremberg, 1471–1528)
*Saint Jerome in His Study*, 1514
Engraving; 9¾ × 7⅜ in.
Gift of the 2012 Collectors Committee, with additional funds provided by the Prints and Drawings Council and Philippa Calnan, M.2012.31

One of Albrecht Dürer's *Meisterstiche*, or Master Engravings, this print evokes ideal scholarly and spiritual reflection. Seated at his writing table, the learned saint works with divine guidance. In the foreground, a lion—tamed after Jerome removed a thorn from its paw, symbolizing the triumph of wisdom over wildness—slumbers peacefully, alongside a dog. Using only engraved lines and black ink, Dürer conjures an astonishing range of tones and textures, from filtered daylight to furry pelts.

Mediterranean Crossings

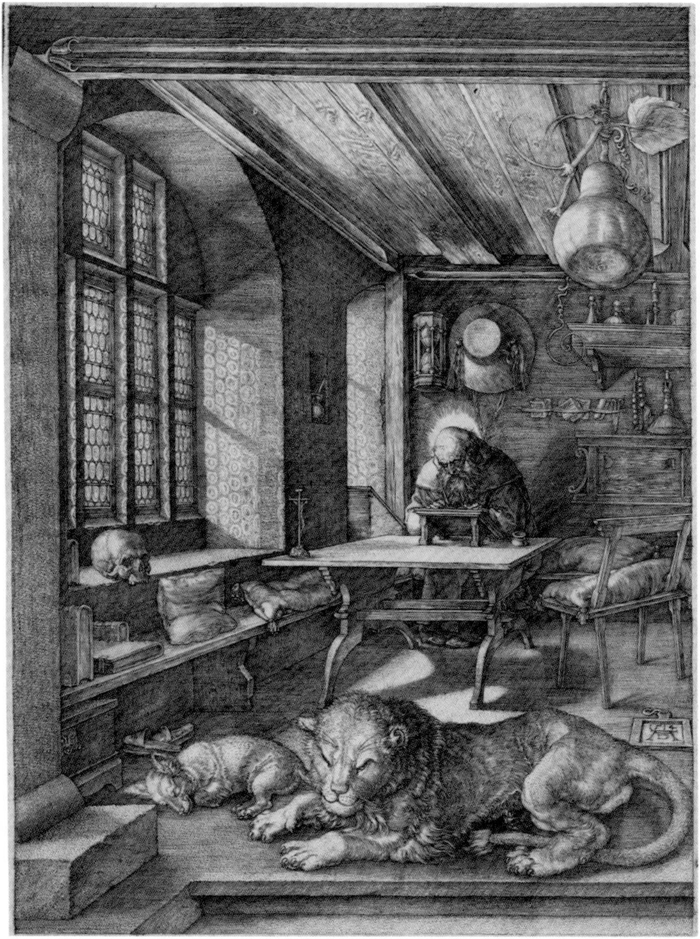

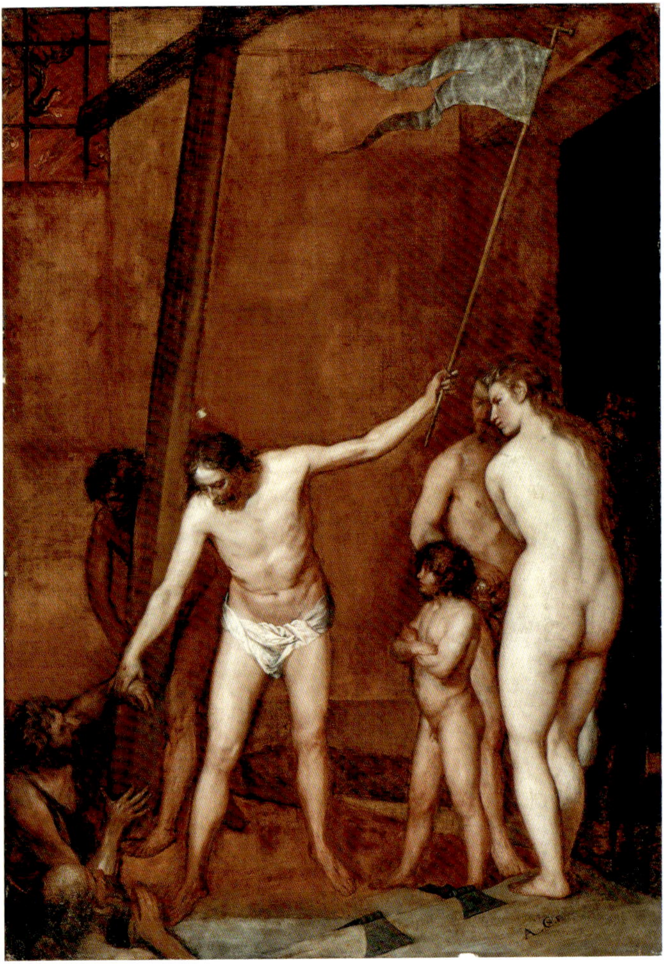

Alonso Cano (Granada, 1601–1667)
*Christ in Limbo*, c. 1655
Oil on canvas; 66 × 47½ in.
Gift of Bella Mabury, M.48.5.1

Alonso Cano, a sculptor and painter by training, depicts the moment when Christ, holding a banner of salvation, hoists a saint from the depths of the underworld. Remarkably, despite the image's powerful religious significance, the artist has also included the figure of a female nude with long flowing hair, her back to the viewer. Cano, who moved to Madrid in 1638, was likely inspired by Italian paintings of classical nudes in the collection of Spanish king Philip IV.

Mediterranean Crossings

Vera Lutter (Germany, b. 1960, active United States)
*Piazza Leoni, Venice, XIV, November 20, 2005*, 2005
Gelatin silver print; 83¼ × 56 in.
The Sir Mark Fehrs Haukohl Photography Collection at the Los Angeles County Museum of Art and the Brooklyn Museum, M.2023.149.12

Vera Lutter's photographs of Venice transform the city's luminous beauty into spectral, timeless visions. Converting a room into a camera obscura by blacking out the windows, she captured long exposures directly onto photographic paper, resulting in negatives that invert light and shadow. The canals, palazzi, and skies appear ghostly and ethereal, as if suspended between presence and memory. In Lutter's hands, Venice becomes both subject and metaphor—an image of transience, reflection, and the fragile persistence of light itself.

Mediterranean Crossings

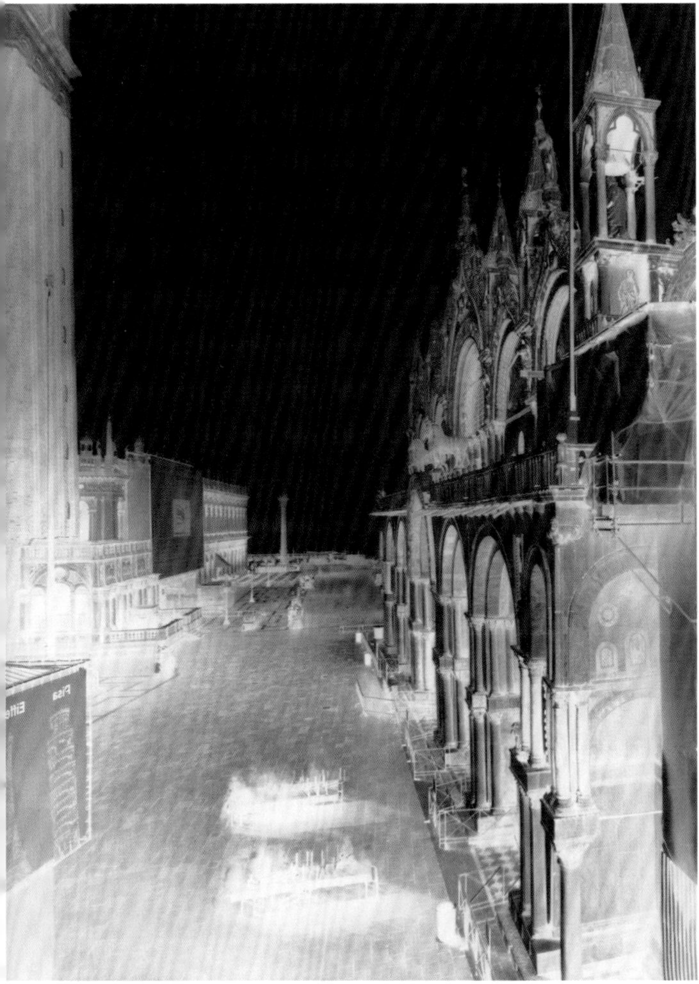

Iznik (Turkey)
Tile, c. 1580–90 (detail)
Fritware, underglaze-painted; 11¼ × 12 × ⅝ in.
Purchased with funds provided by Phil Berg, M.2000.31

Ceramic tableware and tile revetment made in Iznik, in western Turkey, are among the most renowned and influential arts of the Ottoman period. This magnificent and rare surviving tile, with sumptuous flowers and lower border painted to imitate breccia marble, probably comes from the living quarters of Sultan Murad III (r. 1574–95) at the Topkapı Palace, Istanbul, which suffered a devastating fire in 1665. On that account, some of the remaining tiles were dispersed.

Luxury Arts of the Ottoman Empire

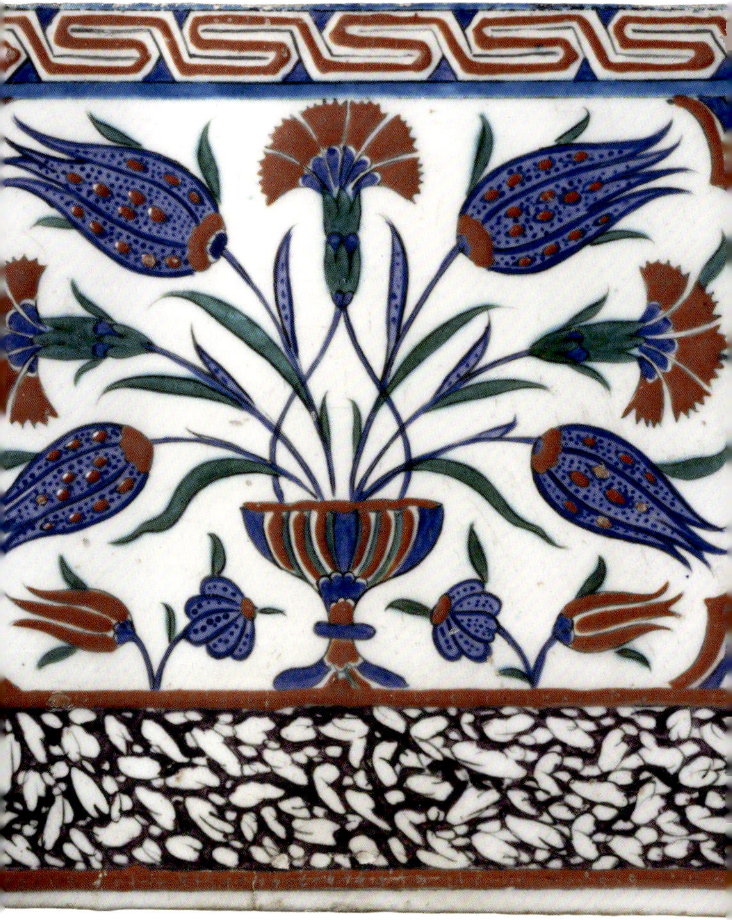

Egypt or Syria
Bracelet, 11th century
Gold, set with rubies and emeralds; diameter: 4⅝ in.
Gift of the Art Museum Council, AC1997.58.1

Just as today, jewelry played an important role in the lives of women in Egypt and Syria under the Fatimid dynasty (969–1171), not only as personal adornment but also as an indicator of affluence and social standing. Surviving trousseau lists indicate that jewelry was the most valuable component of a bride's dowry. Large bracelets such as this one, likely once part of a matched pair, were a spectacular form of wearable wealth and financial security.

Islamic Art and Late Antiquity

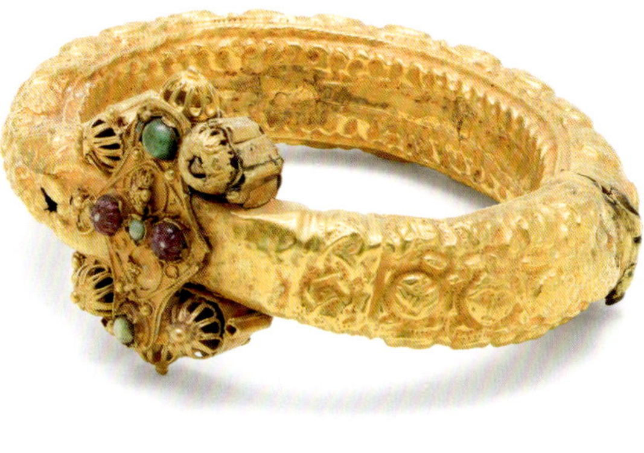

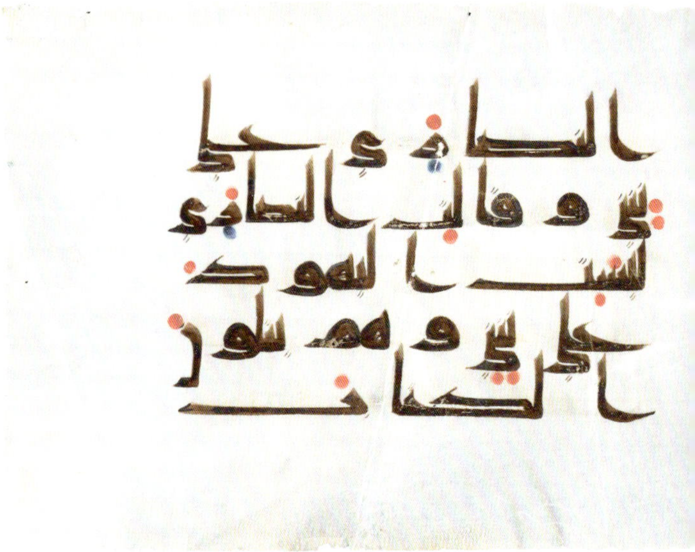

The earliest surviving Qur'an manuscripts, from the second half of the seventh century, were written in a simple form of Arabic script that lacks symbols for short vowels and certain consonants. Scribes of the eighth and ninth centuries gradually introduced a system to mark these letter sounds. The addition

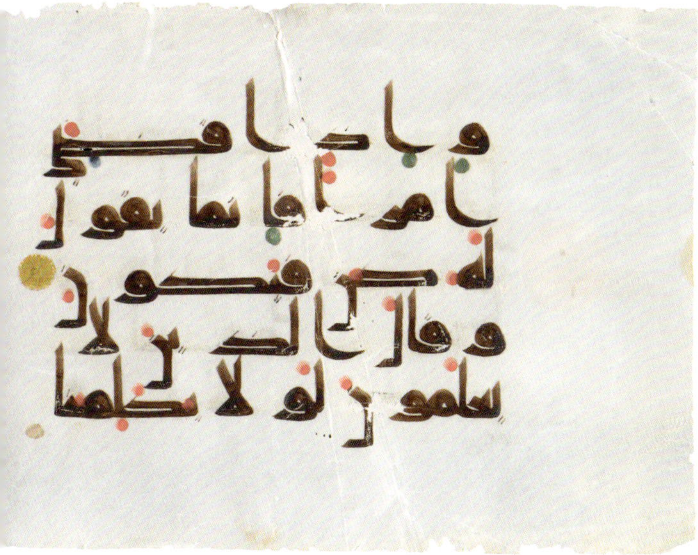

of colored dots and tiny strokes to distinguish certain consonants on this folio reflect this development and help to ensure an accurate recitation of the scripture.

Islamic Art and Late Antiquity

Iraq
Double Folio from a Manuscript of the Qur'an (2:113; 2:113 and 2:116–117; 2:117–118), 9th century
Ink, colors, and gold on parchment; 8¾ × 24½ in.
The Madina Collection of Islamic Art, gift of Camilla Chandler Frost, M.2002.1.349

Egypt or Syria
Hanging Lamp, mid-14th century
Glass, enameled and gilded; 13⅝ × 11¼ in.
William Randolph Hearst Collection, 50.28.4

Spectacular glass lamps such as this one were produced for the many great religious monuments built in fourteenth-century Cairo under the Mamluk dynasty (1250–1517). The Arabic text on the lower section indicates that it was made on the order of Amir Shaykhu, probably for his mosque complex. As is typical and especially appropriate, it is inscribed on the neck with the beginning of a well-known verse from the Qur'an, the Verse of the Light (24:35).

Art of the Word, Word as Art

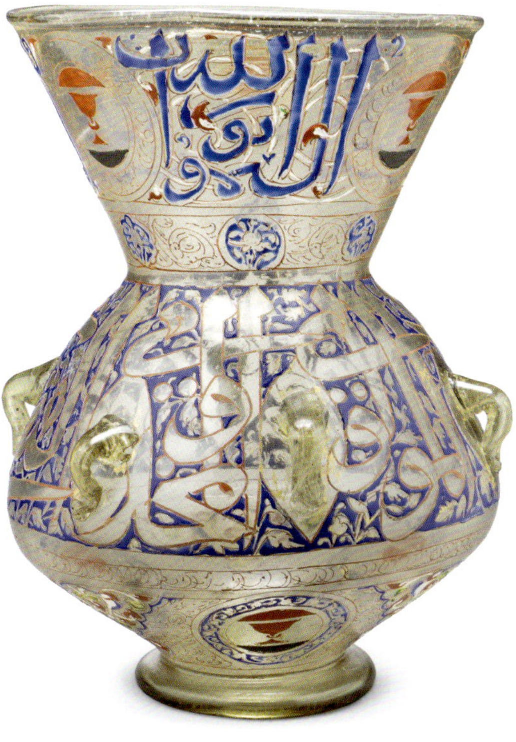

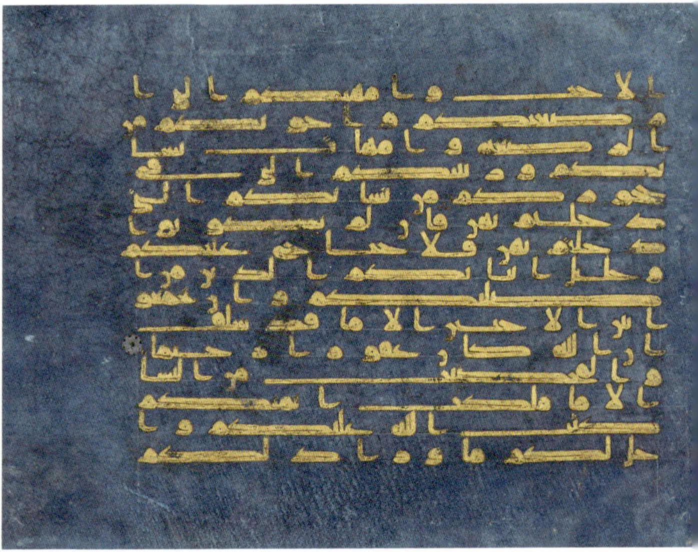

Attributed to Qairawan (Tunisia)
Folio from a Manuscript of the Qur'an (4:23–24; 4:24–25),
late 9th–early 10th century
Gold and silver on indigo-colored parchment; 19⅜ × 24 in.
The Nasli M. Heeramaneck Collection, gift of Joan Palevsky, M.86.196

With its distinctive blue color and use of gold and silver for the kufic script, this page can be identified as part of a spectacular manuscript known as the Blue Qur'an, a multivolume codex that is dispersed among several collections. Here, the entire text is sumptuously rendered in gold, while silver rosettes (now tarnished) separate each verse, the precious metals adding luminosity and contrast to the deep blue of the page, worthy of divine revelation.

Art of the Word, Word as Art

Nasser Al Salem (Saudi Arabia, b. 1984)
*Whoever Obeys Allah, He Will Make for Him a Way Out*, 2012
Corian; 47¼ × 36½ × 5⅛ in.
Purchased with funds by an anonymous donor, M.2015.99

Influenced by Muslim faith and tradition, Nasser Al Salem has developed a unique approach to writing, often employing nontraditional mediums such as neon and video, resulting in multivalent and engaging works. Here, corian is used to execute a contemporary interpretation of square kufic script. Al Salem transforms the Qur'anic verse, "Whoever obeys Allah, he will make for him a way out" (65:3), into a maze, remarkably rendering the words in a way that visually reinforces their meaning.

Art of the Word, Word as Art

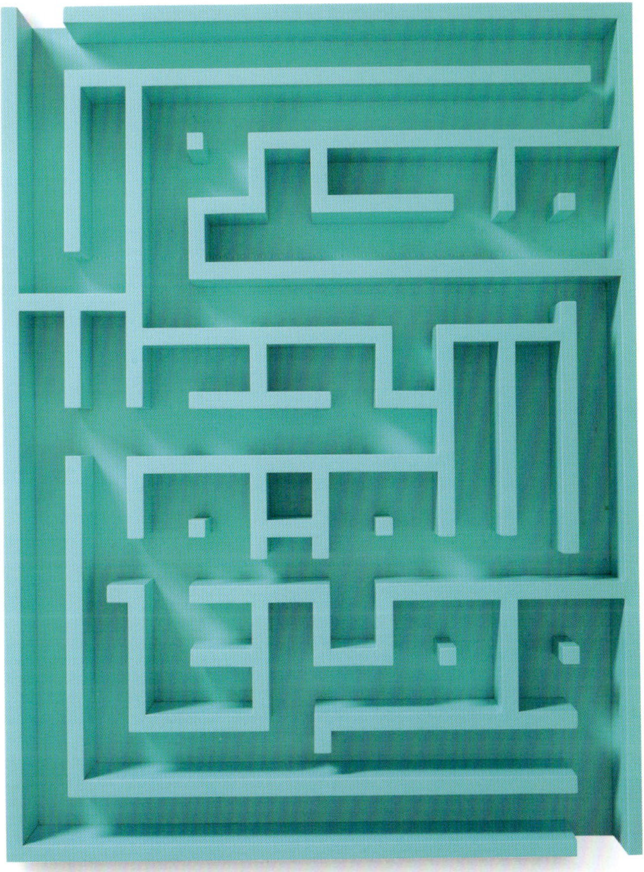

Marcantonio Raimondi (Bologna, b. c. 1470–82, d. 1527–34, active Rome), after Raphael (1483–1520)
*Neptune Calming the Tempest*, or *Quos Ego*, 1515–16
Engraving; 18 × 13⅜ in.
Mary Stansbury Ruiz Bequest, M.88.91.33

Marcantonio Raimondi, a skilled engraver, frequently collaborated with Raphael to translate the latter's paintings into reproducible prints. Here, the narrative source is an episode in Virgil's epic the *Aeneid*, in which the god Neptune—depicted with the dynamic grace characteristic of Raphael—calms the wild seas for the hero Aeneas. The print's multipart format emulates ancient Roman *tabulae iliacae*, sculptural relief carvings arranged to tell stories, often with the culminating scene at the center surrounded by smaller vignettes.

Print Culture: After Raphael

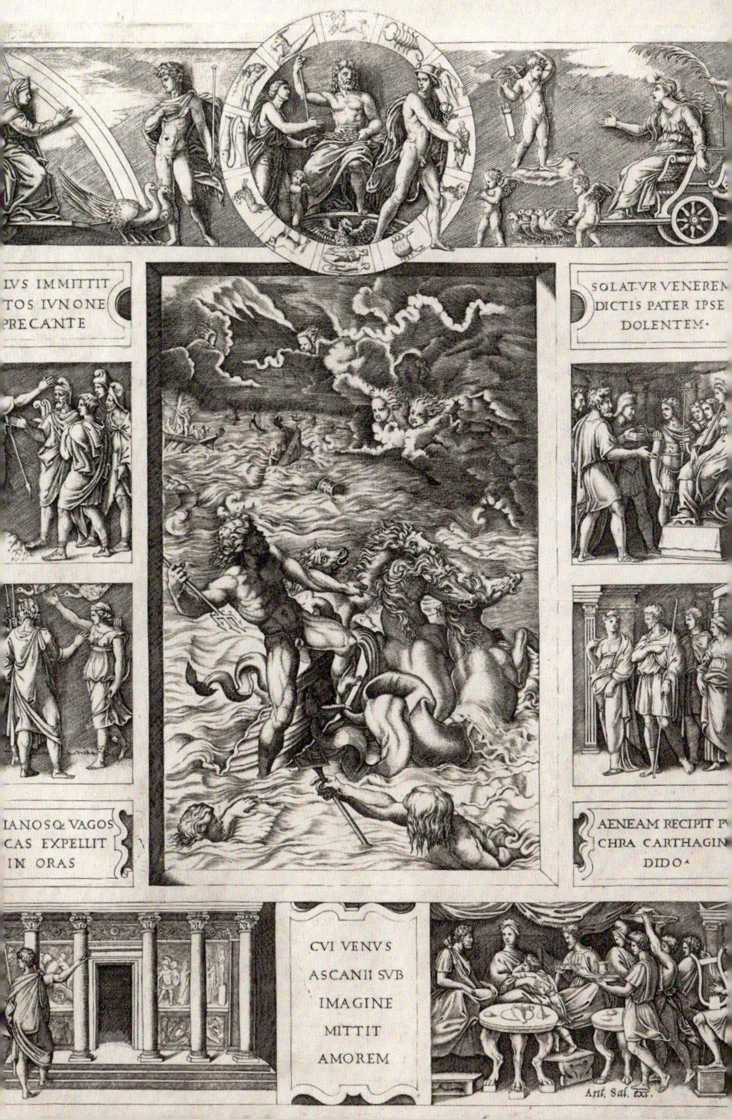
ILVS IMMITTIT
TOS IVNONE
PRECANTE
SOLATVR VENEREM
DICTIS PATER IPSE
DOLENTEM·
IANOSQ VAGOS
CAS EXPELLIT
IN ORAS
AENEAM RECIPIT PV
CHRA CARTHAGIN
DIDO
CVI VENVS
ASCANII SVB
IMAGINE
MITTIT
AMOREM
Ant. Sal. exc.

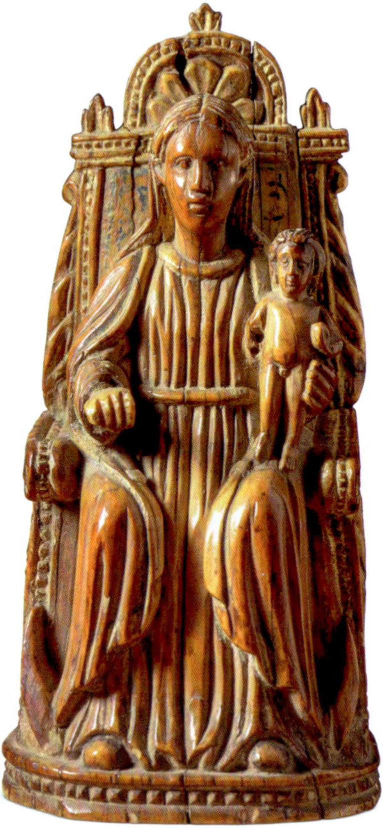

Goa (India)
*Enthroned Madonna and Christ Child (Virgin in Majesty)*, c. 1700
Patinated ivory with paint; 4 7/8 × 2 1/2 × 1 3/4 in.
Gift of Dr. and Mrs. Pratapaditya Pal, M.87.224

The enthroned Madonna and Christ Child, or Virgin in Majesty, was a favorite subject of medieval and early Renaissance theological paintings and sculpture. The Virgin sits formally upon the Throne of Wisdom as the Queen of Heaven. She is uncrowned and unveiled; her hair brushed behind her ears symbolizes her divine perception. Her crescent moon is an ancient symbol of chastity. The Christ Child holds an orb emblematic of his spiritual mastery of the world.

Drawn to Devotion: Piety in Practice

Georges de La Tour (Vic-sur-Seille, 1593–1652)
*The Magdalen with the Smoking Flame*, c. 1635–37
Oil on canvas; 46⅛ × 36⅛ in.
Gift of The Ahmanson Foundation, M.77.73

Mary Magdalen holds a skull on her lap, in front of a table with books, a cross, and a penitential whip, as she contemplates a burning candle, its long plume of smoke unfurling before her. Georges de La Tour's dramatic chiaroscuro makes her psychological state palpable in this haunting rumination on faith, penance, and mortality. The Magdalen was a popular devotional subject in seventeenth-century France; La Tour painted multiple versions of the theme.

Drawn to Devotion: Piety in Practice

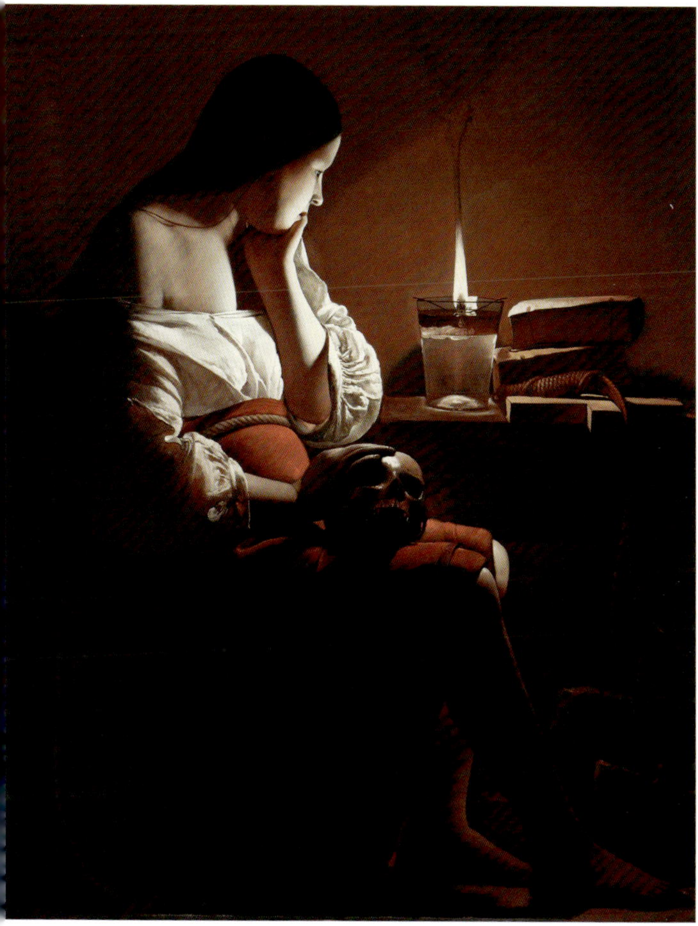

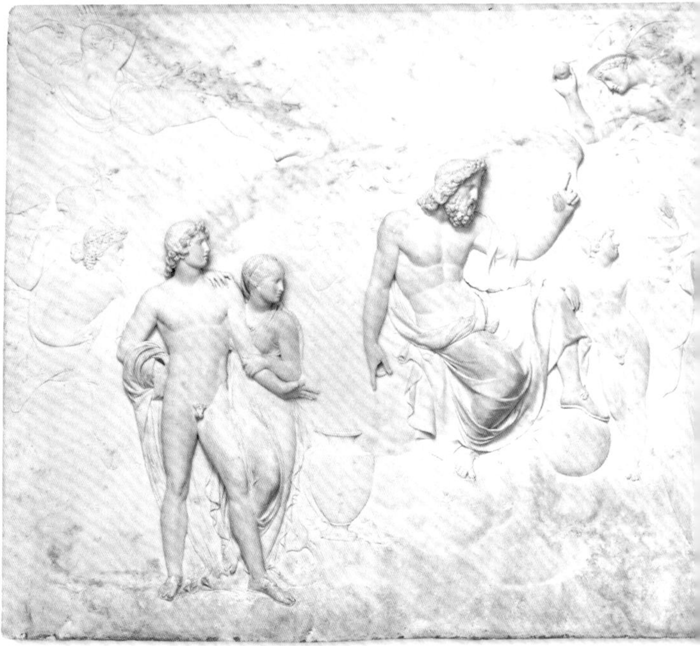

This relief reflects an extraordinary facility for marble carving and compositional arrangement. From the minimally modeled background to the nearly detached foreground figures, John Deare narrates the mythological competition between goddesses that ultimately precipitated the Trojan War, drawn from

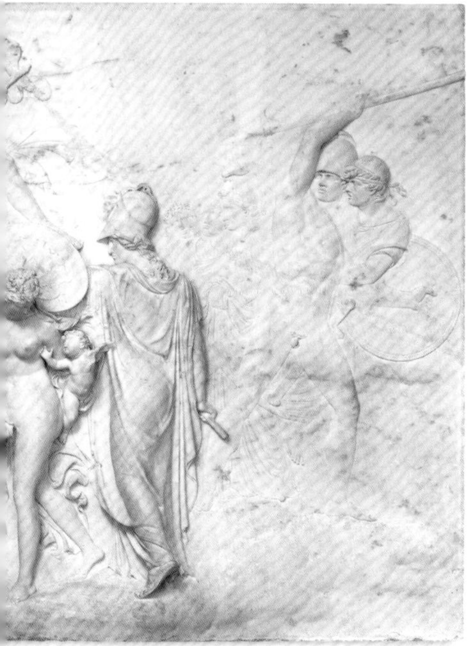

Homer's *Iliad*. Around 1800 in Europe and America, there was a prevailing belief that the study of ancient sources, including recent archaeological discoveries, could lead society to a golden age reminiscent of classical antiquity.

Classical Revivals in Europe and America

John Deare (England, 1759–1798, active Rome)
*Judgment of Jupiter*, 1786–87
Marble; 58¼ × 117¼ × 5 in.
Gift of Anna Bing Arnold, M.79.37

Rome (Italy), Hadrianic period
*The Stowe Vase*, 117–138
Marble; 47 × 40 × 30 in.
William Randolph Hearst Collection, 51.18.8

*The Stowe Vase*—so named because it was displayed for decades in Stowe House, a prominent English country residence—was reconstituted from ancient fragments, most likely by the artist Giambattista Piranesi (1720–1778), who illustrated it in his monumental and well-circulated print album of antiquities. The popularity of the vase, whose pieces were discovered in 1769 near Hadrian's Villa by British archaeologist Gavin Hamilton, was enhanced by its sheer size as well as the circulation of Piranesi's prints. The vase has inspired many reinterpretations, including two at LACMA.

Classical Revivals in Europe and America

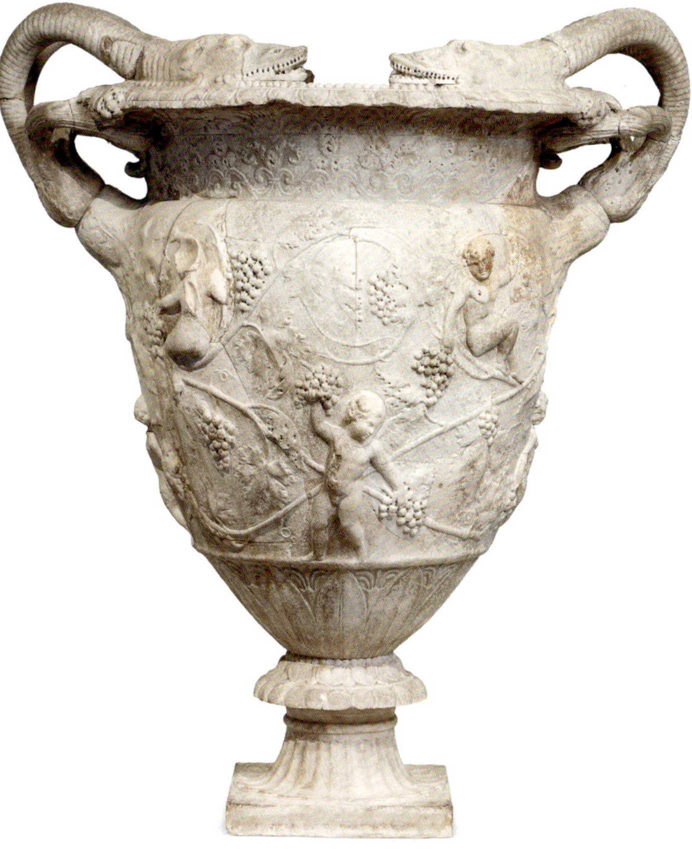

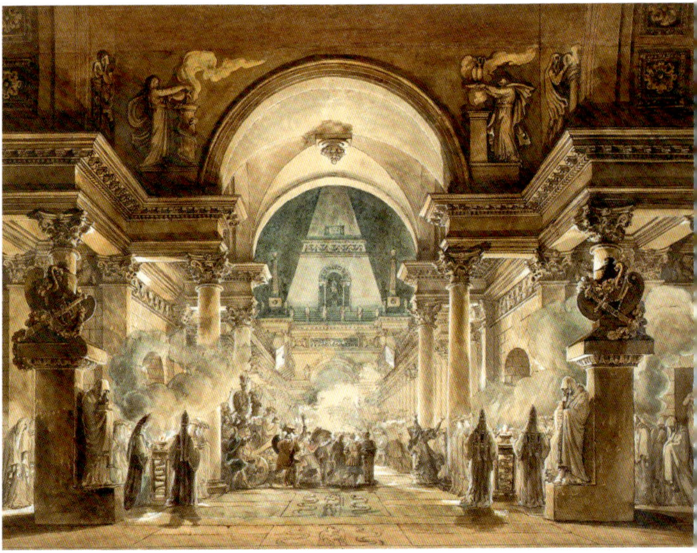

Louis-Jean Desprez (France, 1743–1804, active Sweden)
*The Funeral Procession of Agamemnon*, 1787
Pen and ink, watercolor, and gray and brown washes heightened with gouache on paper; 25½ × 37¼ in.
Purchased with funds provided by the Joseph B. Gould Foundation, M.2004.46

First trained as an architect, Louis-Jean Desprez went on to become the leading theatrical scenographer of his generation, producing set designs for the court of King Gustav III of Stockholm. His architectural expertise—augmented by collaborations with illustrators of *vedute* (Italian cityscapes), including Francesco Piranesi—is readily apparent in this masterful envisioning of an elaborate stage set for a scene from *Agamemnon*, a Greek tragedy from the Oresteia trilogy.

Classical Revivals in Europe and America

William Wetmore Story (United States, 1819–1895, active Italy)
*Cleopatra*, modeled 1858, carved 1860
Marble; 55 × 24 × 48 in.
Gift of Mr. and Mrs. Henry M. Bateman, 78.3

Frozen in a moment of contemplation, William Wetmore Story's *Cleopatra* is charged with meaning derived from both ancient Egypt and the period in which he created the sculpture. Working in Rome on the cusp of the American Civil War, Story was aligned with abolitionist causes, and his work engaged with contemporary debates around slavery and Cleopatra's heritage. Many viewers detected Black African features in Story's rendering of the queen; a deviation from more common Neoclassical representations of white, European subjects.

Classical Revivals in Europe and America

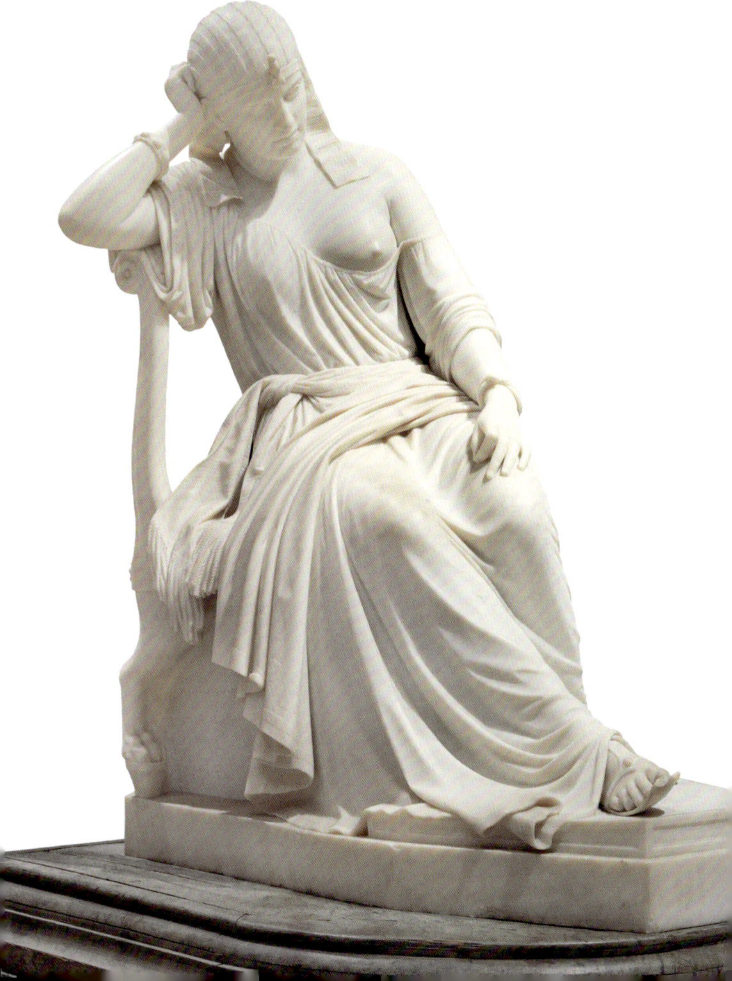

Thomas Sully (England, 1783–1872, also active United States)
*Portrait of the Misses Mary and Emily McEuen*, 1823
Oil on canvas; 44¼ × 34¼ in.
Gift of Jo Ann and Julian Ganz, Jr. in honor of the museum's 40th anniversary, M.2008.222

In this double portrait, painted a year after their father's death, two sisters glance at the viewer in a sentimental moment of familial love. With a portfolio of artwork in one sister's hands and a floral arrangement reminiscent of a Dutch still-life painting on the table beside them, the young women appear cultured and engaged with the world around them. Thomas Sully, who spent most of his career in Philadelphia, was especially celebrated for his portraits.

Classical Revivals in Europe and America

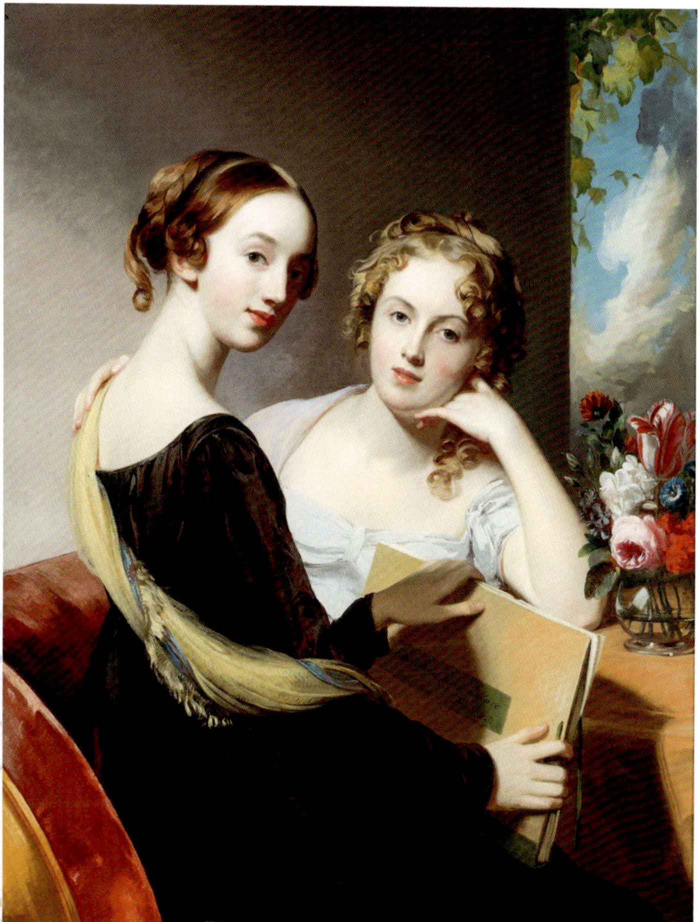

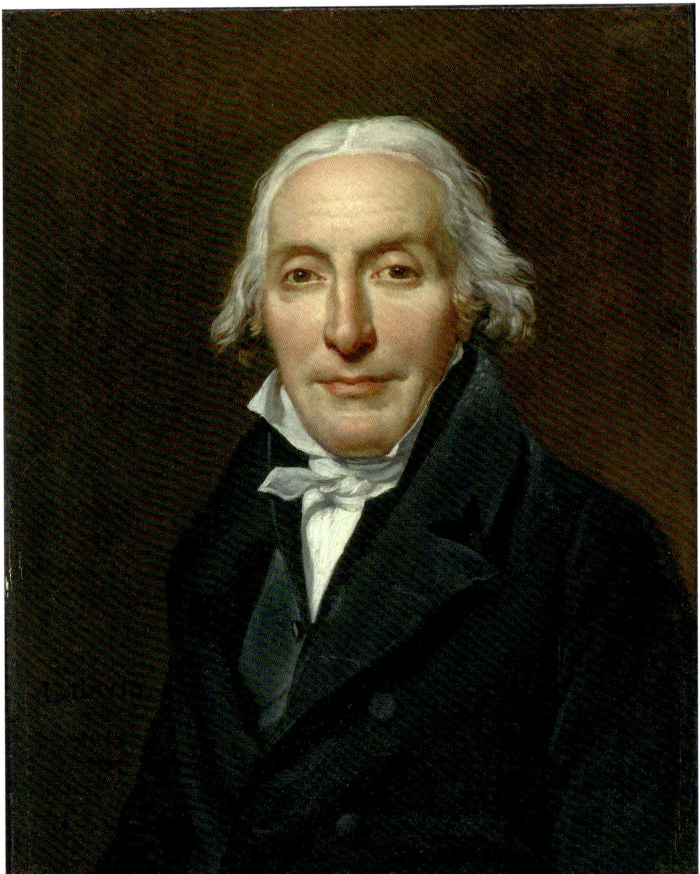

Jacques-Louis David (France, 1748–1825)
*Portrait of Jean-Pierre Delahaye*, 1815
Oil on panel; 24 × 19¼ in.
Gift of The Ahmanson Foundation, M.2006.63

This is the last canvas that Jacques-Louis David produced before leaving for Brussels after Napoleon's defeat and the restoration of the French monarchy. He captures his friend and legal counsel, Jean-Pierre Delahaye, with remarkable intimacy and directness. The sitter gazes outward with an expression that conveys both intelligence and approachability, his unpretentious demeanor rendered through precise brushwork. David likely gifted this work to Delahaye, who handled the exiled artist's legal affairs from France.

Classical Revivals in Europe and America

Guido Reni (Bologna, 1575–1642)
*Bacchus and Ariadne*, c. 1619–20
Oil on canvas; 38 × 34 in.
Gift of The Ahmanson Foundation, M.79.63

The Bolognese artist Guido Reni captures a dramatic moment from Greco-Roman mythology, when Bacchus encounters a distraught Ariadne, daughter of King Minos of Greece, who has just been abandoned by her beloved Theseus. Reni's composition suggests inspiration in seventeenth-century *tableaux vivants* (living pictures), in which actors staged important moments from theatrical performances. The picture is a standout in LACMA's exceptional collection of Italian Baroque paintings, which also includes Reni's striking portrait of Cardinal Roberto Ubaldini nearby.

Model Lives in Baroque Italy

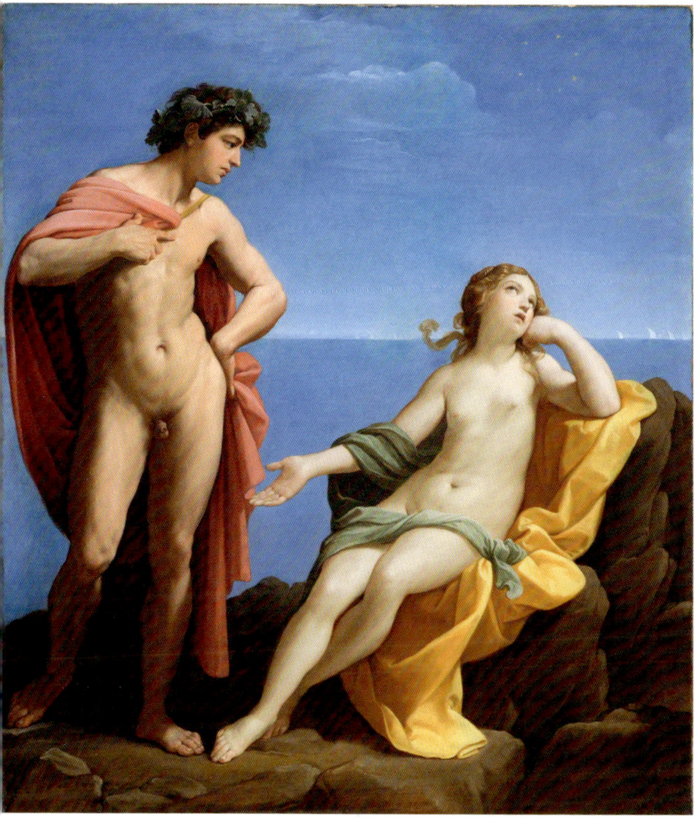

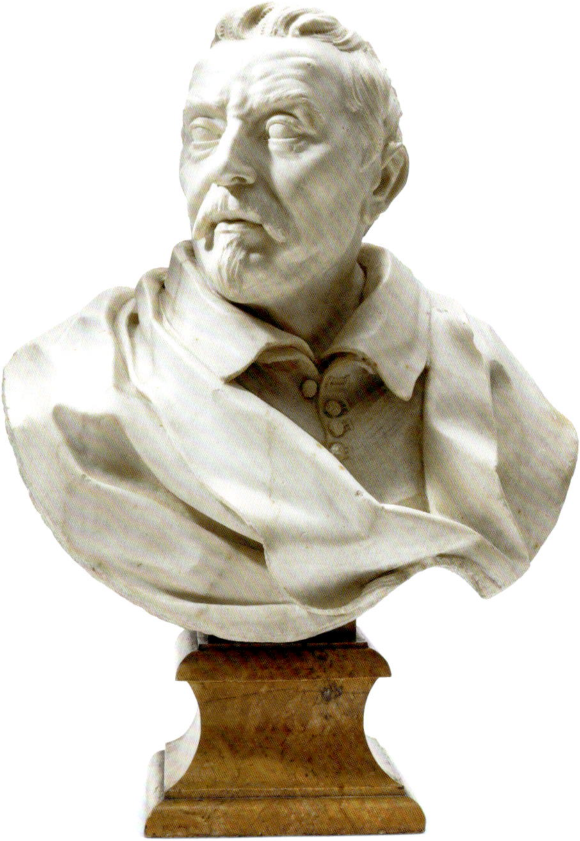

Gian Lorenzo Bernini (Naples, 1598–1680, active Rome)
*Portrait of a Gentleman*, c. 1670–75
Marble; 28 × 22 × 13 in.
Gift of The Ahmanson Foundation in honor of the museum's 50th anniversary, M.2015.4a–b

Created late in Gian Lorenzo Bernini's career, this marble bust by Italy's preeminent Baroque sculptor demonstrates a masterful ability to capture both physical presence and the passage of time. The subject's fixed gaze and furrowed brow suggest power and authority, while folds beneath the eyes and the modulation of skin on the cheeks and neck convey advancing age. The unfinished back and foreshortened composition indicate the bust was designed for viewing from below, likely within a niche.

Model Lives in Baroque Italy

Giovanni Baratta (Carrara, 1670–1747)

*Wealth*, c. 1703–8
Marble; 71 × 29 × 22 in.
Gift of The Ahmanson Foundation, M.2011.81.1

*Prudence*, c. 1703–8
Marble; 71⅝ × 29 × 22 in.
Gift of The Ahmanson Foundation, M.2011.81.2

Commissioned by the nobleman Niccolò Maria Giugni for his Florentine palazzo, these allegorical figures of Wealth and Prudence formed part of an iconographic program affirming Giugni's loyalty to the ruling Medici family. They showcase the exceptional skill of eighteenth-century Italian sculptors, like Giovanni Baratta, especially in the rendering of supple flesh and animated drapery. These works exemplify the artist's early artistic maturity and the elegant stylistic ideals associated with the Medici court.

Model Lives in Baroque Italy

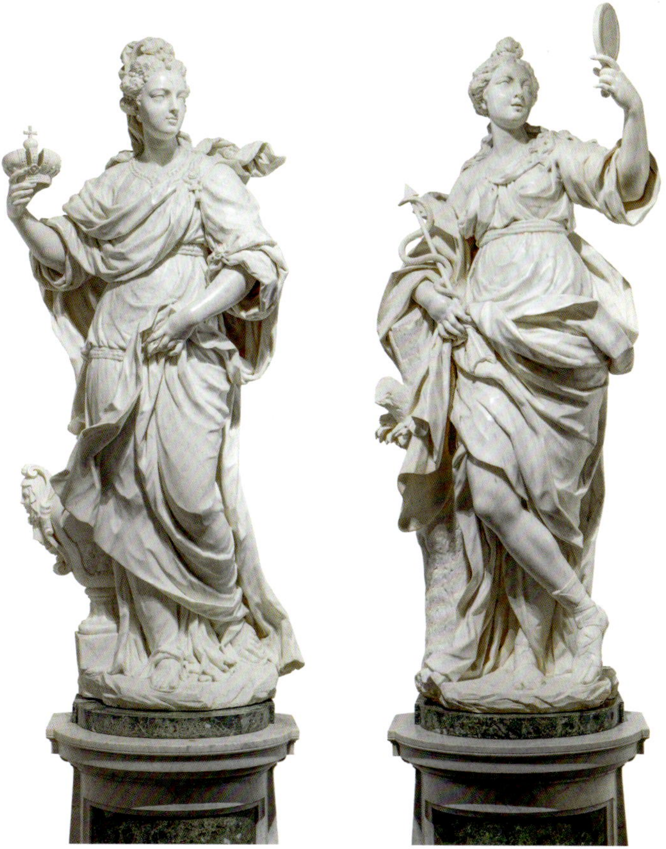

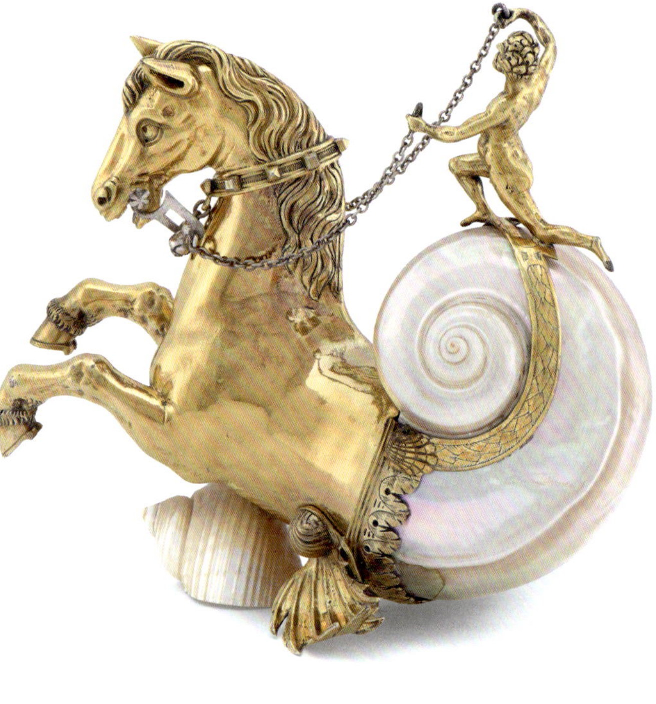

Attributed to Elias Geyer (Saxony, active c. 1572–1618)
Seahorse, c. 1590–1600
Gilded silver and turban shell (*Turbo marmoratus*); 7 × 7⅞ in.
Gift of Varya and Hans Cohn, AC1992.152.108a–b

Goldsmith Elias Geyer transforms a spiraling turban shell (*Turbo marmoratus*) into a fantastical seahorse with Neptune, god of the sea, holding the reins. Native to the Indian and Pacific Oceans, turban shells were prized for their mother-of-pearl interior. While the head of the seahorse can be detached for the hollow body to serve as a drinking cup, such vessels were more often displayed on a banquet table or in a princely cabinet of art and natural wonders.

Shaping Dutch Identity: The Mr. and Mrs. Edward Carter Collection

Rembrandt Harmensz. van Rijn (Leiden, 1606–1669, active Amsterdam)
*The Angel Appearing to the Shepherds*, 1634
Etching, engraving, and drypoint; 10 1/2 × 8 7/8 in.
Gift of William F. and Bradley I. Elterman in memory of Frances and David Elterman, M.2000.120

Rembrandt's dramatic night piece illustrates the announcement of the birth of Christ as described in the Gospel of Luke. Above, an angel appears before a shining celestial vortex, with a dove signifying the Holy Spirit at its center. On earth, the herdsmen and their animals show alarm at the heavenly visitor. The mysterious, shadowy zone Rembrandt etched across the print divides the composition diagonally, heightening the contrast between the angel's serenity and the shepherds' fear.

Shaping Dutch Identity: The Mr. and Mrs. Edward Carter Collection

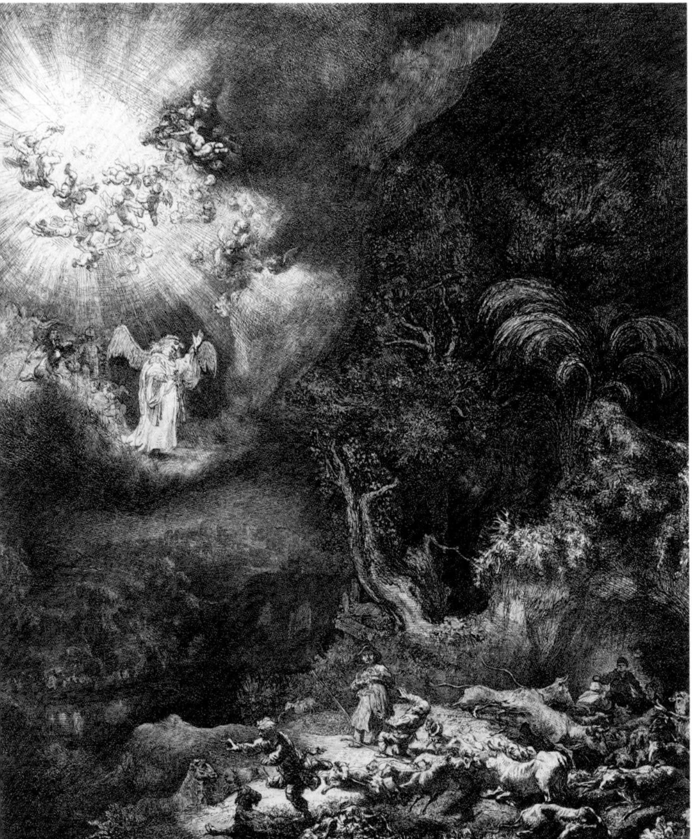

Pieter Jansz. Saenredam (Assendelft, 1597–1665, active Haarlem)
*Interior of the Mariakerk, Utrecht*, 1651
Oil on wood panel; 19⅛ × 14⅛ in.
Gift of Mr. and Mrs. Edward W. Carter, M.2003.108.2

Pieter Jansz. Saenredam's oblique view of the Mariakerk's north aisle, painted fifteen years after his 1636 visit, captures a Romanesque church that no longer exists. Stripped of altarpieces and stained glass during seventeenth-century religious conflicts, the space radiates warmth through ocher, gray, and white tones. The painting's architectural accuracy is based on the artist's meticulous measurements. Edward Carter, LACMA's founding board president, and his wife, Hannah, acquired the work in 1977; they later donated their collection of seventeenth-century Dutch paintings, among the finest in America, to the museum.

Shaping Dutch Identity: The Mr. and Mrs. Edward Carter Collection

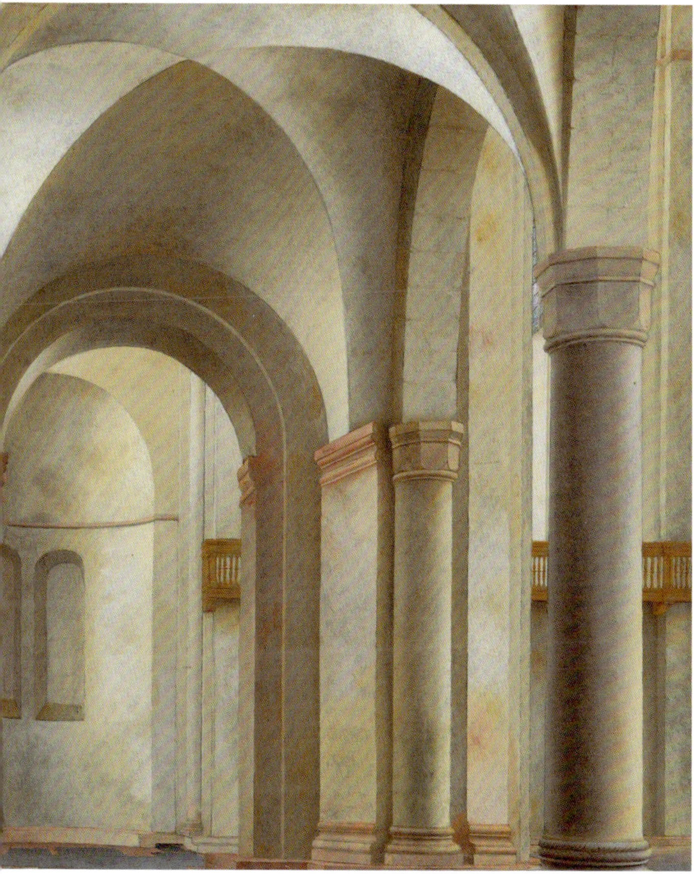

Rembrandt Harmensz. van Rijn (Leiden, 1606–1669, active Amsterdam)
*The Raising of Lazarus*, c. 1630–32
Oil on wood panel; 37⅜ × 32 in.
Gift of H. F. Ahmanson and Company, in memory of Howard F. Ahmanson, M.72.67.2

This is Rembrandt's only known painting of the miracle in which Christ raises his friend Lazarus from the dead, although he made drawings and etchings of the same subject. Painted during the early part of his career, Rembrandt's dramatic composition features Christ standing above Lazarus's tomb, while onlookers reveal their surprise at the miracle unfolding before them. Theatrically staged characters are illuminated with a bright light, while the rest of the scene is obscured in shadow.

Shaping Dutch Identity: The Mr. and Mrs. Edward Carter Collection

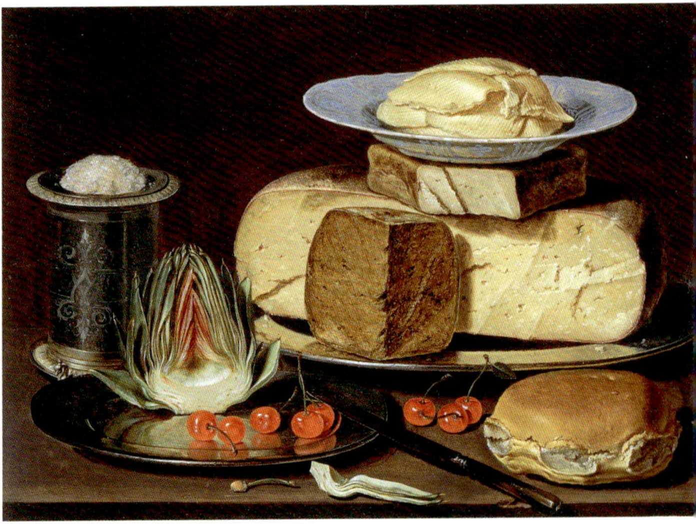

Clara Peeters (probably Antwerp, c. 1588/90–1636)
*Still Life with Cheeses, Artichoke, and Cherries*, c. 1625
Oil on wood panel; 13⅛ × 18⅜ in.
Gift of Mr. and Mrs. Edward W. Carter, M.2003.108.8

This bountiful still life showcases staples of the Dutch diet and reflects a global economy beyond the confines of its intimate domesticity. Salt—extracted first from Europe and later Africa and the Americas—was refined in Zeeland and exported on Dutch ships. It was a vital commodity used in fish preservation and cheese production. Peeters also includes a butter-filled Kraak ware plate, a type of Chinese export porcelain, perched atop cheese wedges.

Shaping Dutch Identity: The Mr. and Mrs. Edward Carter Collection

Hendrick Avercamp (Amsterdam, 1585–1634, active Kampen)
*Winter Scene on a Frozen Canal*, c. 1620 (detail)
Oil on wood panel; 14½ × 25¾ in.
Partial gift of Mr. and Mrs. Edward William Carter and purchased with funds provided by The Ahmanson Foundation, the Paul Rodman Mabury Collection, the William Randolph Hearst Collection, the Michael J. Connell Foundation, the Marion Davies Collection, Mr. and Mrs. Lauritz Melchior, Mr. and Mrs. R. Stanton Avery, the Estate of Anita M. Baldwin by exchange, and Hannah L. Carter, M.2009.106.23

The painter Hendrick Avercamp depicts life on a frozen canal during one of the brutally cold winters of the Little Ice Age, a period of cooling that peaked in Europe in the seventeenth century. Old and young pursue leisure activities such as ice skating, sledding, and colf (an early form of golf), but social distinctions are revealed in the details: an enslaved Black African child carries colf sticks and a Romani woman, from a marginalized itinerant community associated with fortune telling, reads palms.

Shaping Dutch Identity: The Mr. and Mrs. Edward Carter Collection

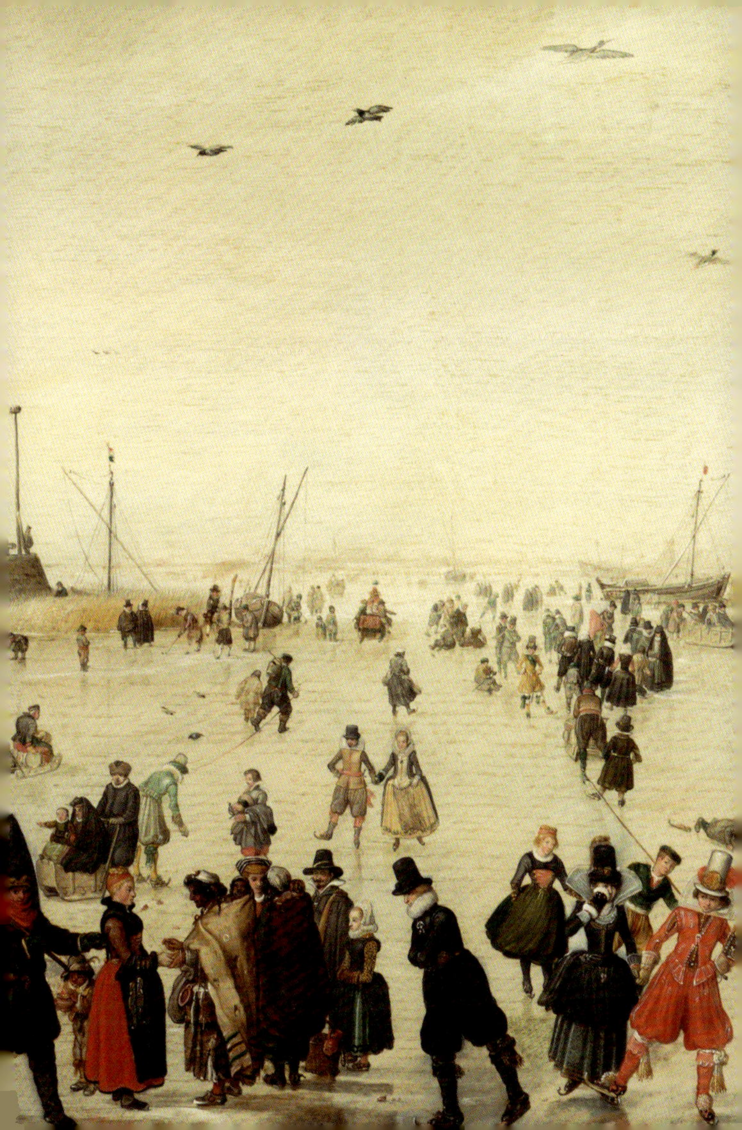

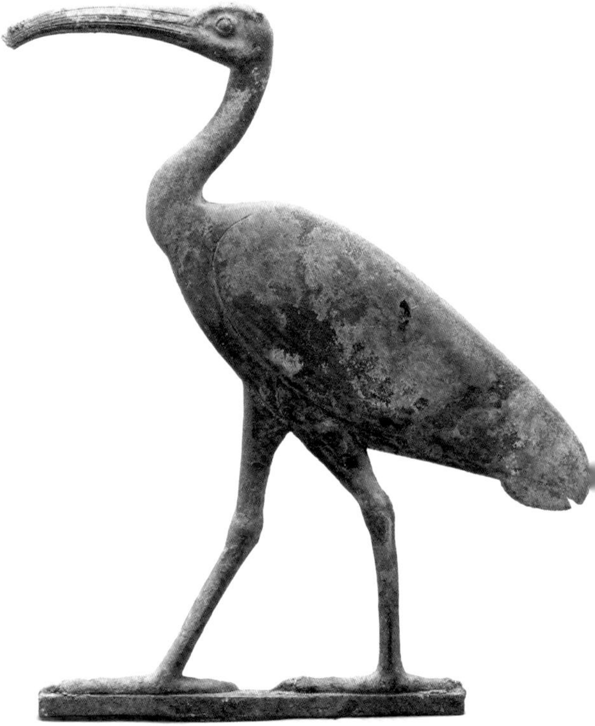

Egypt, Late Period, 26th dynasty
Ibis Processional Standard, 664–525 BCE
Bronze; 15 × 11¼ × ⅝ in.
Art Museum Council Fund, M.91.73

This bronze processional standard depicts the ibis form of Thoth, the Egyptian god of writing, intelligence, and the moon. Standards such as this represented regional deities and were carried in religious festivals, rituals, and public processions. Although frequently shown in temple and tomb scenes, surviving examples are rare. Cast by the lost-wax method, this standard once had eyes that were overlaid with gold. Its stylized feet, shown in profile, emphasize clarity and visibility rather than naturalistic detail.

The Ancient Mediterranean: Merging Beliefs

Egypt, Late Period, 26th dynasty
Bastet, 664–525 BCE
Bronze; 6¾ × 2⅝ × 4¼ in.
Gift of Varya and Hans Cohn, AC1992.152.50

The goddess Bastet, daughter of the sun god Re, appeared in ancient Egypt as both a fierce lioness protectress and a gentler domestic cat guardian of households and granaries. This beautifully proportioned bronze figure displays naturalistic details: upraised ears pierced for gold earrings, a tail curved gracefully around the front paws, and an incised collar with beaded rows and a *wadjet* pendant symbolizing health. Probably too small to contain a mummified cat, the bronze likely adorned a sacred animal coffin.

The Ancient Mediterranean: Merging Beliefs

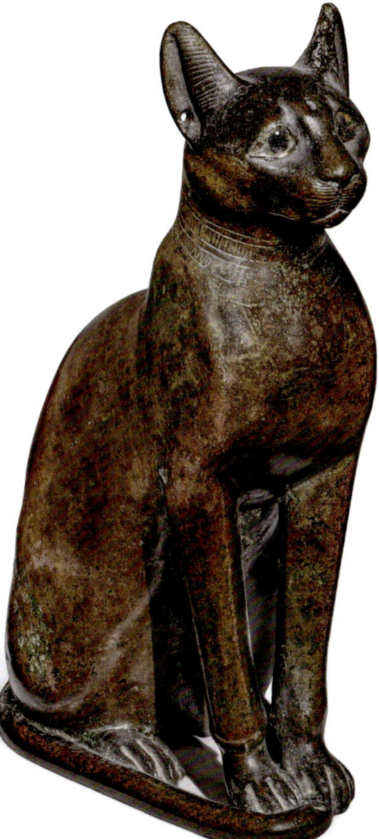

Attributed to the Deepdene Painter (Attica, active c. 475–450 BCE)
Amphora with Athena Pouring Wine for Herakles, and a Woman Pouring Wine for Dionysos, c. 470–460 BCE
Red-figure ceramic; height: 8½ in.
William Randolph Hearst Collection, 50.8.21

This amphora exemplifies the ancient Greek pottery technique known as the red-figure style, where slip (liquified clay) that blackens during firing surrounds figures that remain in the red-orange color of clay. The side of the vessel visible here depicts Athena, the goddess of wisdom, pouring wine for Herakles, the mythical figure famed for his strength. On the other side, a female follower of Dionysos, the god of wine and revelry, similarly fills his cup.

The Ancient Mediterranean: Gods and Goddesses

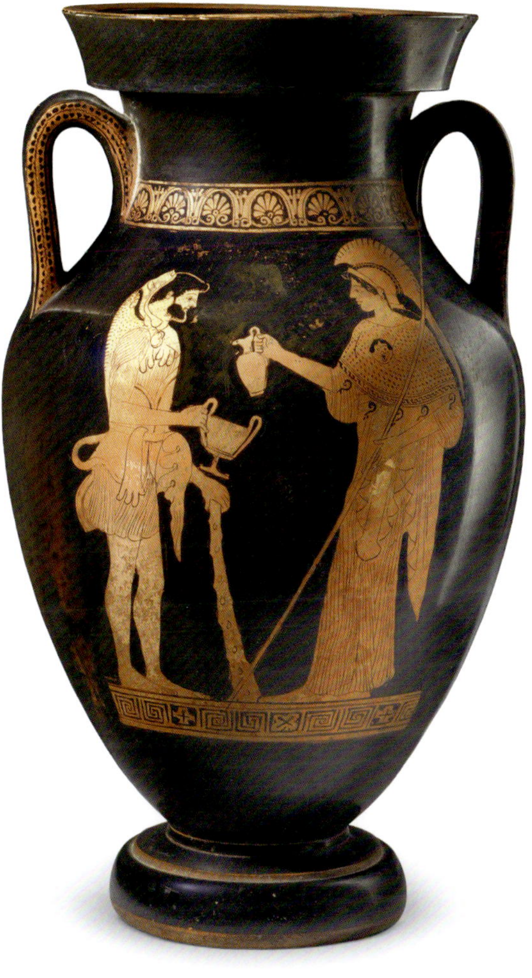

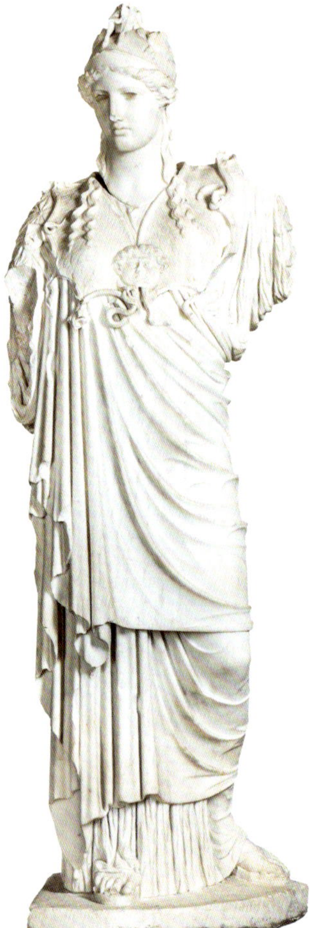

Roman artist
Excavated near Ostia, Rome
*The Hope Athena*, 2nd-century CE copy after a Greek original
Marble; 86 × 30 × 19 in.
William Randolph Hearst Collection, 51.18.12a–b

This larger than life-size sculpture of Athena represents the Greek goddess of wisdom and war. She is identified through her helmet, animal-skin cloak fringed with snakes, breastplate decorated with Medusa, and long tunic. *The Hope Athena* featured in two prominent British collections in the hundred years following its excavation near Rome in 1797 including that of Thomas Hope. In the 1930s, it was acquired by William Randolph Hearst, who gifted it to LACMA, among many other Greek and Roman antiquities.

The Ancient Mediterranean: Gods and Goddesses

Egypt
Mummy Mask, 1st century
Cartonnage, gilding, and pigments; 20 × 12 × 11 in.
Partial gift of Yves and Cynthia Courbet, and purchased with funds provided by the Ancient Art Deaccession Fund and the Ancient Art Acquisition Fund, M.2019.396

During the early Roman Period in Egypt, painted cartonnage masks formed of layered linen and plaster became the predominant method for protecting a mummy's head and face in elite burials. This well-preserved example features a youthful face gilded to imitate the imperishable golden skin of the gods. The wig displays symmetrical images of the funerary god Osiris holding his crook and flail, rows of protective cobras and deities, and adjacent jackal-headed Anubis figures reclining on shrines.

Life and Afterlife: Imagery of Early Egypt

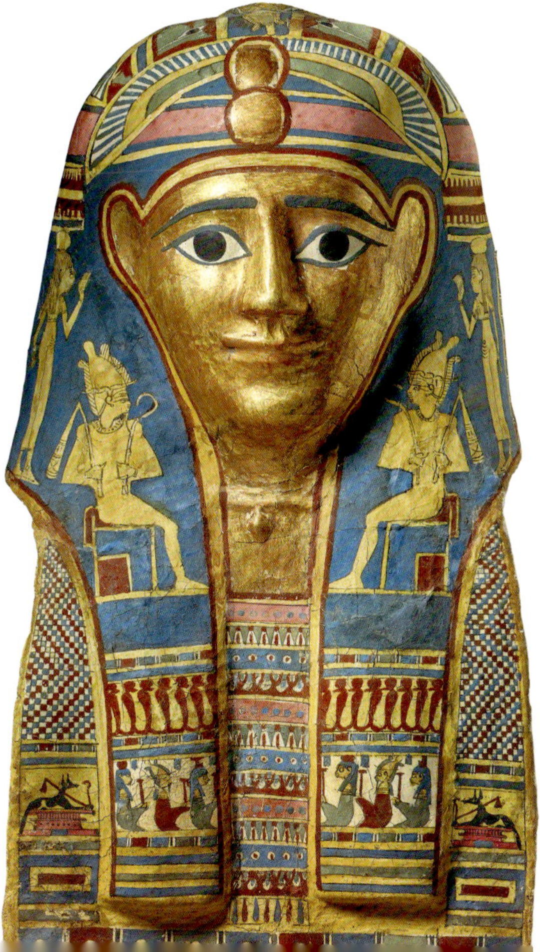

Unidentified sculptor and polychromer (Guatemala)
*Saint Michael Vanquishing the Devil*, second half of 18th century
Polychromed and gilded wood, silver gilt, bone, and glass;
20 × 14½ × 8½ in.
Purchased with funds provided by the Bernard and Edith Lewin Collection of Mexican Art Deaccession Fund, M.2021.1a–b

This image of Saint Michael demonstrates the refinement that made Guatemalan sculpture legendary. The triumphant archangel stands over the fallen demon, rendered naturalistically with hairy skin, bulging glass eyes, and bone teeth. The *encarnaciones* (flesh tones) make the saint more lifelike. Carved from a single block of wood, the sculpture bears a bewildering array of *estofados*, painted and incised patterns made to emulate fine fabrics. Small sculptures, such as this one, were generally intended for private devotional use.

Picturing the Divine in Spanish America

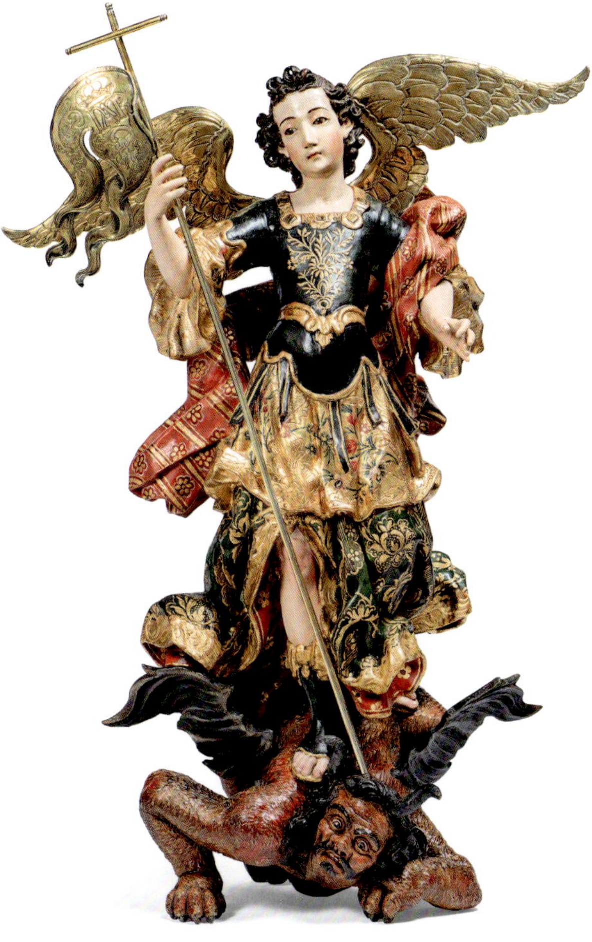

Manuel de Arellano (Mexico, 1662–1722)
and Antonio de Arellano (Mexico, 1638–1714)
*Virgin of Guadalupe*, 1691
Oil on canvas; 71½ × 48⅝ in.
Purchased with funds provided by the Bernard and Edith Lewin Collection of Mexican Art Deaccession Fund, M.2009.61

Our Lady of Guadalupe is one of the most copied images of the Christian world. This version by Antonio de Arellano and his son Manuel de Arellano depicts the Virgin surrounded by four vignettes. The scenes narrate her appearances to the Indigenous commoner Juan Diego in 1531 and culminate in the miracle that imprinted her image on his cloak. The inscription *tocada a la original* ("touched to the original") emphasizes that their copy was endowed with the power of the original icon.

Picturing the Divine in Spanish America

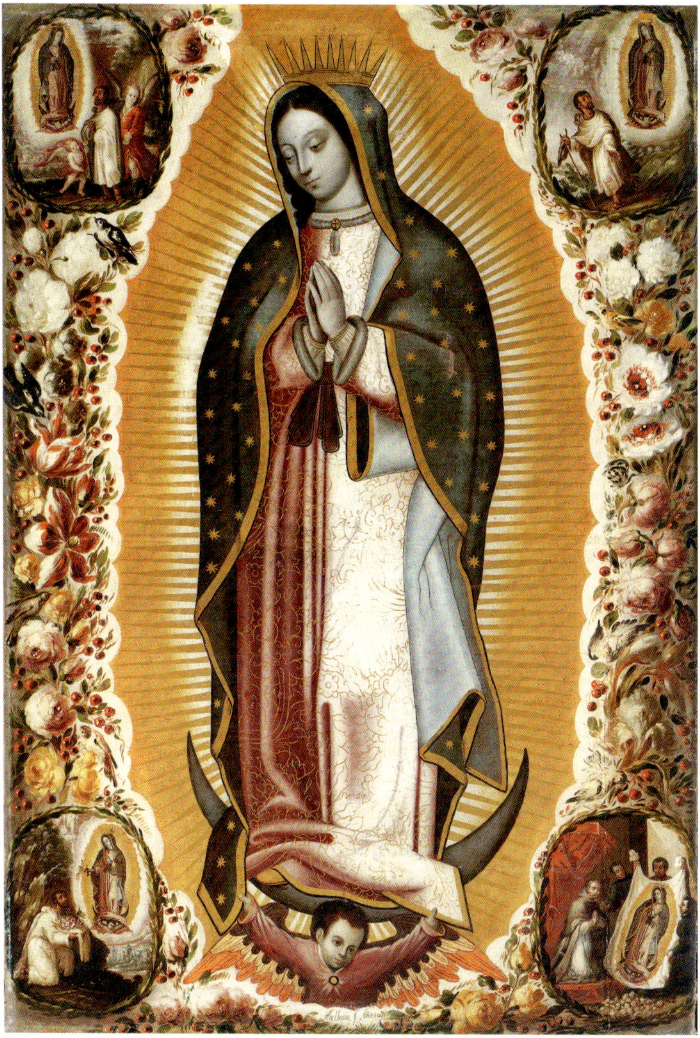

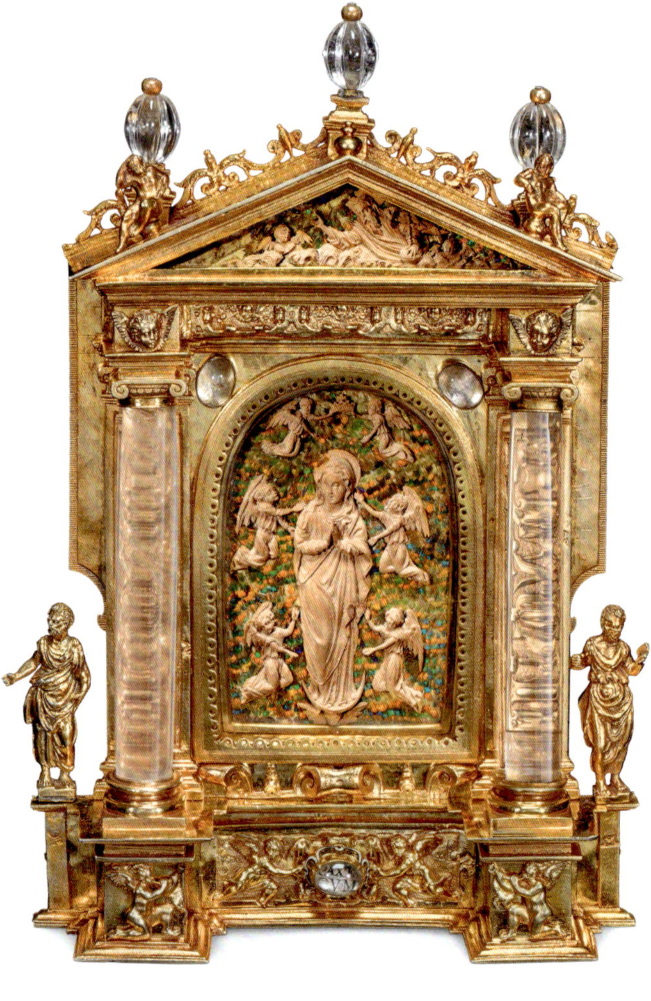

Nahua artists (Mexico)
Pax with the Assumption and Coronation of the Virgin, c. 1575–78
Silver gilt, rock crystal (quartz), wood, feathers, and enamel;
12¾ × 8⅞ × 5¾ in.
Gift of the 2024 Collectors Committee, M.2024.36

A pax is an object decorated with Christian subjects and used in the "kiss of peace" ritual as part of the Mass. This remarkable work was created by Indigenous artists during the turbulent years after the conquest of Mexico City. It combines precious metals, iridescent feathers, wood microcarvings, and rock crystal. Long used by Indigenous artists and invested with sacred meanings, these materials were redeployed in post-Conquest times to create Christian objects, demonstrating the persistence of Indigenous traditions under Spanish rule.

Picturing the Divine in Spanish America

Luisa Roldán, called La Roldana (Spain, 1652–1706)
*The Education of the Virgin*, 1680s
Polychromed wood; 30 × 24⅞ × 17 in.
Gift of the 2019 Collectors Committee with additional funds from Linda Borick and Bill Davidson on behalf of the Louis L. Borick Foundation, M.2019.235

This painted wood sculpture depicts Saint Anne tenderly teaching her young daughter, the Virgin Mary, to read scripture. It is a powerful portrayal of female intellect and literacy, at a time when only a small portion of the population could read. Born in Seville, Roldán apprenticed with her father and later started her own workshop, completing commissions for churches, confraternities, and private clients. She would become the most significant female sculptor of seventeenth-century Spain.

The Iberian World: From Spain to Spanish America

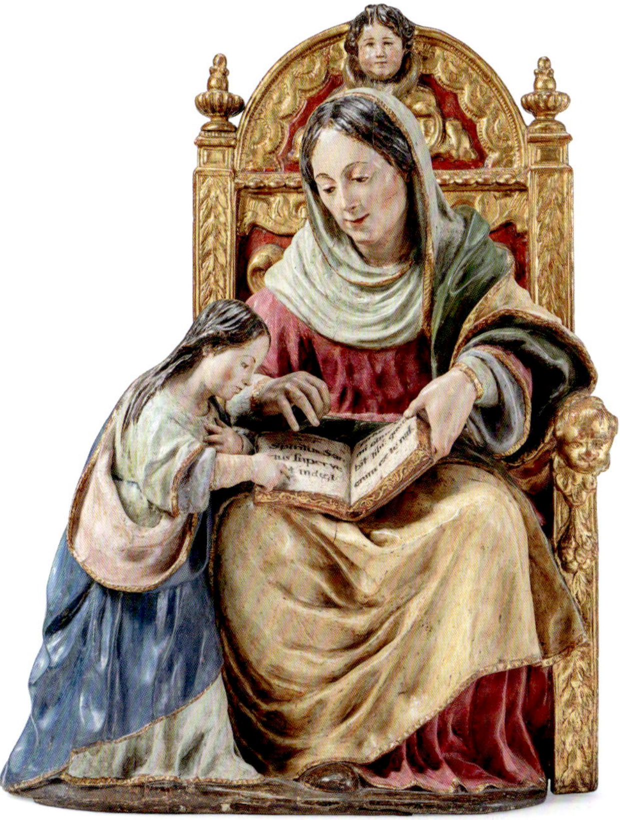

Manuel de Arellano (Mexico, 1662–1722)
*Creole Woman from the City of Guadalajara*, c. 1710
Oil on canvas; 41 × 31 in.
Gift of the 2025 Collectors Committee with additional funds from an anonymous donor, M.2025.32.1

This painting is not a specific portrait but rather a depiction of a racial type. Together with a companion painting of a Creole man, it provides a glimpse of Mexico's diverse population and inventive sartorial practices. The woman wears a combination of local and foreign-style clothing, including a sumptuous Indigenous blouse (*huipil*) and pearls, which symbolize local riches. Manuel de Arellano painted these works during a period of mounting social and racial tensions in Mexico City. The images construct a view of a mixed yet orderly and prosperous society to send to Europe.

The Iberian World: From Spain to Spanish America

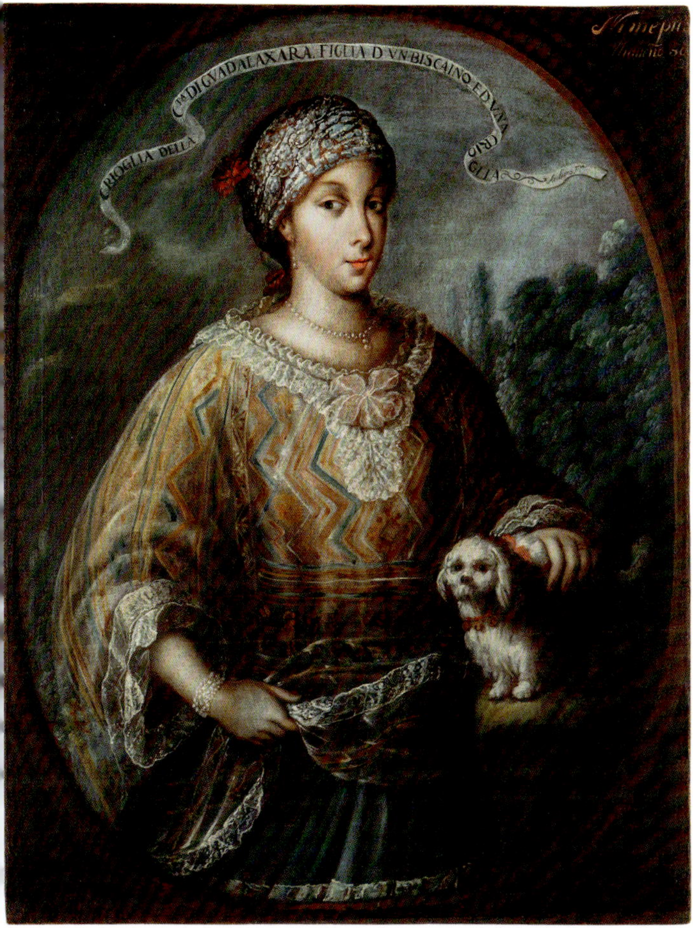
CRIOGLIA DELLA Cta DI GVADALAXARA, FIGLIA D VN BISCAINO E D VNA CRIOGLIA

Juan Patricio Morlete Ruiz (Mexico, 1713–1772)
*View of the Old Port of Toulon*, from the series *Ports of France*, 1771 (detail)
Oil on canvas; 39¾ × 60⅞ in.
Purchased with funds provided by the Bernard and Edith Lewin Collection of Mexican Art Deaccession Fund, M.2007.197.2

This detailed French seascape was painted by the Mexican artist Juan Patricio Morlete Ruiz. Scenes of the ports of France were widely known through fashionable prints after Claude-Joseph Vernet's sweeping canvases. Copying and modifying these compositions allowed Morlete Ruiz to demonstrate his virtuosity and position himself in relation to a transatlantic community of artists with shared interests. The inscription on this painting reads "copied in Mexico by Juan Patricio Morlete Ruiz the year 1771," signaling his claim of authorship.

Juan Patricio Morlete Ruiz: Seascapes and Copies

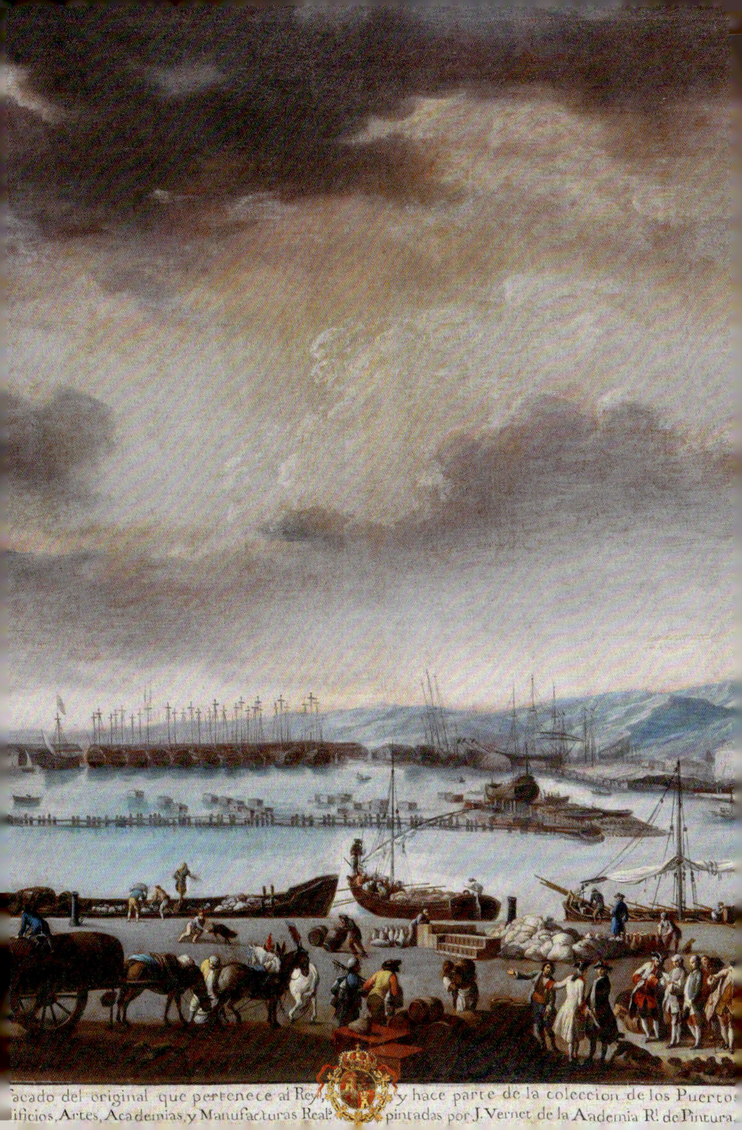
acado del original que pertenece al Rey, y hace parte de la coleccion de los Puertos
ificios, Artes, Academias, y Manufacturas Realˢ pintadas por J. Vernet de la Aademia Rl. de Pintura.

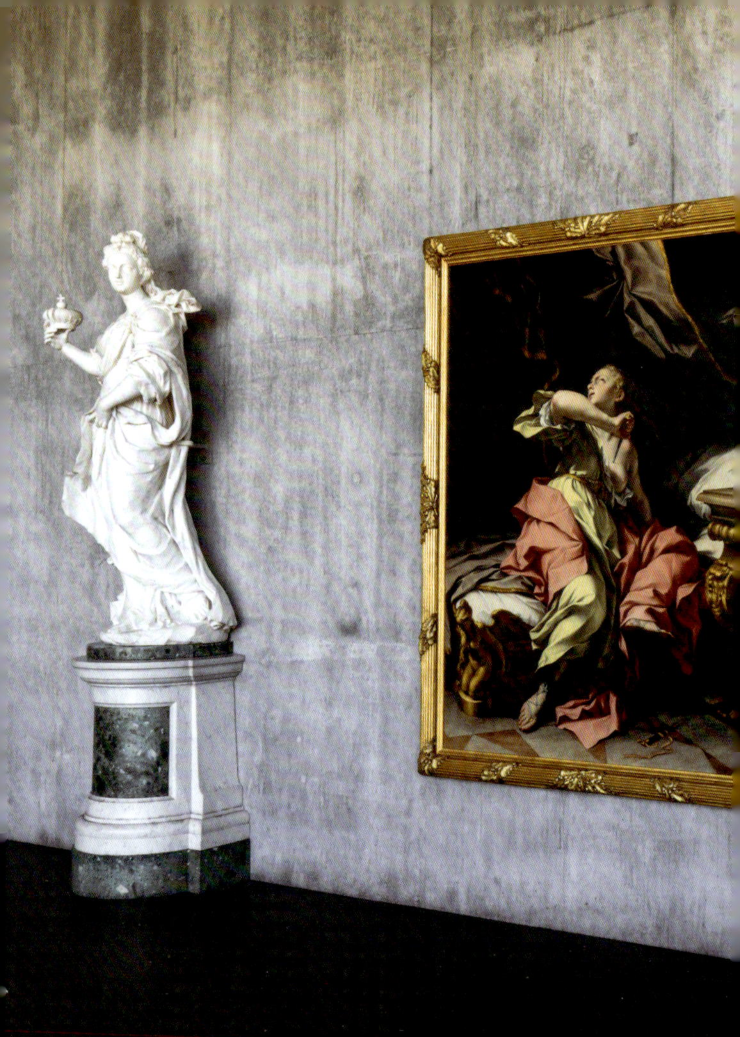

Ludovico Mazzanti's *The Death of Lucretia* (c. 1735–37) flanked by Giovanni Baratta's *Wealth* and *Prudence* (both c. 1703–8)

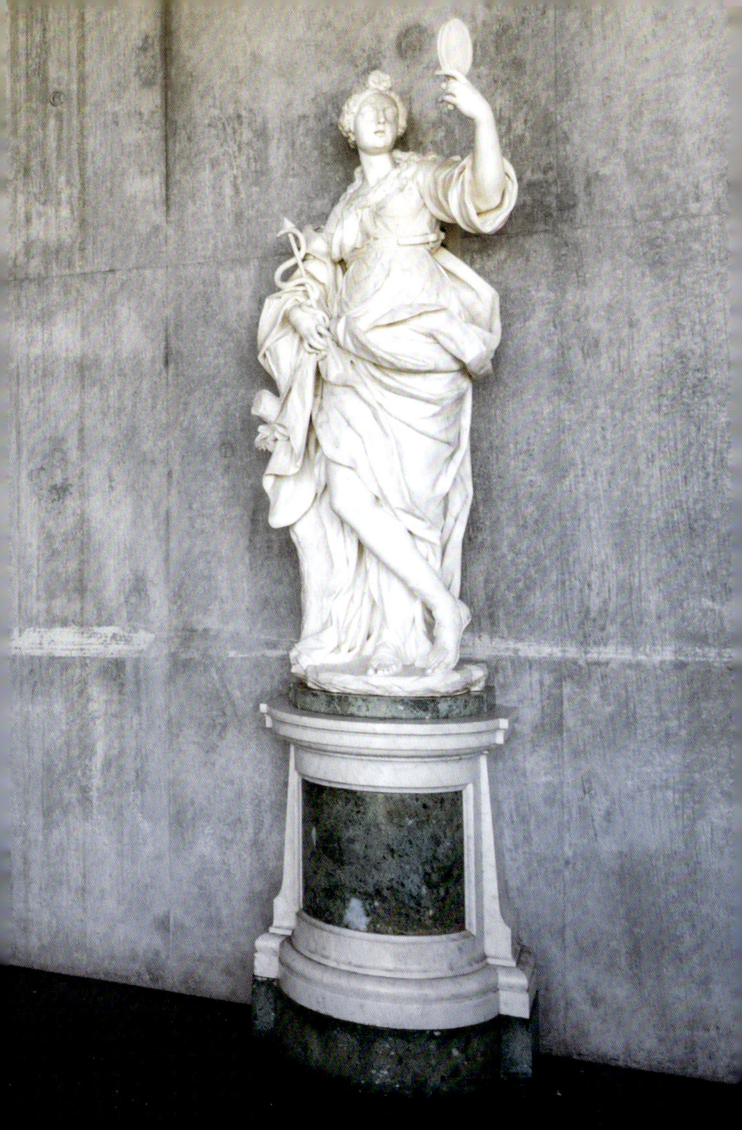

# Atlantic Ocean

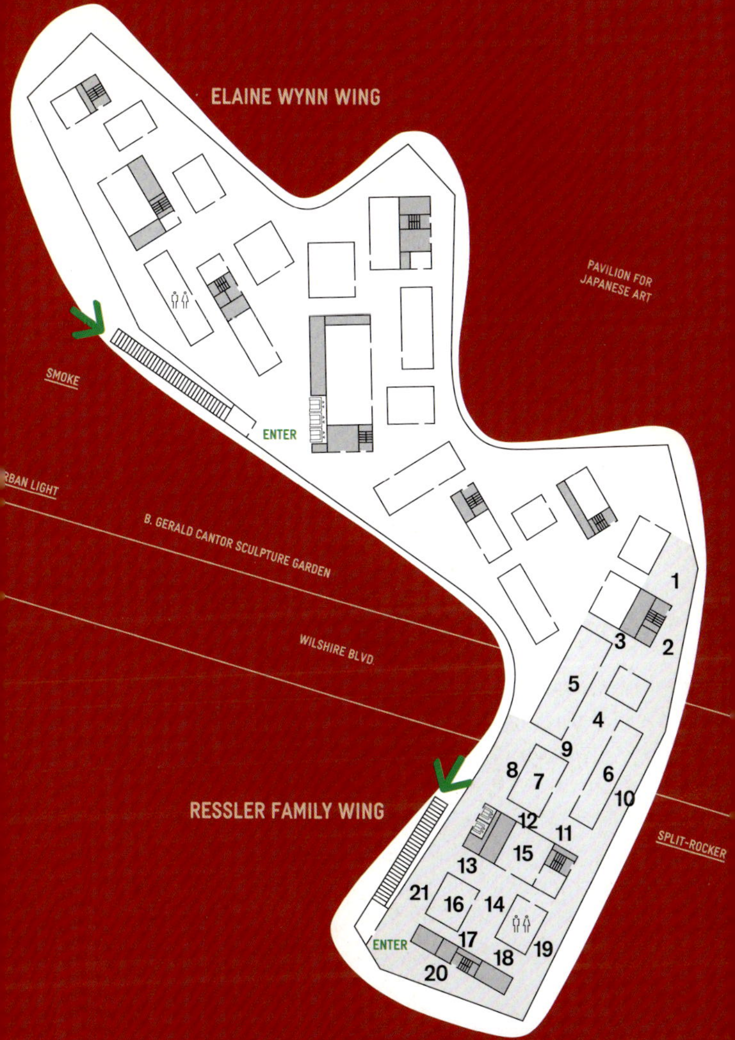
ELAINE WYNN WING
PAVILION FOR JAPANESE ART
SMOKE
ENTER
RBAN LIGHT
B. GERALD CANTOR SCULPTURE GARDEN
WILSHIRE BLVD.
RESSLER FAMILY WING
SPLIT-ROCKER
ENTER
1
2
3
4
5
6
7
8
9
10
11
12
13
14
15
16
17
18
19
20
21

# Atlantic Ocean

Before the sixteenth century, the Atlantic rim supported distinct artistic traditions that developed independently for millennia. West African kingdoms—Benin, Kongo, Asante—possessed advanced bronze casting using the lost-wax technique and textile weaving that produced kente and raffia cloth. Indigenous American civilizations maintained equally complex traditions: Aztec featherwork and codex production, Inca architectural stonework and textile arts, and Maya astronomical knowledge that informed sculptural work and earthwork construction. European powers developed oil painting techniques, printmaking, and Renaissance humanism.

Columbus's 1492 arrival in the Caribbean initiated permanent European-American contact, transforming trade and cultural production throughout the Atlantic basin. The Atlantic Ocean's moderate size and circular current patterns—trade winds flowing east to west, westerlies returning west to east—created conditions that enabled efficient triangular circuits: European manufactured goods were sold in West

Africa, enslaved Africans were transported to the Americas, and American plantation staples were shipped to Europe. Spain, Portugal, France, Great Britain, and other European colonial powers built maritime networks that systematically extracted natural resources, cultural production, and enslaved labor from Africa and the Americas while funneling wealth to European capitals. This system shaped everything people made—from the gold that funded Portuguese church decoration to the luxury goods produced by enslaved artisans who received no credit for their skill.

The Atlantic Ocean galleries display artworks from these regions, with a focus on movement across the ocean. Here you will find African and Black American textiles in conversation; modern Latin American paintings, sculpture, and furniture; LACMA's deep holdings of twentieth-century photography; art of the United States across media; and highlights of our expansive collection of decorative arts and design.

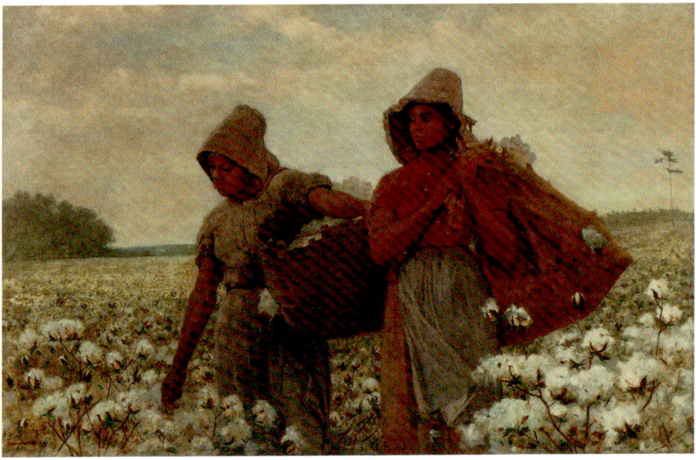

Winslow Homer (United States, 1836–1910)
*The Cotton Pickers*, 1876
Oil on canvas; 24 × 38⅛ in.
Acquisition made possible through Museum Trustees: Robert O. Anderson, R. Stanton Avery, B. Gerald Cantor, Edward W. Carter, Justin Dart, Charles E. Ducommun, Camilla Chandler Frost, Julian Ganz, Jr., Dr. Armand Hammer, Harry Lenart, Dr. Franklin D. Murphy, Mrs. Joan Palevsky, Richard E. Sherwood, Maynard J. Toll, and Hal B. Wallis, M.77.68

Based on Winslow Homer's travels to Reconstruction-era Virginia, *The Cotton Pickers* is a poignant depiction of life for newly emancipated Black Americans in the South. While one woman reaches down to pick a boll of cotton, the other gazes into the distance, poised on the brink of an uncertain future. Her apron snags on a branch below, physically connecting her to the crop that enriched white fortunes and fueled the translatlantic slave trade.

Transatlantic Exchange and Its Legacies

United States
"Lady of the Lake" Quilt, c. 1840 (detail)
Cotton, pieced and quilted; 98½ × 98½ in.
American Quilt Research Center Acquisition Fund, M.87.226.2

The "Lady of the Lake" quilt pattern seen here—defined by pieced squares composed of two large central half-square triangles framed with smaller half-square triangles—originated around 1820 in Vermont. The quilter deftly deployed dark and light half-squares in an alternating fashion, both vertically and horizontally, intensifying a sense of visual movement.

Transatlantic Exchange and Its Legacies

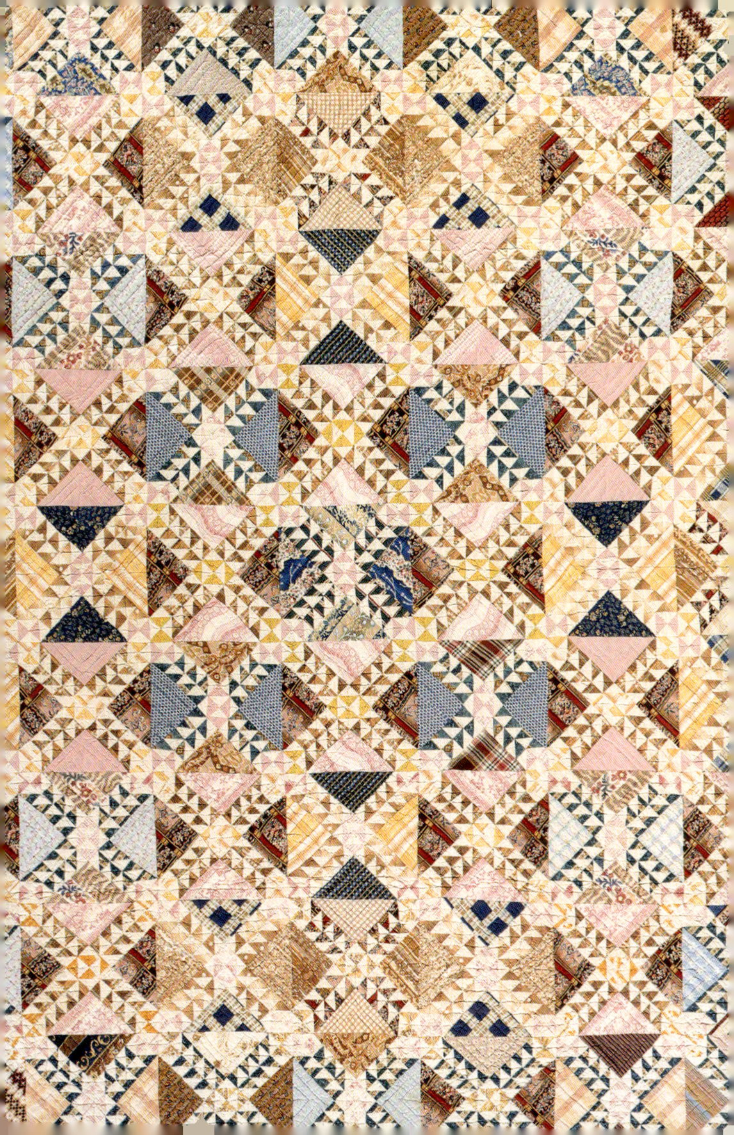

Betye Saar (United States, b. 1926)
*I'll Bend But I Will Not Break*, 1998
Vintage ironing board, flat iron, chain, white bedsheet, wood clothespins, and rope; 80 × 96 × 36 in.
Gift of Lynda and Stewart Resnick through the 2018 Collectors Committee, M.2018.76.1–.5

Betye Saar's sculptural tableau is an iconic statement on race and women's work. The ironing board—itself a traditional symbol of female labor—is borrowed from a well-known eighteenth-century print showing how scores of Africans were packed into slave ships to cross the Atlantic. The work also refers to the marking of enslaved persons with branding irons, and their chaining in transit or as punishment. "KKK" appliquéd to the sheet denotes the white-supremacist Ku Klux Klan, still active today in the United States.

Transatlantic Exchange and Its Legacies

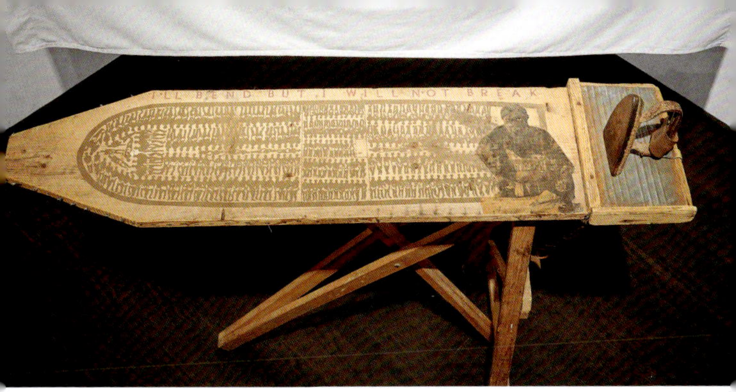
I'LL BEND BUT I WILL NOT BREAK

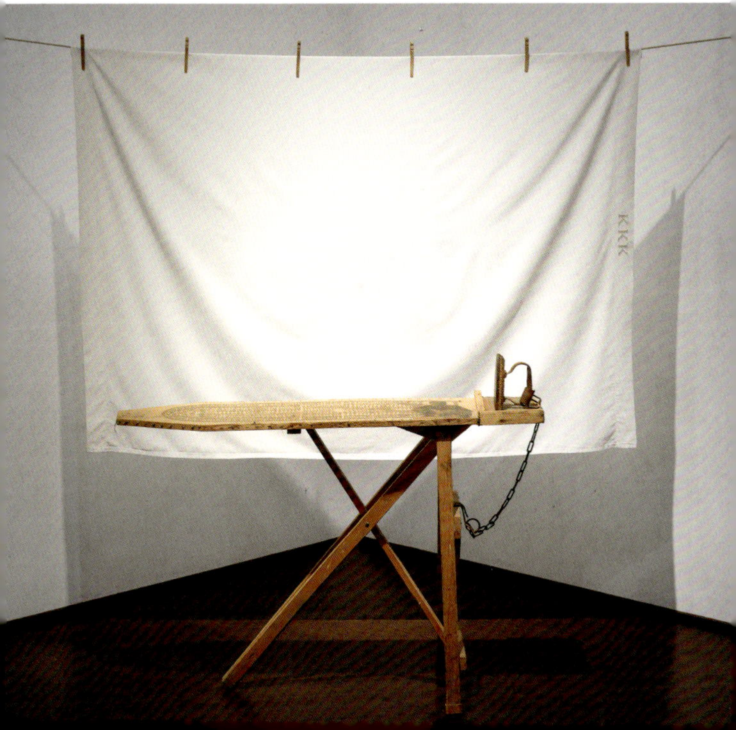
KKK

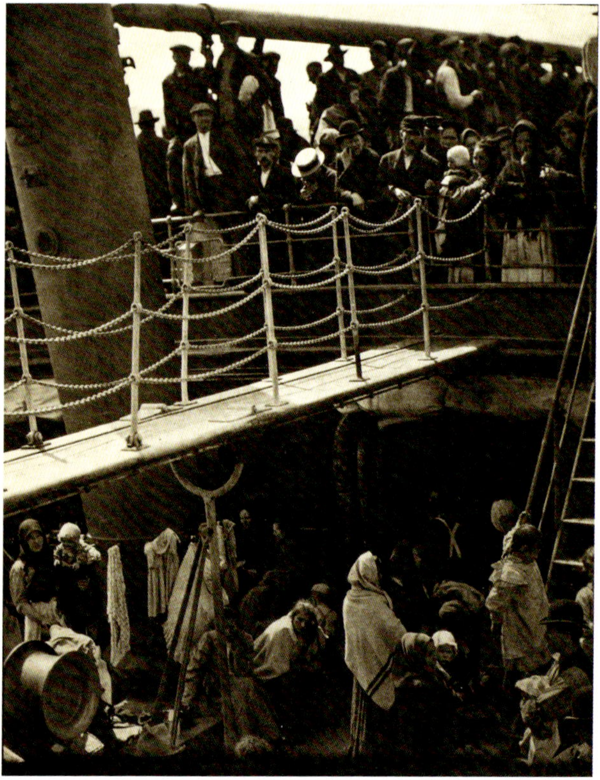

300 Atlantic

Alfred Stieglitz (United States, 1864–1946)
*Steerage*, 1907
Photogravure; 13⅛ × 10½ in.
The Marjorie and Leonard Vernon Collection, gift of the Annenberg Foundation, acquired from Carol Vernon and Robert Turbin, M.2008.40.2043

Stieglitz's most iconic photograph captures social status during his 1907 voyage to Europe, with the upper-class travelers in suits and hats shown above, and the lower-class women and children wrapped in shawls below. The composition transforms human figures into geometric shapes that merge with the vessel's infrastructure of stairways, beams, and a bisecting wood plank. Contrast between oceanic light and cavernous shadow creates a modernist study in form. Though often interpreted as depicting European immigrants arriving in America, the ship actually traveled from New York to Europe, carrying immigrants refused entry and craftspeople returning home.

Mary Cassatt (United States, 1844–1926, active France)
*The Child's Bath*, 1880
Oil on canvas; 39½ × 25⅞ in.
Mrs. Fred Hathaway Bixby Bequest, M.62.8.14

The only American-born artist who exhibited with the French Impressionists, Mary Cassatt showed in four of the group's eight exhibitions, displaying this work in their fifth show in 1880. The painting is among her earliest depictions of modern women and children—a subject that earned her international recognition. Compressed into the picture's foreground, the caregiver and child are composed of rapidly applied brushstrokes, and the quickness of Cassatt's execution reinforces the fleeting nature of this intimate moment.

Labor and Leisure in the American Metropolis

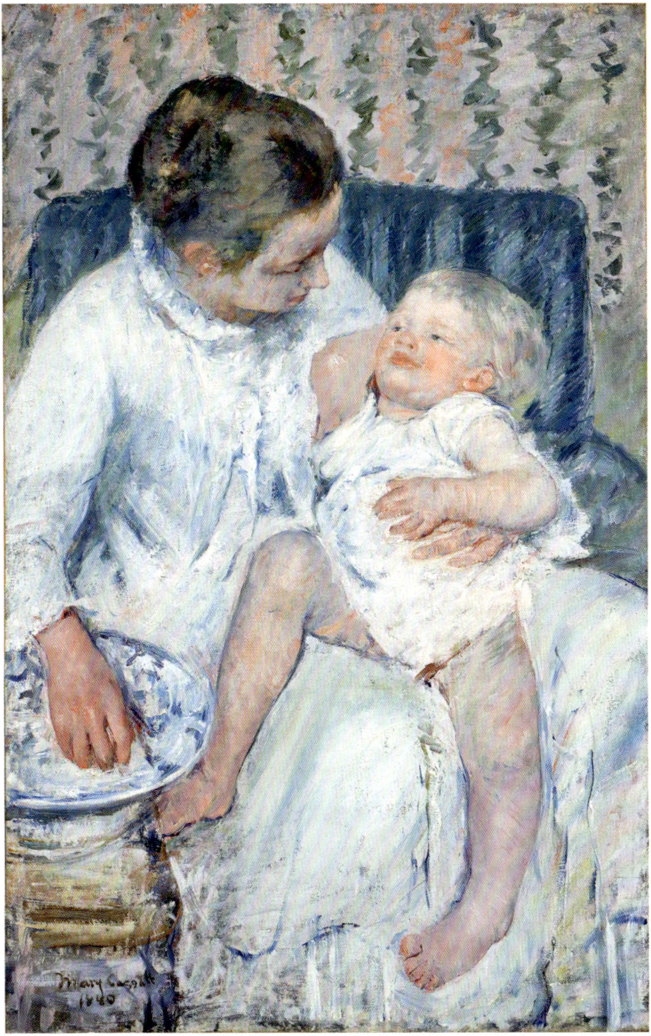
Mary Cassatt
1880

Tiffany Studios (United States, 1902–32)
Louis Comfort Tiffany (United States, 1848–1933)
"Pond Lily" Lamp, 1902–10
Leaded glass and bronze; 27¼ × 18 in.
Gift of Mr. David Geffen, M.85.128a–b

A leading proprietor of American Art Nouveau glass, Tiffany Studios was famous for its then-radical innovation of depicting nature using the color and texture of glass itself rather than applied paint. The firm was renowned for its opalescent glass, which here suggests the gentle movements of rippling water. This rare "Pond Lily" lamp features an integrated design of gracefully descending lilies and overlapping lily pads on its cast bronze base. The alternation of mottled blue-green and brown-orange glass evokes the tranquil water of a pond.

Labor and Leisure in the American Metropolis

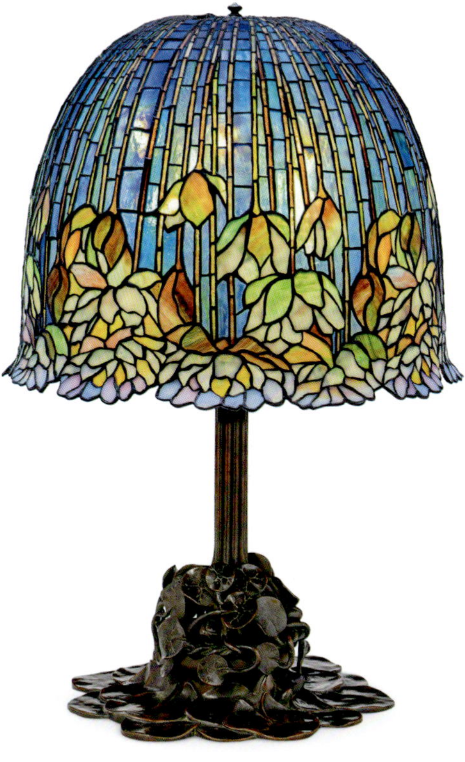

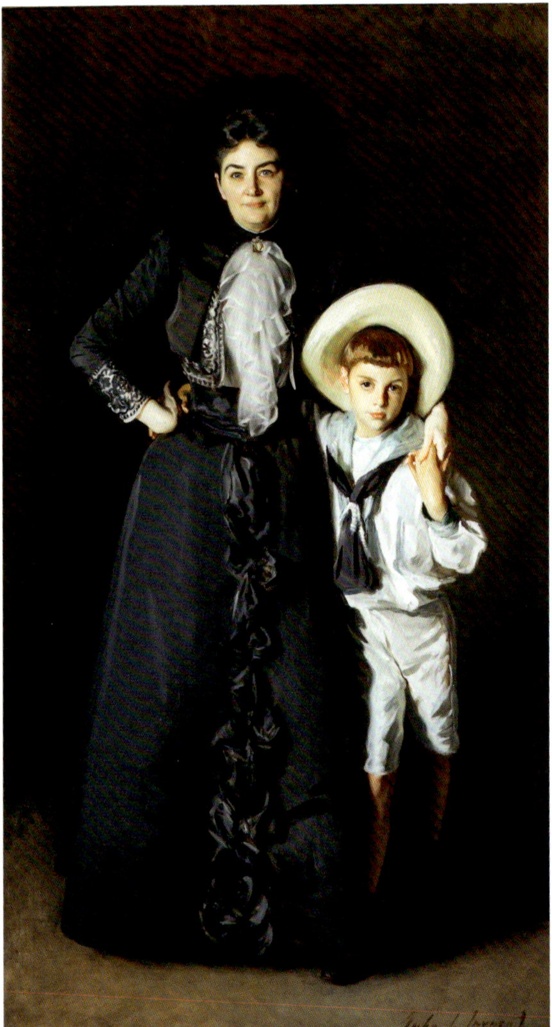

John Singer Sargent (Italy, 1856–1925, active France, England, and United States)
*Portrait of Mrs. Edward L. Davis and Her Son, Livingston Davis*, 1890
Oil on canvas; 86⅛ × 48¼ in.
Frances and Armand Hammer Purchase Fund, M.69.18

In 1889, after establishing his reputation as a premier portrait painter in Paris and London, John Singer Sargent returned to the United States. He was immediately inundated with commissions from wealthy patrons, including for this portrait of Maria Robbins Davis and her son, who posed for the artist in their carriage house in Worcester, Massachusetts. Sargent omitted any indication of the setting, instead focusing his virtuoso brush on their intimate embrace and fashionable black and white ensembles.

Labor and Leisure in the American Metropolis

George Bellows (United States, 1882–1925)
*Cliff Dwellers*, 1913
Oil on canvas; 40¼ × 42 in.
Los Angeles County Fund, 16.4

In 1916, the museum purchased George Bellows's *Cliff Dwellers*—one of the first works acquired for the collection. The artist was among a generation of painters, later dubbed the Ashcan School, who depicted modern urban life amid dramatic social and economic change. In this view of an overcrowded tenement on New York City's Lower East Side, Bellows adopted a somber color palette and rough brushwork to convey the harsh realities of life in immigrant and working-class communities.

Labor and Leisure in the American Metropolis

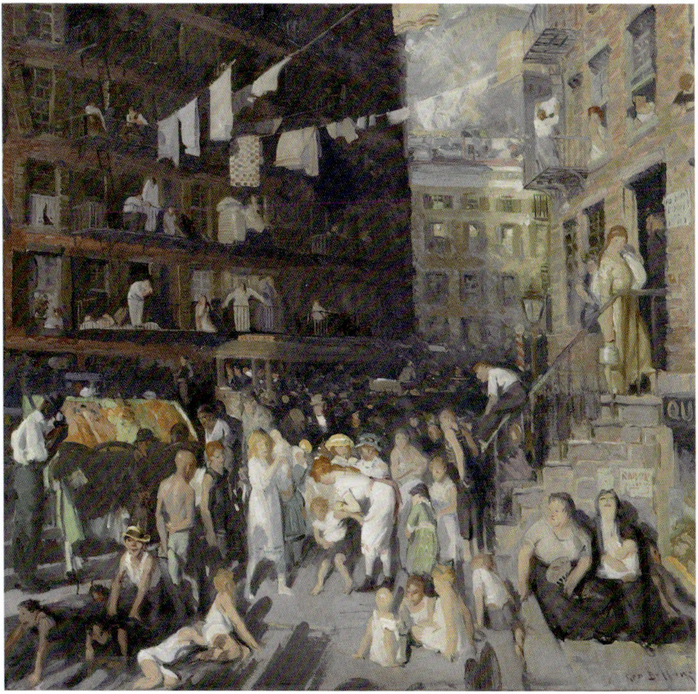
QU

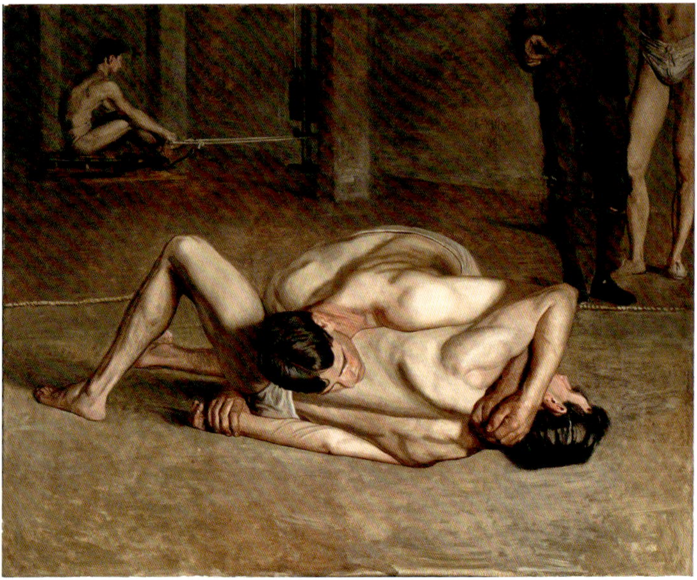

Thomas Eakins (United States, 1844–1916)
*Wrestlers*, 1899
Oil on canvas; 48⅜ × 60 in.
Gift of Cecile C. Bartman and The Cecile and Fred Bartman Foundation, M.2007.1

A lifelong enthusiast of wrestling, Thomas Eakins began attending matches in the 1870s, as the popular bourgeois sport offered ample opportunity to study male bodies in states of tremendous exertion, contortion, and duress. In preparation for this painting—his last great sporting picture—Eakins photographed wrestlers in his Philadelphia studio, carefully juxtaposing clothed and unclothed bodies, wrinkled and taut flesh. Although the work underscores his academic study of classical sculpture, his wrestlers are not particularly heroic, capturing instead an awkward entanglement of bodies.

Labor and Leisure in the American Metropolis

James Van Der Zee (United States, 1886–1983)
*Atlantic City*, 1930, printed c. 1974
Gelatin silver print; 6½ × 4 in.
Gift of Emerald and Harriet Merrill, M.83.315.5

Van Der Zee's 1930 photograph captures three Black women sunbathers arranged in a triangular composition on the beach, their bodies gracefully intermingling. The central figure, farthest from the lens, wears a swimming cap and rests her hand confidently on her hip, while the two women in the foreground embrace more affectionately. The location is likely Missouri Avenue Beach, an unofficial Blacks-only destination during Atlantic City's era of racial segregation that was a vibrant cultural spot for families as well as performers and celebrities. The photograph exemplifies Van Der Zee's documentary approach to capturing Black social life beyond his Harlem portrait studio.

Labor and Leisure in the American Metropolis

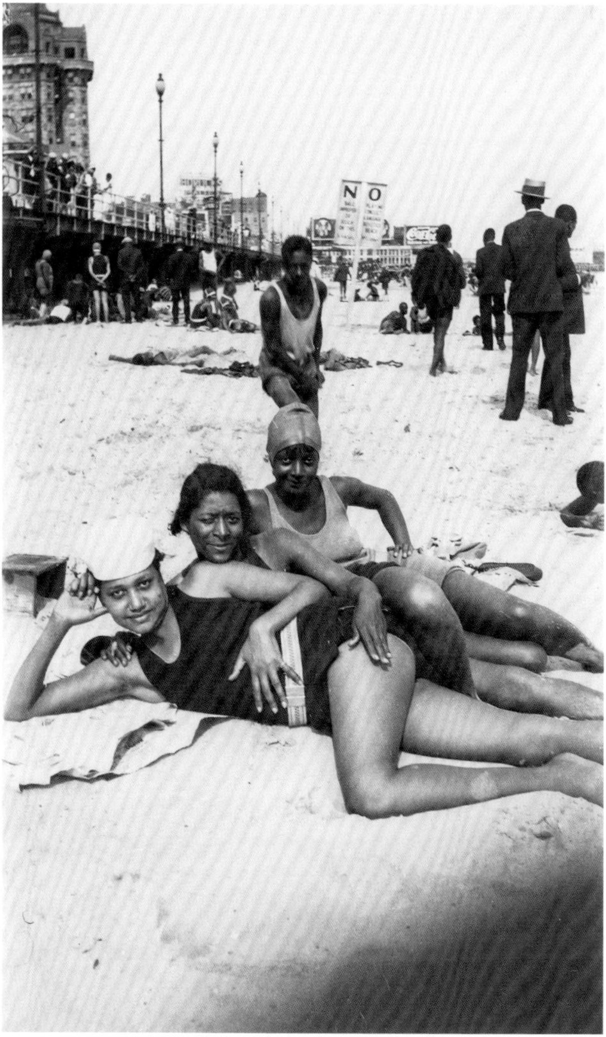
NO
NO

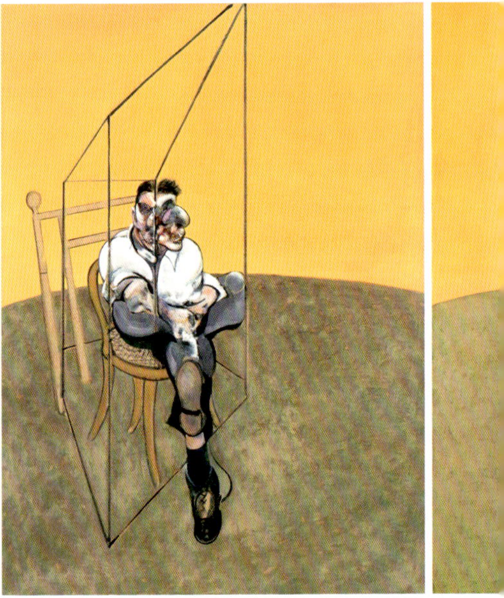

Francis Bacon was lauded for his raw, distorted images that convey physical and psychological intensity. Among his most celebrated works are the triptychs, which he likened to cinematic sequences. In this life-size triptych, Bacon's friend and rival,

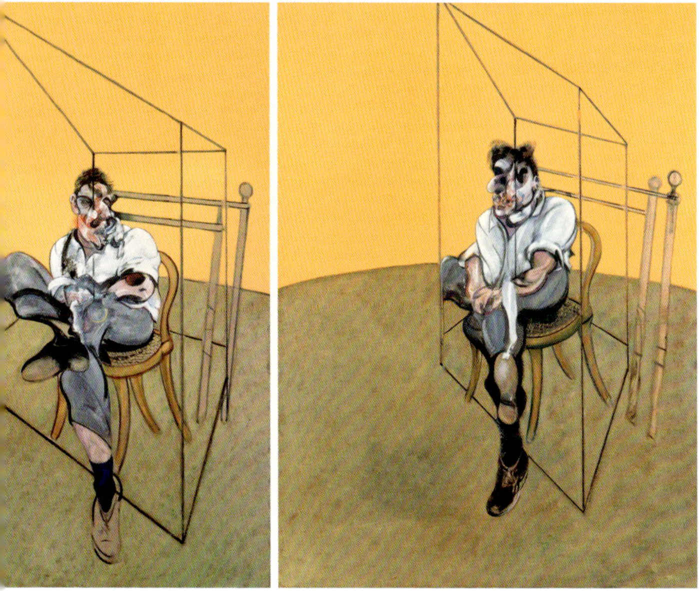

artist Lucian Freud, seems both awkward and self-assured; he twists from panel to panel within a stagelike frame. Bacon painted from photographs rather than life, distilling likeness into abstraction.

Francis Bacon: *Three Studies of Lucian Freud*

Francis Bacon (Ireland, 1909–1992, active England)
*Three Studies of Lucian Freud*, 1969
Oil on canvas; each 77⅞ × 58⅛ in.
Gift of Elaine P. Wynn, M.2025.63a–c

Claude Monet (France, 1840–1926)
*The Artist's Garden, Vétheuil*, 1881
Oil on canvas; 39⅜ × 32¼ in.
Gift of A. Jerrold Perenchio, M.2025.64.20

By the time Claude Monet began to paint this extraordinary view of his garden at Vétheuil on the outskirts of Paris, he had secured personal and professional success. This is one of four versions of the scene, and the only one to include two children, one of whom is the artist's son. The painting reads as a triumphant pronouncement of the height of summer, bursting with sunflowers and quivering with the effects of the stark midday sun.

The A. Jerrold Perenchio Collection of Impressionist and Modern Art

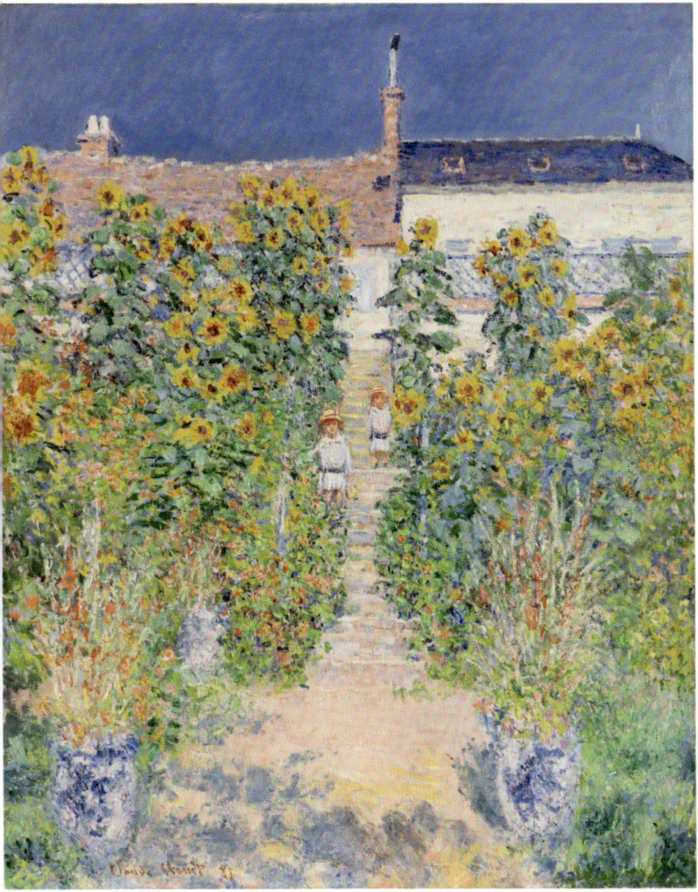

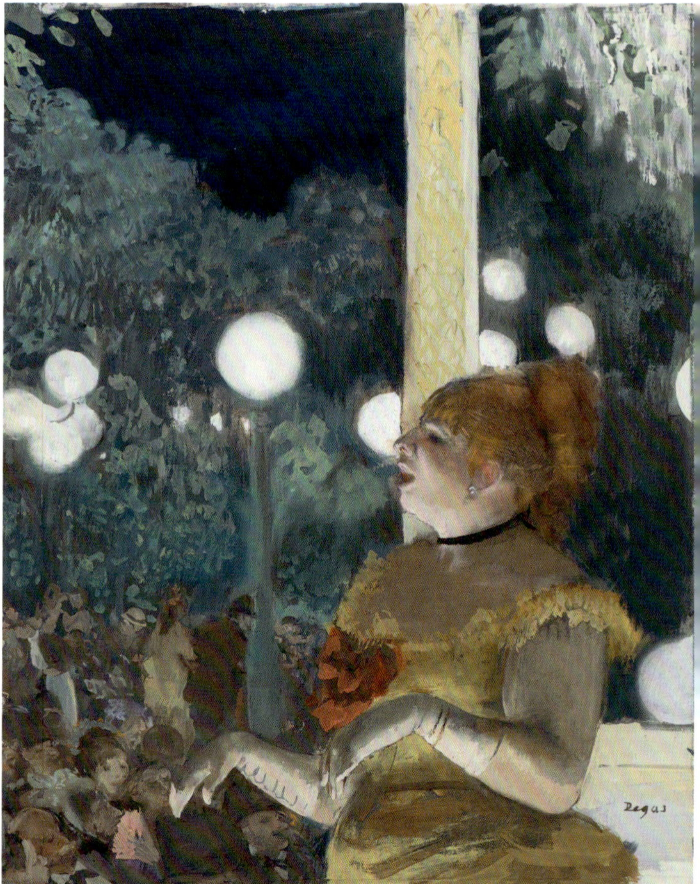
Degas

Edgar Degas (France, 1834–1917)
*At the Café-Concert: The Song of the Dog*, c. 1876–77
Gouache and pastel over monotype on joined paper; 22⅛ × 17⅛ in.
Gift of A. Jerrold Perenchio, M.2025.64.2

Among his Impressionist colleagues, Edgar Degas was arguably the most dedicated to exploring the intricacies of modern urban life. Here, under the harsh, artificial glow of gas lamps at a café-concert on the Champs-Élysées, the artist captures the wildly popular singer Thérésa before a crowd of cavorting and caricatured men and women. The singer is caught open-mouthed, performing a whimsical song that required her to impersonate a dog.

The A. Jerrold Perenchio Collection of Impressionist and Modern Art

René Magritte (Belgium, 1898–1967)
*Dangerous Liaisons*, 1935
Oil on canvas; 28¾ × 21½ in.
Gift of A. Jerrold Perenchio, M.2025.64.25

René Magritte's technical skill allowed him to engage deeply with visual games involving illusion and artifice, and quite often he plays with these qualities in their relationship to image making. Here, a nude female impossibly reflects herself in a mirror she holds, and yet she is still beguilingly hidden. This back and forth, found literally in the figure's position and metaphorically in the imagined nature of the image, lies at the heart of Magritte's painting.

The A. Jerrold Perenchio Collection of Impressionist and Modern Art

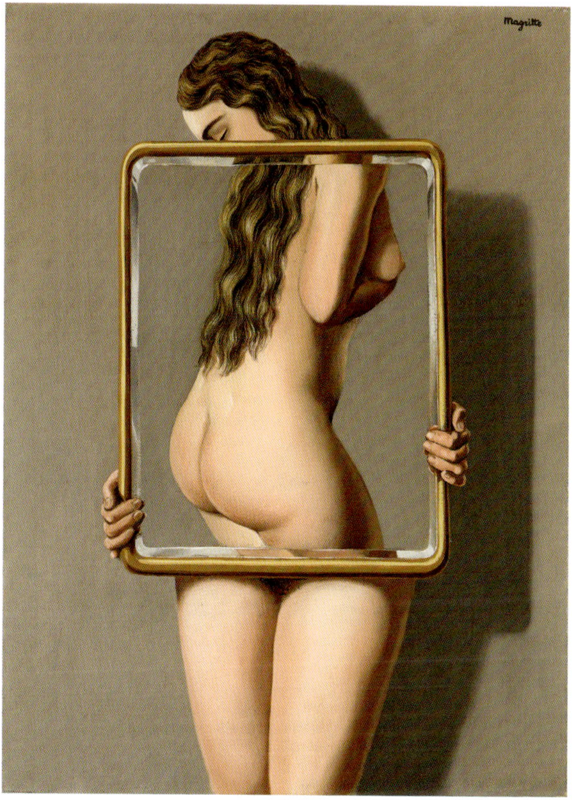
Magritte

Vincent van Gogh (Netherlands, 1853–1890, active France)
*Tarascon Stagecoach*, 1888
Oil on canvas; 28 1/8 × 36 1/2 in.
Gift of the Henry and Rose Pearlman Foundation and Family, M.2025.139

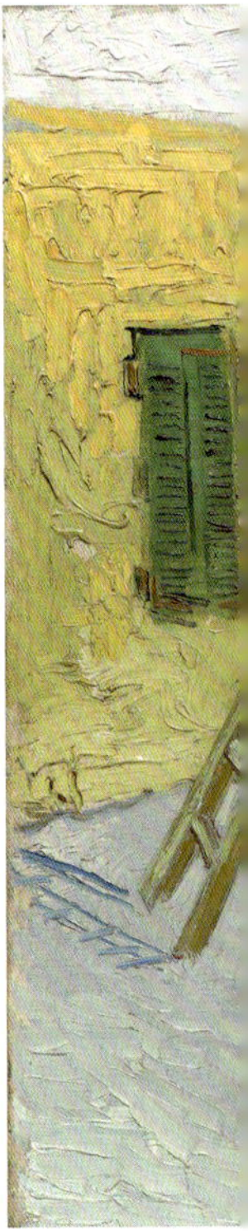

After moving from Paris to the quiet town of Arles in the south of France, Vincent van Gogh began to explore the expressive possibilities of color in his work. This vibrant painting, the first by the artist to enter LACMA's collection, is essentially a portrait of a stagecoach—an outmoded form of transport long supplanted by the railroad. Van Gogh's nostalgic evocation betrays a yearning for a simpler, vanishing way of life.

Responses to Industrialization

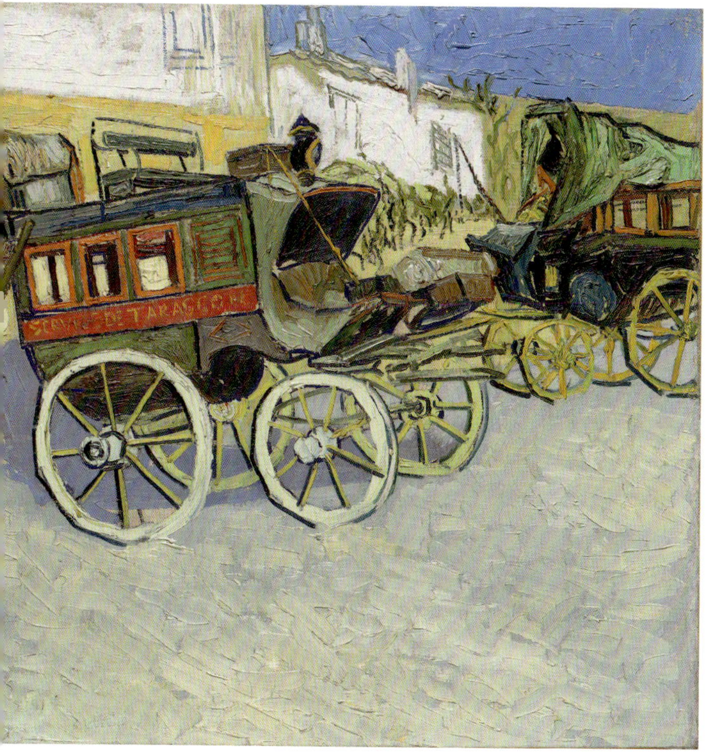

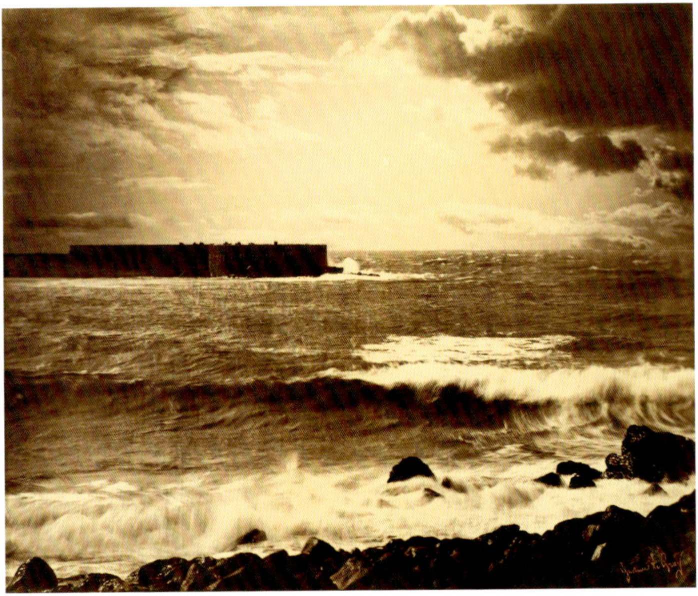

Gustave Le Gray (France, 1820–1884)
*The Great Wave, Sète*, 1857
Albumen silver print; 13⅜ × 16½ in.
The Marjorie and Leonard Vernon Collection,
gift of the Annenberg Foundation and Carol Vernon and Robert Turbin,
M.2008.40.1284

A master of early photographic technique, Gustave Le Gray specialized in *marines*, or sea pictures, a popular genre in painting but one that seemed impossible in photography, since the emulsions of the period could not capture both bright skies and darker landscapes simultaneously. Le Gray overcame this limitation by combining two separate negatives—one exposed for the dramatic sky, another for the churning Mediterranean waters—onto a single sheet of paper. The result is seamless, constructed yet convincing.

Bruno Paul (Germany, 1874–1968)
Candelabrum, designed 1901, manufactured 1901–4
Designed for United Workshops for Art in Handicraft (Germany)
Manufacturer: K. M. Seifert & Co. (Germany)
Brass; 16⅜ × 27½ × 9⅛ in.
Purchased with funds provided by Debbie and Mark Attanasio,
M.2008.19.2

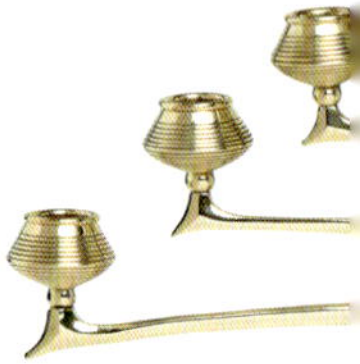

This dramatic but largely undecorated candelabrum marks Bruno Paul's shift from Art Nouveau's sinuous curves toward a more functionalist aesthetic. As a cofounder of Munich's Vereinigte Werkstätten für Kunst im Handwerk (United Workshops for Art in Handicraft), Paul helped lead the city's flourishing design community at a time when industrial production had upended traditional ways of making in Germany. The organization embraced rational forms and machine work while advocating for designers' active role in production and distribution.

Responses to Industrialization

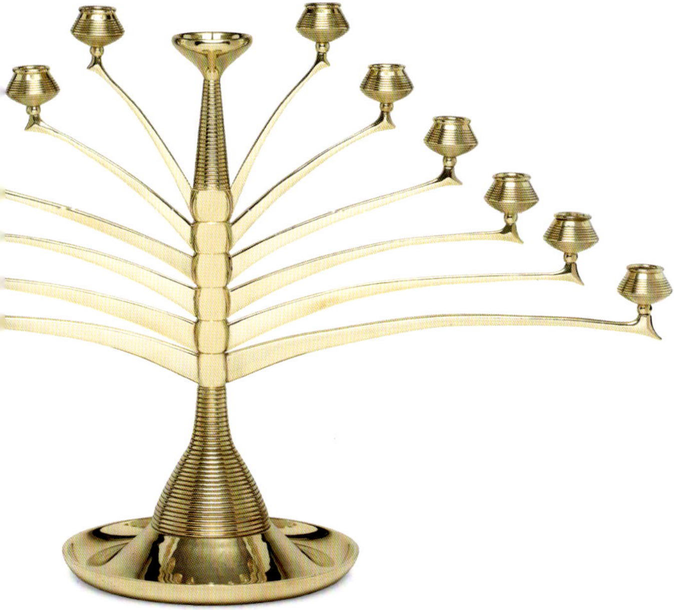

Wassily Kandinsky (Russia, 1866–1944, active Germany)
*The Mirror*, 1907
Linocut; 12¾ × 6¼ in.
The Robert Gore Rifkind Center for German Expressionist Studies, M.82.288.106

Wassily Kandinsky's linocut demonstrates his early interest in Russian and Bavarian folk cultures. The woman's medieval clothing and the fairy-tale-like setting suggest an atmosphere more than a narrative. The mirror of the title reflects not her face but the stylized landscape beyond; her skirt's starburst pattern gradually transforms into flowers dotting the field below her feet, merging figure and ground. Adopting the decorative simplification of folk traditions, Kandinsky forged his own path toward modernist abstraction.

Responses to Industrialization

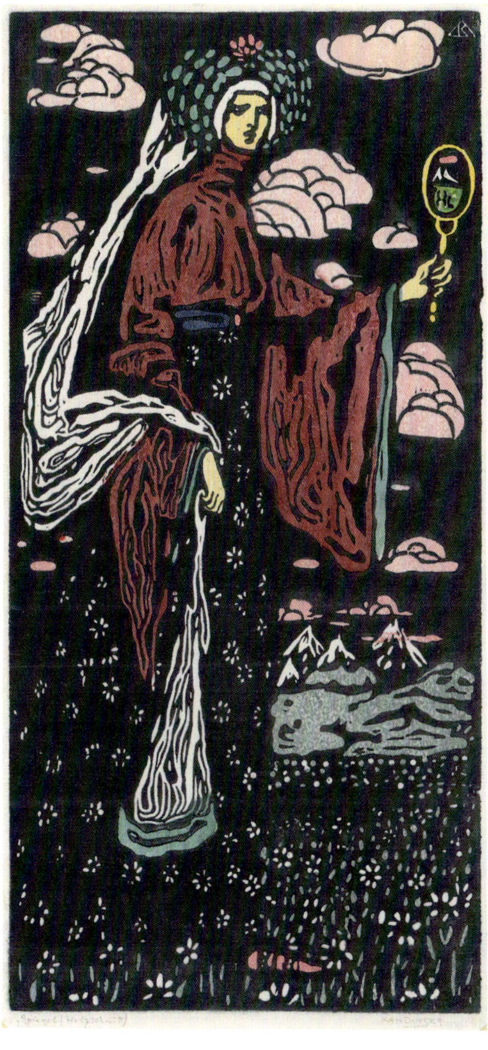

Spiegel (Holzschnitt)
KANDINSKY

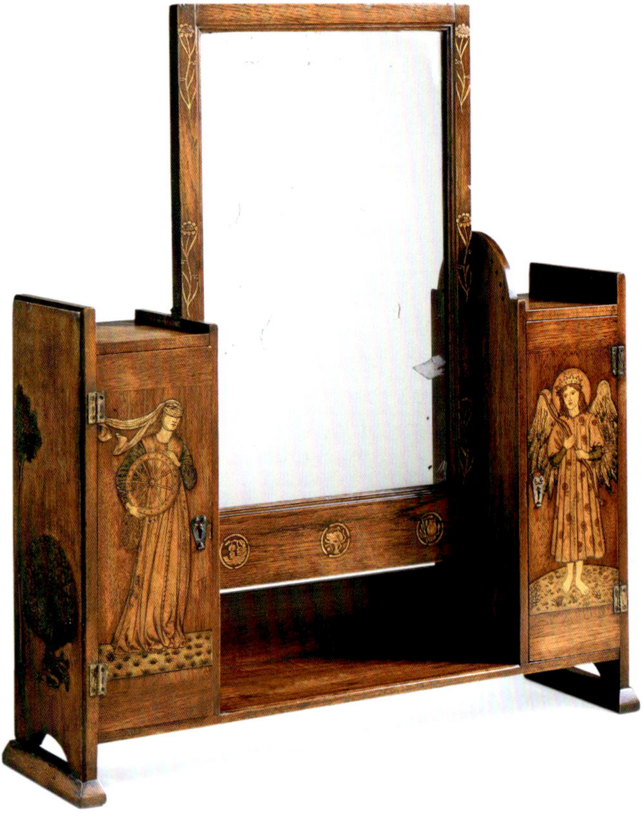

Morris, Marshall, Faulkner & Co., later Morris & Co. (England)
Philip Webb (England, 1831–1915) and Edward Burne-Jones (England, 1833–1898), designers
Toilet Mirror for Warrington Taylor, 1862
Walnut, gesso, paint, gilding, glass, and brass; 33 × 29 × 8¼ in.
Purchased with funds provided by Mr. and Mrs. Russell McKinnon and other donors, M.2001.19.1

Of all Arts and Crafts movement protagonists, William Morris had the most far-reaching influence. This toilet mirror, one of the earliest objects produced by his firm, embodies the movement's goal of collaborative equality between architects and artists, with Philip Webb providing the design and Edward Burne-Jones the gesso and painted decoration. Made for Webb's friend (and soon the company's business manager), it demonstrates the Arts and Crafts embrace of the handmade, together with vernacular forms and medieval-inspired decoration.

Charles Rennie Mackintosh (Scotland, 1868–1928)
*The Scottish Musical Review*, 1896
Lithograph; 96½ × 39⅛ in.
Gift of the 2014 Collectors Committee, with additional funds provided by Kitzia and Richard Goodman, J. Ben Bourgeois and Andrew Rhoda, Viveca Paulin-Ferrell and Will Ferrell, and Olivier and Zoë de Givenchy, M.2014.90

While Charles Rennie Mackintosh is internationally renowned for his architecture and furniture design, his graphic design is much less recognized. In this towering poster for *The Scottish Musical Review*, an androgynous, elongated figure is conflated with an abstract, flowering tree of life. The halo surrounding the figure suggests transcendence; the songbirds refer to the subject of the magazine; and the purple, indigo, and green evoke the Scottish landscape. All illustrate Symbolist themes of spiritual transformation and renewal.

Responses to Industrialization

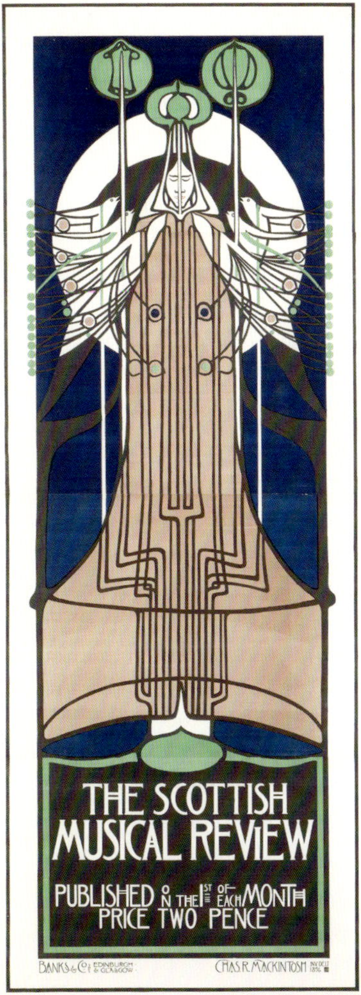
THE SCOTTISH
MUSICAL REVIEW
PUBLISHED ON THE 1ST OF EACH MONTH
PRICE TWO PENCE
BANKS & Co EDINBURGH & GLASGOW
CHAS R. MACKINTOSH INV DELT 1896

Arthur Heygate (A. H.) Mackmurdo (England, 1851–1942)
Chair, c. 1883
Made for the Century Guild
Made by Collinson & Lock (England)
Mahogany, leather, and brass; 38½ × 19½ × 19½ in.
The Los Angeles County Museum of Art and The Huntington Library, Art Museum, and Botanical Gardens, purchased jointly with funds provided by Max Palevsky and Jodie Evans, the Decorative Arts and Design Council, the Frances Crandall Dyke Bequest, the Schweppe Art Acquisitions Fund, and MaryLou Boone, M.2009.115

A founder of the Century Guild, Mackmurdo declared that this loose collective of designers would restore the decorative arts "to their rightful place beside painting and sculpture." His iconic design for this chair, with its long, undulating plantlike forms, is now considered a key precedent of Art Nouveau and was included in virtually every history of the style. In addition to furniture and buildings, guild members produced metalwork, textiles, stained glass, and an influential journal.

Responses to Industrialization

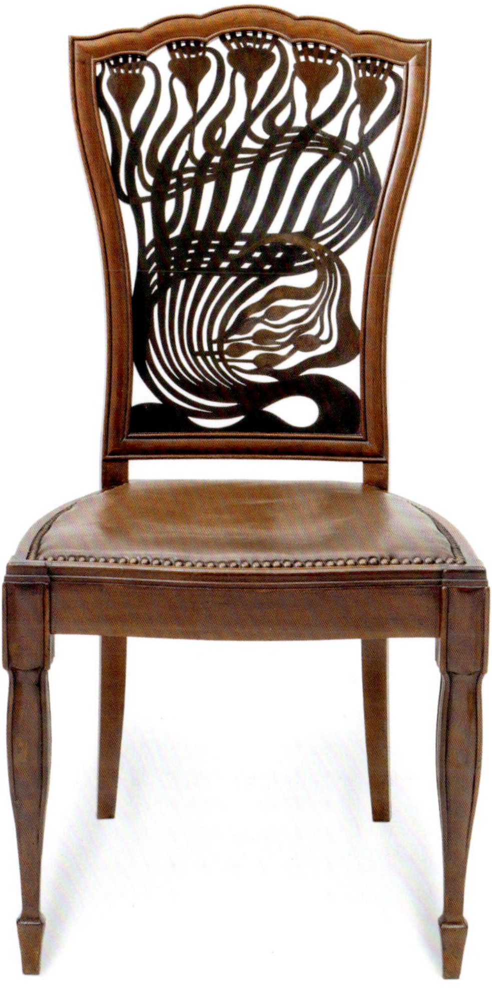

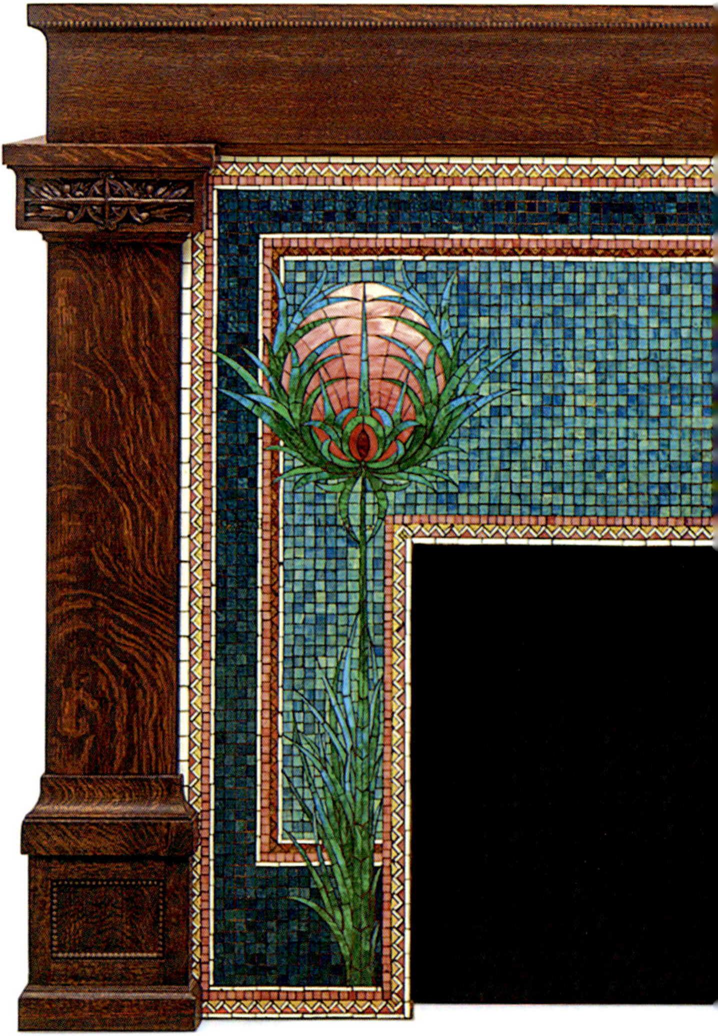

George Washington Maher (United States, 1864–1926)
Fireplace Surround from the Patrick J. King House, Chicago, 1901 (detail)
Made by the firm of Louis J. Millet (United States)
Oak, glass, and enamel; 58½ × 84 × 13½ in.
Gift of Max Palevsky and Jodie Evans in honor of the museum's 25th anniversary, M.89.151.8a–d

Prairie School architects embraced the ideal of design unity, and none more fervently than George Washington Maher. He developed what he called the "motif rhythm theory"—the constant repetition of an image drawn from nature, preferably one unique to the site or meaningful to the client. This motif would, he opined, "bind the design together." The stylized thistle on the fireplace surround from the Patrick King house in Chicago is found throughout the interior.

Mary Cottenham Yeats (Ireland, 1867–1947)
Chest with Scenes of Hy Brazil, c. 1901
Painted pine and wrought iron; 19 × 66 × 26 in.
Purchased with funds provided by Bruce Newman, M.2017.313

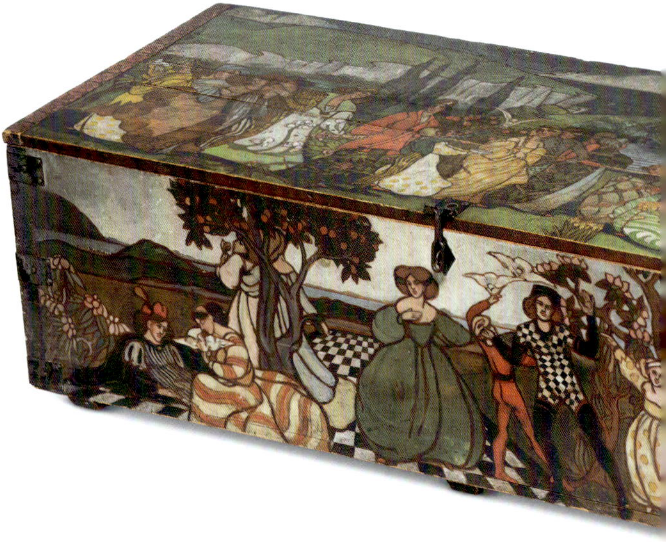

This chest depicts an idyllic scene on the mythic Irish island of Hy Brazil (Isle of the Blest). The pastoral lore appealed to Mary Cottenham Yeats, whose artistic circle—including her brother-in-law, poet W. B. Yeats—promoted Irish identity and national aspirations in the decades before the establishment of an independent state. In response to an increasingly industrialized society, these artists sought refuge in creating beautiful handcrafted objects, founding a guild that celebrated Irish history and traditional techniques.

Responses to Industrialization

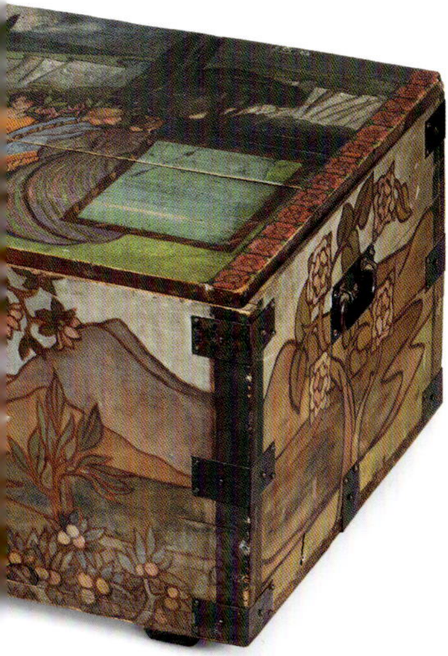

Frank Lloyd Wright (United States, 1867–1959)
Table Lamp for the Susan Lawrence Dana House, Illinois, 1902–4
Made by Linden Glass Company (United States)
Leaded glass, bronze, brass, and zinc; 23 × 29 × 29 in.
Gift of Max Palevsky, M.2000.180.44a–b

Wright's goal for the Prairie style was complete design unity—the total work of art created when building, furnishings, and setting form an environmental whole. He called this philosophy "organic design," insisting that a building "associate with the ground and become natural to its prairie site." The overhanging eaves of the Dana house were inspired by the low horizon of the prairie, as was the lamp's shade. And the glass, in earthy tones of amber, moss green, terracotta, and creamy white, echoes prairie colors.

Responses to Industrialization

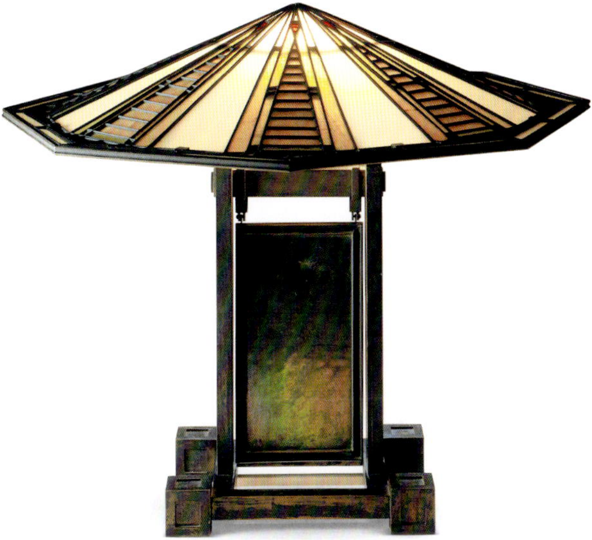

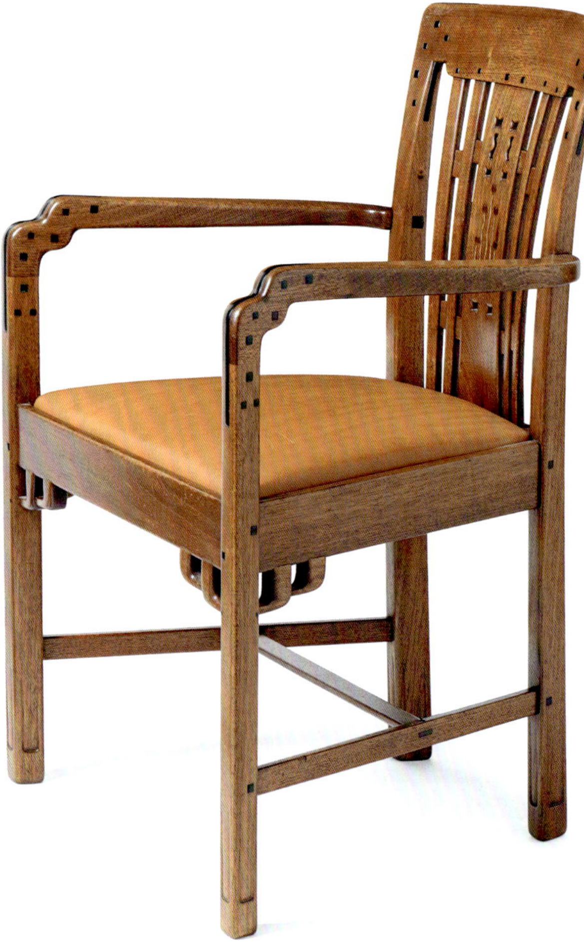

Charles Sumner Greene (United States, 1868–1957)
and Henry Mather Greene (United States, 1870–1954)
Made by Peter Hall Manufacturing Company (United States)
Armchair for the Robert R. Blacker House, Pasadena, California, 1907
Mahogany, ebony, oak, and upholstery (replaced); 33⅜ × 24¼ × 21⅝ in.
Gift of Max Palevsky and Jodie Evans, M.89.151.4

This armchair from one of the Greene brothers' most ambitious commissions embodies Arts and Crafts principles: total design unity (the Greenes were responsible for both the house and its furnishings), exaltation of fine craftsmanship, and Asia as a revered design source, manifest in the chair's "cloud lift" brackets. Unlike the typical use of local, sturdy white oak, however, the Blacker furniture was made with expensive, imported mahogany and ebony, explaining why the house has been called "the ultimate California bungalow."

Josef Hoffmann (Austria-Hungary, 1870–1956, active Austria), designer
Made by the Wiener Werkstätte (Austria)
Tea Set, 1922–23
Silver and ivory; teapot: 9¼ × 3 in.; creamer: 4⅛ × 6¼ × 2¾ in.;
sugar bowl and lid: 3¾ × 3⅞ in.; tray: 2½ × 24 × 4¾ in.
Gift of the 2007 Collectors Committee, M.2007.52.1–.4

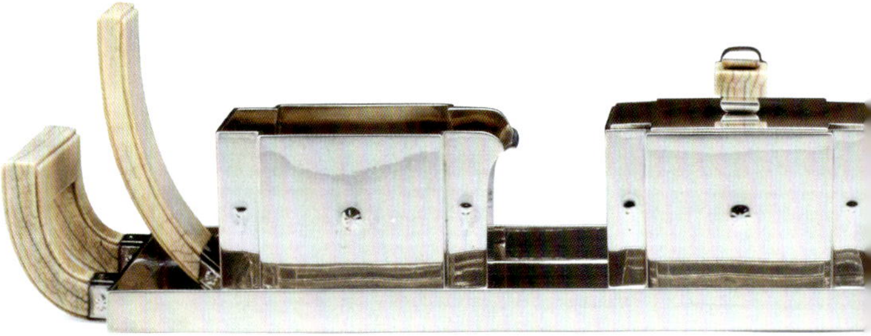

Josef Hoffmann was cofounder of the Wiener Werkstätte, the cooperative workshop at the center of avant-garde design in Austria. His work in countless mediums celebrated rigorous geometry—the repetition and creative interplay of circles and squares. This tea set, one of only three made, also demonstrates the influence of Viennese art in the United States after World War I. Proudly displayed at the short-lived outpost of the Werkstätte in New York, it was purchased by Oscar-winning screenwriter Frances Marion and brought to Los Angeles.

Responses to Industrialization

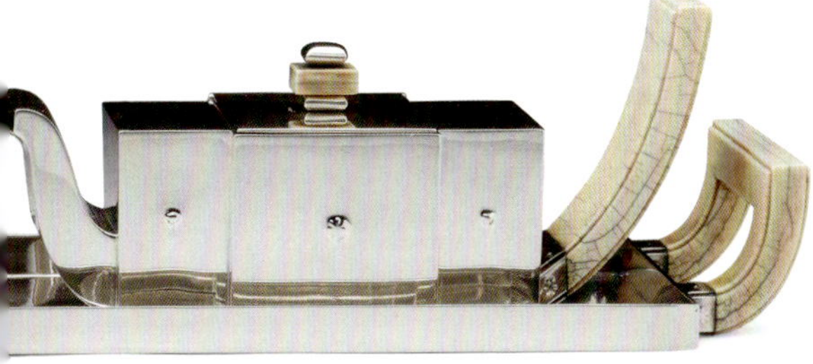

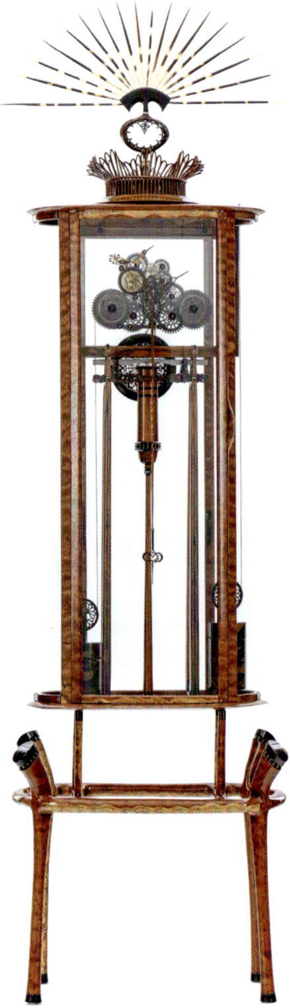

346 Atlantic

Frank E. Cummings III (United States, b. 1938)
*Only Time Will Tell* Clock, 2011–13
Curly and spalted bubinga, walnut, rosewood, ebony, African blackwood, oak root, 18k gold, glass, garnets, tourmalines, sapphire, topaz, rubies, diamonds, curved and etched mirror, porcupine quills, black pearls, and ivory; 88½ × 25¼ × 15½ in.
Gift of Frank E. Cummings III through the 2022 Collectors Committee, M.2022.174

Cummings's clock is a meditation on time, reflecting both the two years required to hand make nearly every component and the decades of artistic practice that led to this culminating work. A master woodworker and self-taught horologist, he created only two clocks, each marking a pivotal moment in his career. This second and final example incorporates precious materials Cummings saved and intricate motifs he'd perfected over many years, reflecting his assertion that "all of my works are vessels for my life."

Benedetto Buglioni (Florence, 1459/60–1521)
and Santi Buglioni (Florence, 1494–1576)
*The Buonafede Nativity*, c. 1520
Lead-glazed earthenware; 96⅛ × 78 × 10 in.
William Randolph Hearst Collection, 48.24.9

This large-scale altarpiece featuring the Nativity and the Adoration of the Shepherds was commissioned by Florentine cleric Leonardo Buonafede. The predella panels below the central scene contain images of his patron saints and coats of arms. Archival records reveal he commissioned several glazed terracotta sculptures from the popular Buglioni workshop in Florence. Run by cousins Benedetto and Santi Buglioni, the workshop produced objects in pieces that could be easily transported from Florence to other locations and reassembled upon arrival.

Grandeur in Sacred Spaces

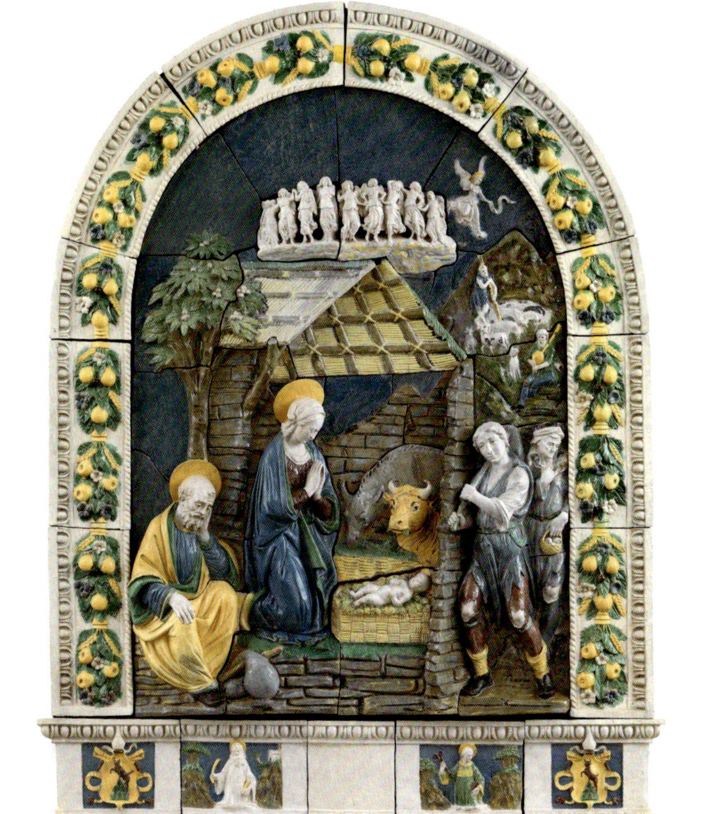

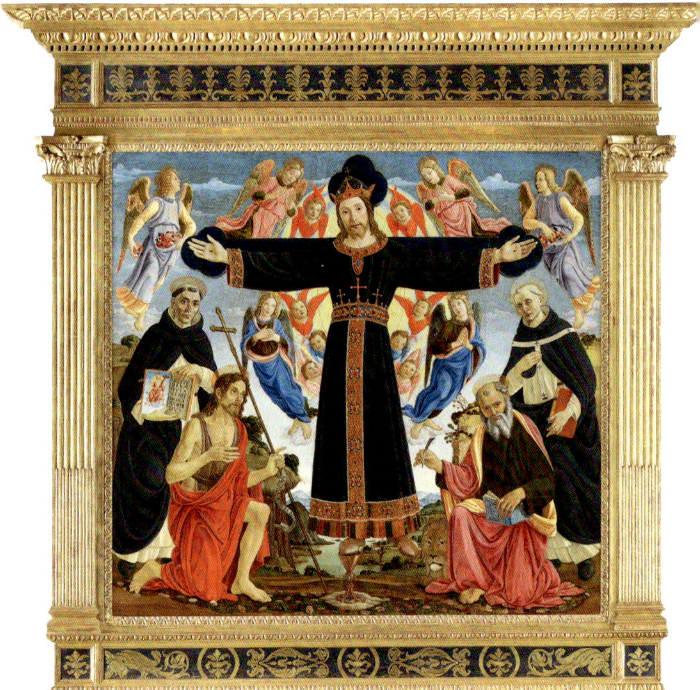

Master of the Fiesole Epiphany (Florence, active c. 1450–1500)
*Christ on the Cross with Saints Vincent Ferrer, John the Baptist, Mark, and Antoninus*, c. 1491–95
Tempera and possibly oil on panel; 72¾ × 79¾ in.
Gift of The Ahmanson Foundation, M.91.242

The Master of the Fiesole Epiphany depicts Christ affixed to a cross and flanked by four saints specific to the Dominican church of San Marco in Florence. The painting honors a miraculous wooden sculpture of the Holy Face of Lucca, purportedly carved by the biblical figure Nicodemus and completed by angels. The sculpture in the Cathedral of Lucca was adorned with an imperial crown and elaborate ankle-length tunic (colobium) whose detail in this painting reflects Lucca's importance as a center for silk production.

Grandeur in Sacred Spaces

Possibly Middelburg (Netherlands)
Heraldic Panel, 1620–25 (detail)
Glass, lead came, enamel, and silver stain; 33¼ × 17¾ in.
William Randolph Hearst Collection, 45.21.57

This stained-glass panel, one of a series of six, likely decorated a mercantile building in Middelburg, an important port city of the Dutch East India Company. Ships returning from their voyages to Asia and Africa often first docked in Middelburg. The panel's imagery features several references to global transoceanic trade, including a seascape with ships flying Dutch tricolor flags, a Semper Augustus tulip originally from Turkey, and a golden chrysanthemum from China.

Heraldry in European Decorative Arts

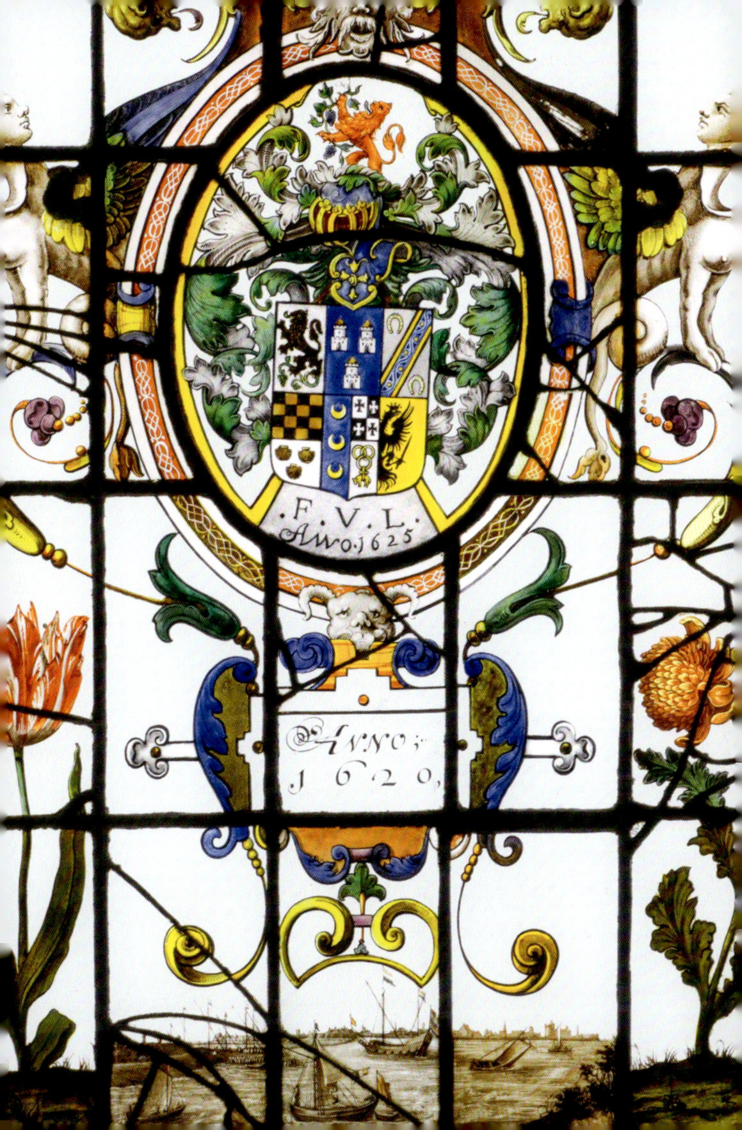

.F.V.L.
Anno.1625
Anno.
1620.

Giovanni di Paolo (Siena, c. 1395/99–1482)
*Triptych with the Enthroned Virgin between Saints*, c. 1427–30
Tempera and gold on panel; 25¾ × 22⅛ in.
Gift of The Ahmanson Foundation, AC1996.139.1a–b

This triptych by the Sienese artist Giovanni di Paolo depicts the Madonna and Christ Child atop a carpet whose stylized animal figures were inspired by textiles. Elsewhere are religious figures and saints with instruments of their martyrdom. The triptych was likely commissioned as a devotional object for a wealthy patron. Its base includes a notch for a candle, whose flickering light would have transformed the gilded surface into an otherworldly experience.

Gold-Ground Painting in Europe

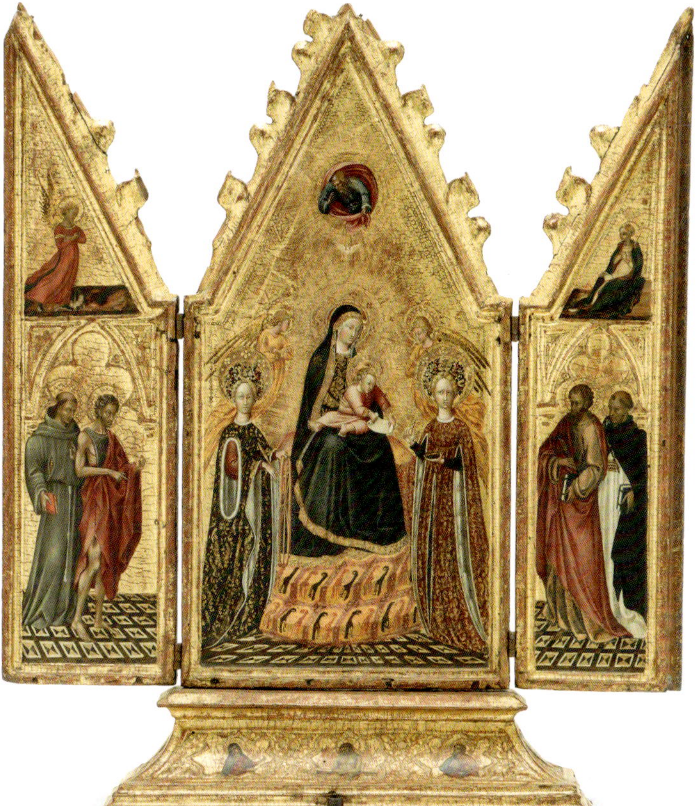

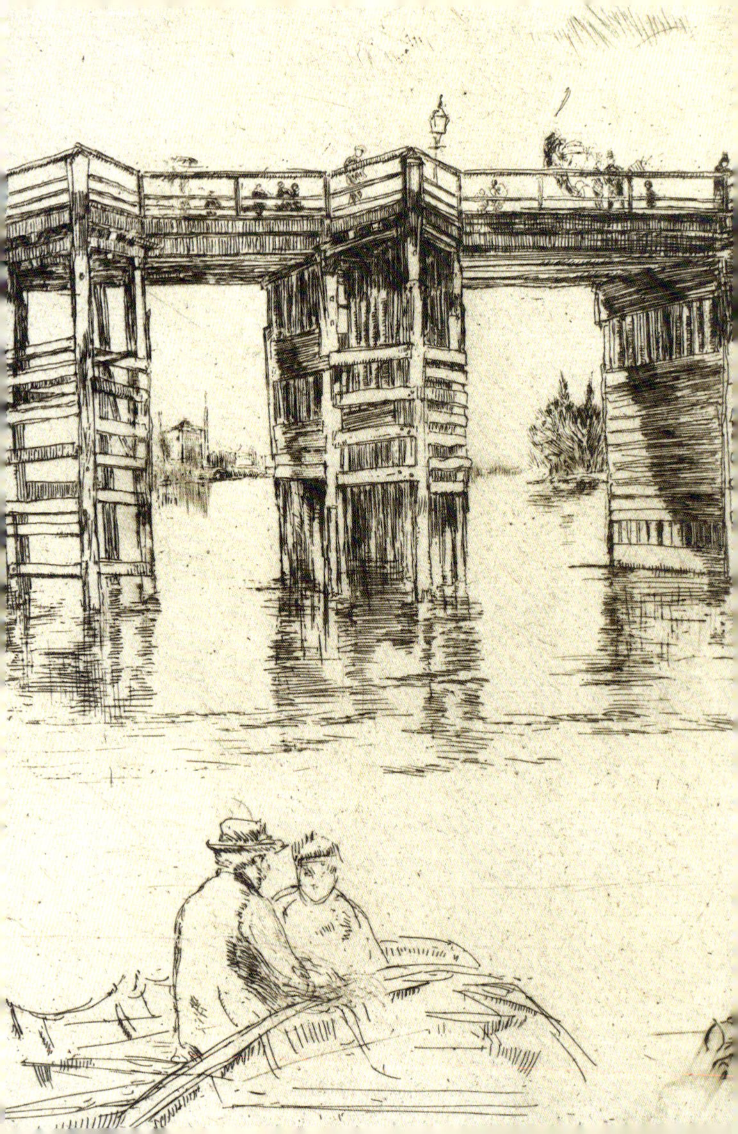

James McNeill Whistler (United States, 1834–1903, active England)
*Old Putney Bridge*, 1879 (detail)
Etching and drypoint; 8 × 11⅝ in.
The Julius L. and Anita Zelman Collection, AC1992.234.9

In this Thames view, James McNeill Whistler captured the wooden Fulham (or "Old Putney") Bridge shortly before its replacement by a stone bridge in 1886. He established the structure's piers with emphatic inking, and animated the span with figures and carriages crossing above. In the foreground, two lightly sketched flat-bottomed boats lead the eye across the water to the richly detailed bridge, suggesting the artist's own vantage point.

In Conversation: James McNeill Whistler and Japan

Frederick Hurten Rhead (England, 1880–1942, active United States)
University City Pottery (United States)
Vase, 1911
Glazed earthenware; height: 17¼ in.
Gift of Max Palevsky and Jodie Evans, M.91.375.44

British émigré Frederick Hurten Rhead was among America's leading ceramists in the early twentieth century. His career included many kinds of production, ranging from his own studio work to designs for prominent commercial potteries. One was the University City Pottery in Missouri, where elite ceramists were invited to experiment free from financial imperatives. The short-lived venture enabled Rhead to create ambitious, unique works like this vase, which showcases his virtuosic incised design and expertise in matte glazes.

International Currents in Ceramics

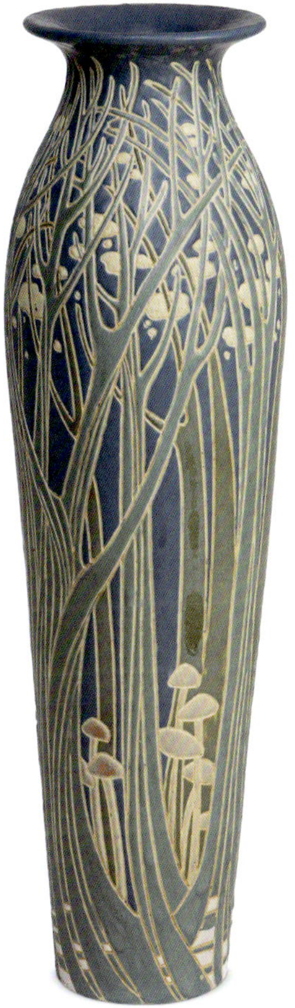

Ladi Kwali (Nigeria, 1925-1984)
Water Jar, c. 1962
Stoneware with porcelain slip; 14¾ × 15¼ × 15¼ in.
Gift of the 2024 Collectors Committee, M.2024.82.1

Nigerian ceramist Ladi Kwali was renowned for combining Indigenous ceramic traditions and European practices. Trained in her native village, she then studied with British potter Michael Cardew, who introduced her to new clays and glazes that gave her work durability and a shimmery, almost iridescent luster. Here, the incised motifs record the natural world of northern Nigeria—fish, birds, scorpions, and lizards. Kwali became a national hero—for the past fifty years, her image has graced a Nigerian banknote, and she has inspired many younger artists in her country and beyond.

International Currents in Ceramics

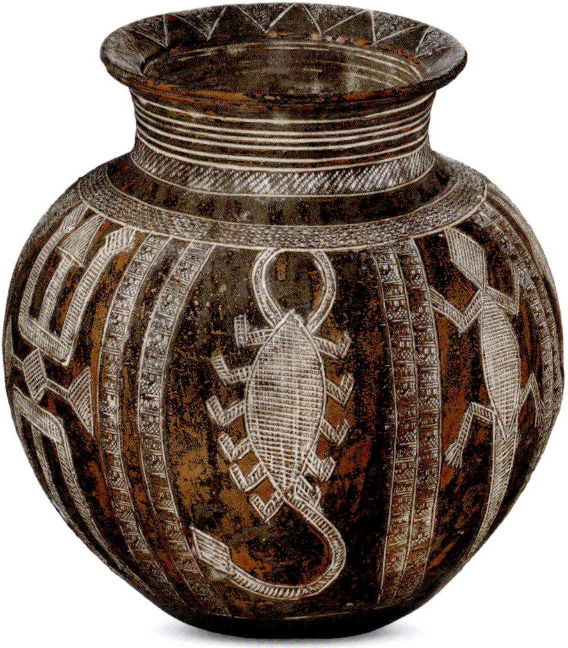

Marianne Brandt (Germany, 1893–1983)
Ashtray, 1924
Designed at the Bauhaus Metal Workshop (Germany)
Brass alloy and nickel-plated brass; 2¾ × 4¾ × 4¼ in.
Gift of the 2024 Decorative Arts and Design Acquisitions Committee ($DA^2$)
with additional support from Suzanne Kayne, M.2024.105.1

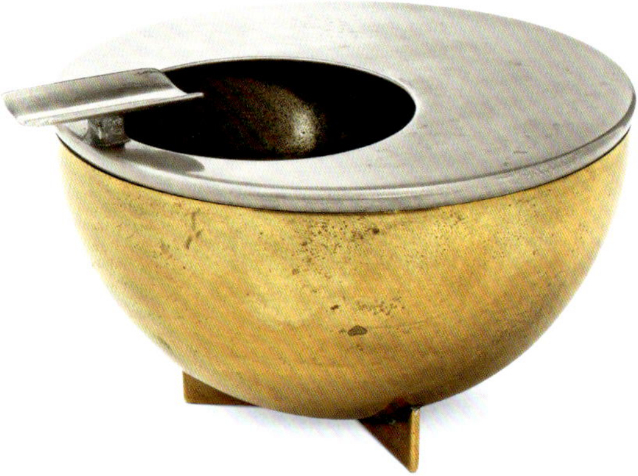

Marianne Brandt was a student and later head of the Metal Workshop at the Bauhaus in Germany, the progressive Weimar-era school of art and design. In this ashtray, she reduced the object to its essential, geometric forms (a partial cylinder above a half-sphere), suitable for mass production. All of Brandt's works, including this ashtray, so exemplified the Bauhaus ideal of creating modern goods for the modern world that they became symbolic of the school itself.

Modernism in the Marketplace

Walter Dorwin Teague (United States, 1883–1960)
*Nocturne* Radio, 1934
Manufacturer: Sparton Corporation (United States)
Mirrored glass and chrome-plated and lacquered metal; 46 × 43½ × 12 in.
Decorative Arts and Design Council Fund in honor of Joel Chen receiving the 2012 Design Leadership Award, Debbie and Mark Attanasio, Waldo Fernandez, Carole Gaba, Ric and Suzanne Kayne, Evans Y. Lam, Shau-Wai and Marie Lam Family Foundation, Lee Family, Los Angeles Modern Auctions (LAMA), Off The Wall Antiques, Susan and Eric Smidt, Michael S. Smith, Priscilla and Curtis Tamkin, David and Deborah Trainer, and Margaret Weitzman, M.2012.115

A towering console of chrome and mirrored cobalt glass, the *Nocturne* radio was intended to dazzle with its unusual circular form. It embodies the machine aesthetic of the 1930s, which, in the depths of the Depression, became a comforting metaphor for speed and progress. Geometric abstraction was considered appropriate for the radio, the most advanced communication technology of its time. The *Nocturne* originally retailed for $350 ($9,000 today), far beyond the means of most Americans, and therefore was mostly found in upscale hotel lobbies.

Modernism in the Marketplace

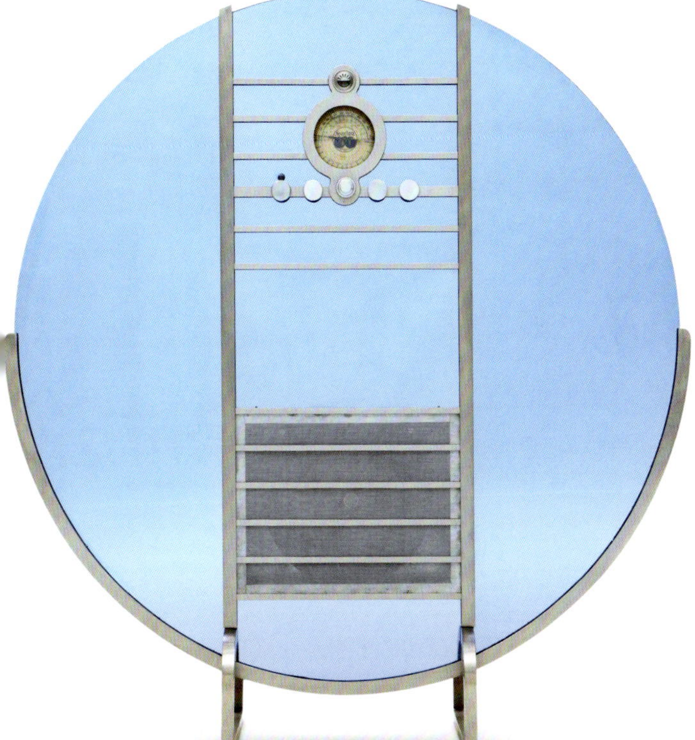

Edward Weston (United States, 1886–1958)
*Armco, Ohio*, 1922
Gelatin silver print; 9⅝ × 7⅝ in.
Anonymous gift, 46.61.24

Just before relocating to Mexico in 1922, Edward Weston visited Middletown, Ohio, where his brother-in-law worked in the steel industry. Captivated by the stark beauty of the American Rolling Mills Company factory, he photographed abstracted images of pipes, smokestacks, and utility poles against a white winter sky. This photograph marked a pivotal shift from Weston's earlier soft-focus Pictorialist style toward the sharp, direct modernism that would define his later career.

Pictorialism to Modernism in Photography

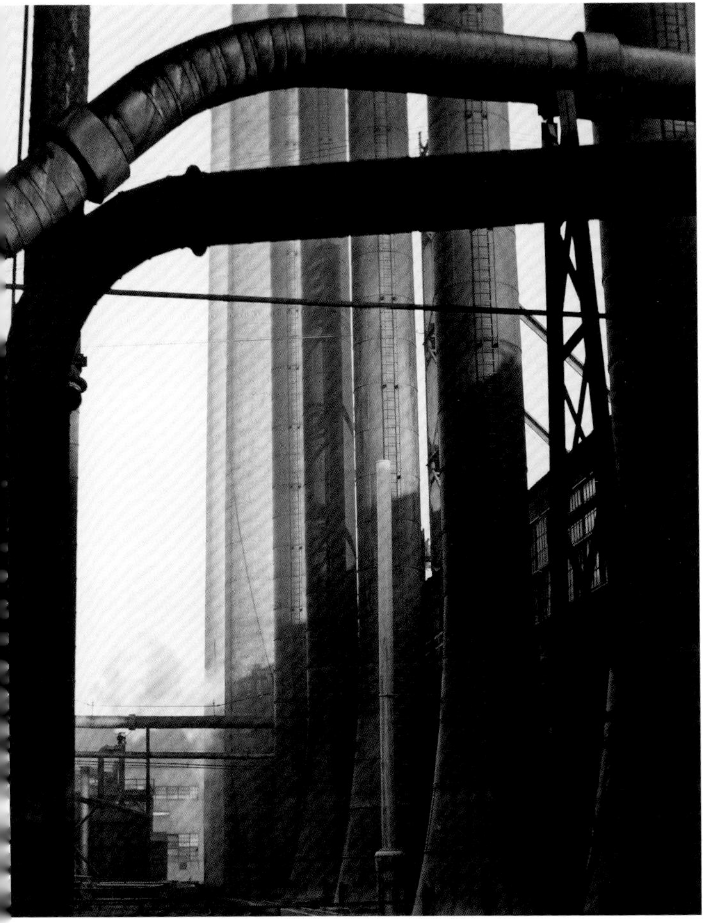

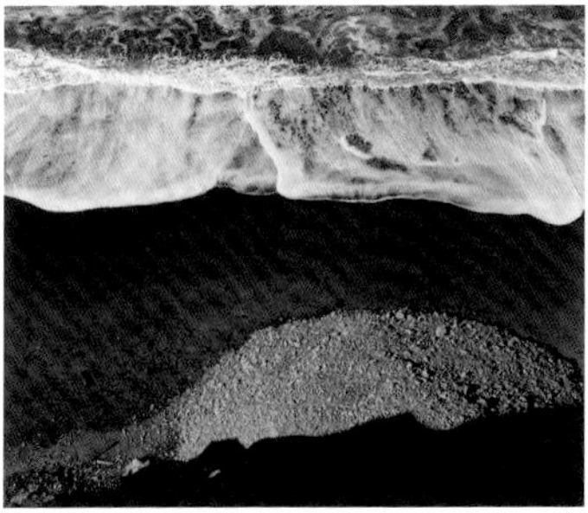

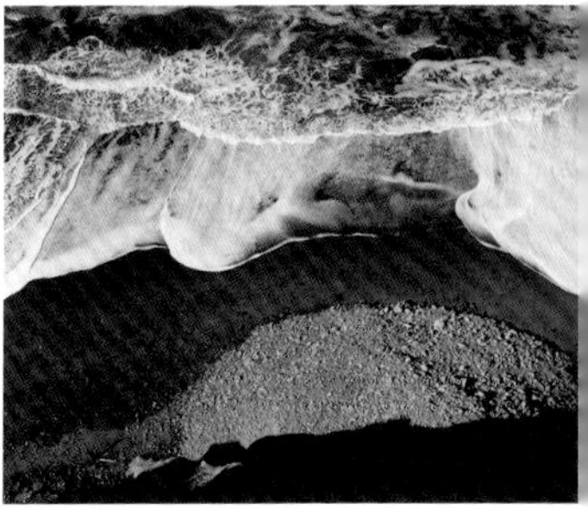

Driving along Highway 1 in San Mateo County early one morning, Ansel Adams stopped to photograph the Pacific Ocean. Using a 4 × 5-inch view camera, he made a sequence of five exposures while waves continually crawled up over the sandy beach just to the edge of the rocks. The resulting gelatin silver prints abstract the larger seascape into repeating patterns that echo rhythmic sequences, a reflection of Adams's musical training.

Tonal Variations: Photography and Music

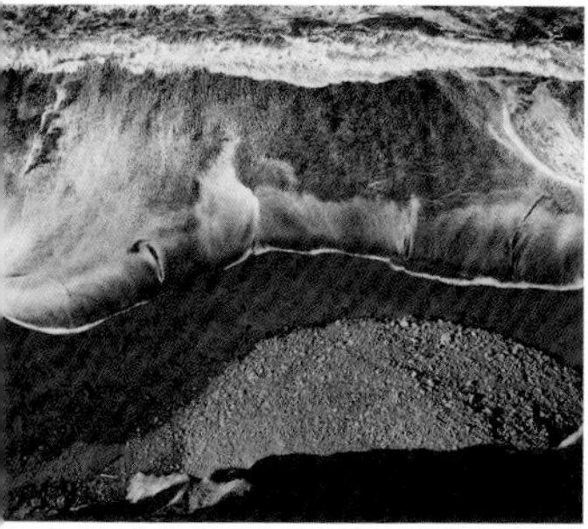

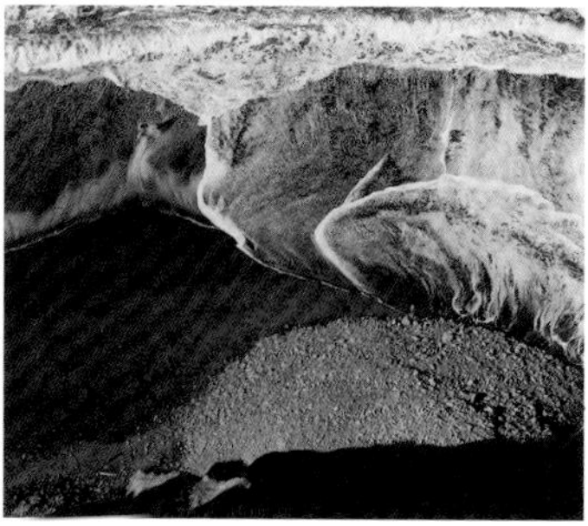

Ansel Adams (United States, 1902–1984)
*Surf Sequence*, c. 1940, printed after 1972 (4 of 5 shown)
Gelatin silver prints; each 11 × 13⅛ in.
The Marjorie and Leonard Vernon Collection, gift of the Annenberg Foundation and Carol Vernon and Robert Turbin, M.2008.40.49.1–.5

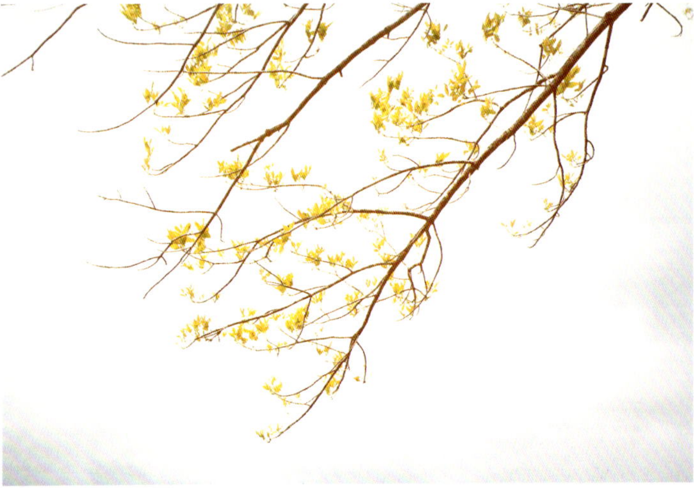

William Eggleston (United States, b. 1939)
*Untitled*, c. 1976
Dye coupler print; 10⅛ × 15 in.
Gift of Caldecot Chubb, M.2011.196.4

A pioneer of color photography, William Eggleston helped establish the medium as fine art beginning in the early 1970s. Here, an isolated tree branch with budding yellow flowers appears against puffy white and gray clouds. Eggleston's oblique upward angle and off-kilter perspective abstract the scene, transforming an ordinary Southern landscape into a study in color and form. The composition recalls Alfred Stieglitz's early twentieth-century cloud photographs, the *Equivalents*, which marked photography's first intentional move toward abstraction.

Tonal Variations: Photography and Music

Thomas Joshua Cooper (United States, b. 1946, active Scotland)
*Looking toward Antarctica and Dreaming—Drake Passage, Cabo de Hornos/Cape Horn, #1, Isla Hornos, Islas Hermite, Antártica Chilena, Chile, Very near the South-Most Point of All South America*, 2006, printed 2017
Gelatin silver chlorobromide print, toned with selenium; 40 × 54 in.
Gift of Lannan Foundation, M.2020.82.43

Since the early 1970s, Thomas Joshua Cooper has been photographing outdoors, traveling to remote sites and exposing one negative per location using a nineteenth-century view camera. Here, the waves have created a white arrow directing viewers toward the Drake Passage—a dangerous trade route connecting the Atlantic and Pacific Oceans named for the sixteenth-century English explorer Sir Francis Drake. While Cooper's approach has cartographic aspects, he is ultimately devoted to generating psychological impact.

Thomas Joshua Cooper: Atlantic Basin Photographs

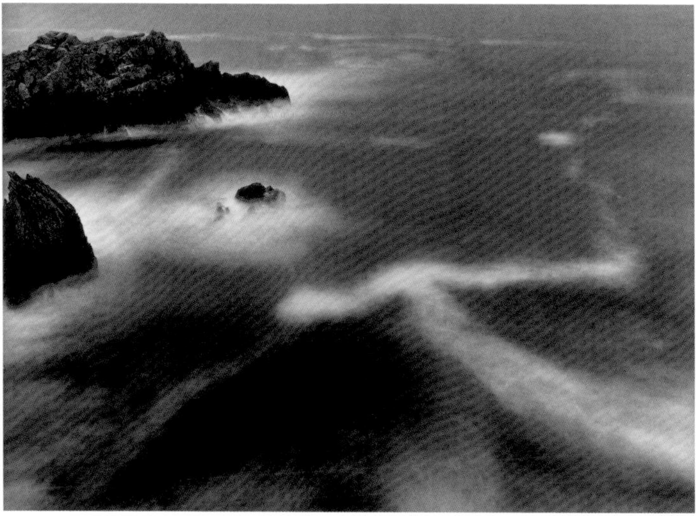

Joaquim Tenreiro (Portugal, 1906–1992, active Brazil)
Three-Legged Chair, c. 1947–60
Ivorywood (*pau marfim*), Brazilian Angel's Heart (*angelim pedra*);
21¼ × 29⅛ × 26⅜ in.
Purchased with funds provided by the Bernard and Edith Lewin Collection of Mexican Art Deaccession Fund, M.2020.11.1

This gently curved seat with a striped design is made from two alternating woods, showcasing Joaquim Tenreiro's masterful command of woodworking. The first version of the chair was commissioned by Brazilian playwright José Silveira Sampaio for the set of his satirical play *On the Necessity of Being Polygamous*, in which the seat's three legs reference the plot's central love triangle. The chair became one of Tenreiro's most acclaimed midcentury designs, incorporating different Brazilian woods to create its vibrant pattern.

Turmoil and Optimism in Latin America

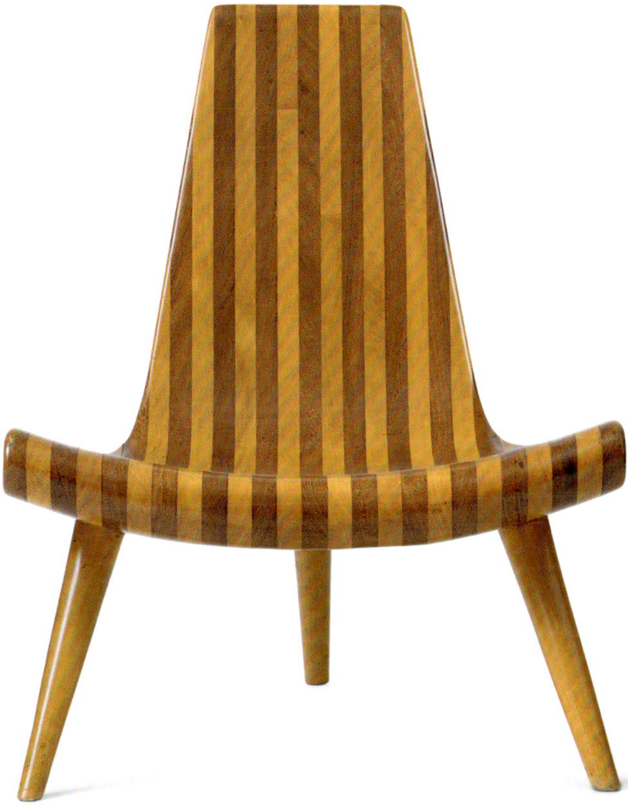

Julio Le Parc (Argentina, b. 1928, active France)
*Mural: Virtual Circles*, 1964–66 (detail)
Wood, aluminum, stainless steel, and polished metal; 80 1/2 × 165 1/4 × 14 in.
Purchased with funds provided by Debbie and Mark Attanasio, Jane and Marc Nathanson, Jane and Terry Semel, The Loreen Arbus Foundation, Janet Dreisen Rappaport and Herb Rappaport, an anonymous donor, Alyce Woodward Oppenheimer, and the Bernard and Edith Lewin Collection of Mexican Art Deaccession Fund through the 2013 Collectors Committee, M.2013.115a–g

Seen from the front, this work is deceptively static but becomes fully activated with the slightest movement of the viewer. Julio Le Parc was a prominent member of the Op and kinetic art movements. In 1960, two years after moving to Paris, he cofounded the Groupe de Recherche d'Art Visuel (GRAV). The group's goal was to break from traditional art by creating playful, participatory works that destabilized viewers' perceptions—what Le Parc called a "plastic kinetic adventure."

Turmoil and Optimism in Latin America

Oscar Niemeyer (Brazil, 1907–2012) and Anna Maria Niemeyer (Brazil, 1929–2012)
Rio Chaise, 1978
Manufacturer: Tendo Brasileira (Brazil)
Lacquered plywood, cane, and leather; 24 × 67 × 35 in.
Purchased with funds provided by the Bernard and Edith Lewin Collection of Mexican Art Deaccession Fund, M.2020.206

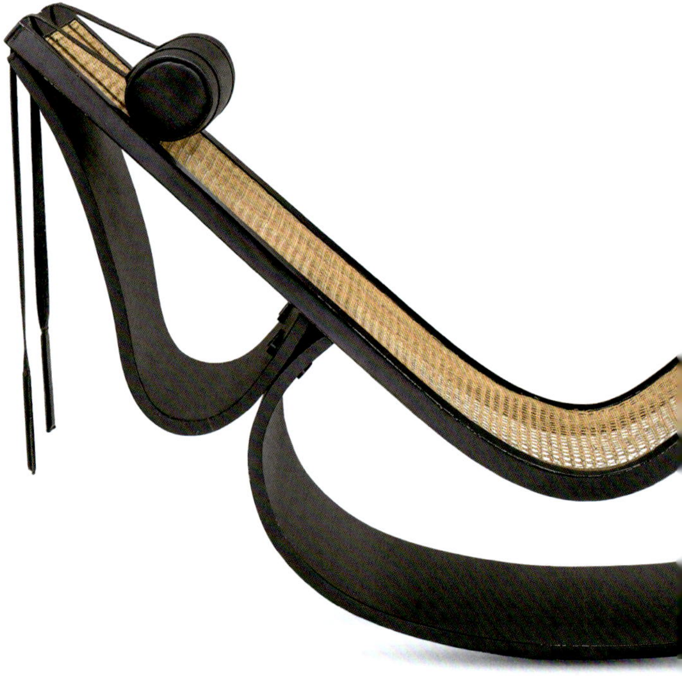

The Brazilian architect Oscar Niemeyer designed this chaise in collaboration with his daughter Anna Maria Niemeyer. The materials are skillfully balanced to produce a functional and sculptural form that resembles a drawing in space. His preference for organic forms is reflected in the chair's sinuous lines. "I am not attracted to straight angles or to the straight line, hard and inflexible, created by man," Niemeyer stated. "I am attracted to free-flowing, sensual curves.... Curves make up the entire universe."

Turmoil and Optimism in Latin America

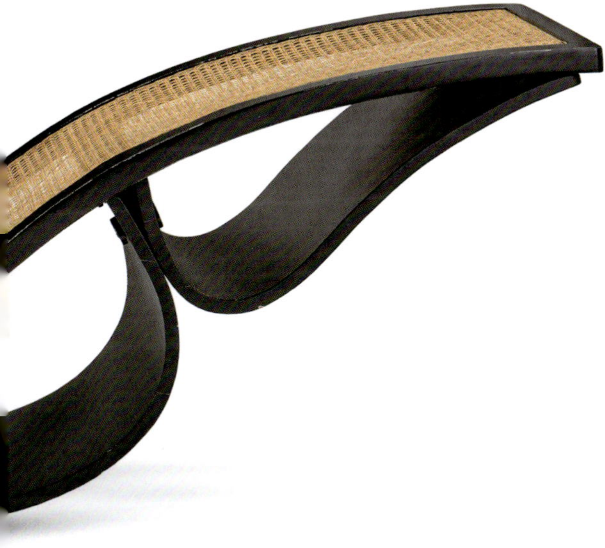

Bamana blacksmith (Republic of Mali)
*Gwandansu* (Mother and Child for the Gwan Association), c. 1279–1395
Wood; 38 × 11½ × 12 in.
Gift of the 2013 Collectors Committee, with additional funds provided by Kelvin Davis and Bobby Kotick, M.2014.19

This rare Bamana mother-and-child figure embodies fertility, protection, and generational continuity. Gwan sculptures, among the largest in Bamana art, support women through childbirth and honor the spiritual force associated with new life and iron smelting. With elongated proportions, serene poise, and an infant clinging to her torso, the figure conveys dignity and strength. The worn, richly patinated surface reflects centuries of ritual washing, anointing, and offerings during annual Gwan celebrations. Radiocarbon dating places the work in the thirteenth to late fourteenth century.

The Power of Objects in West and Central Africa

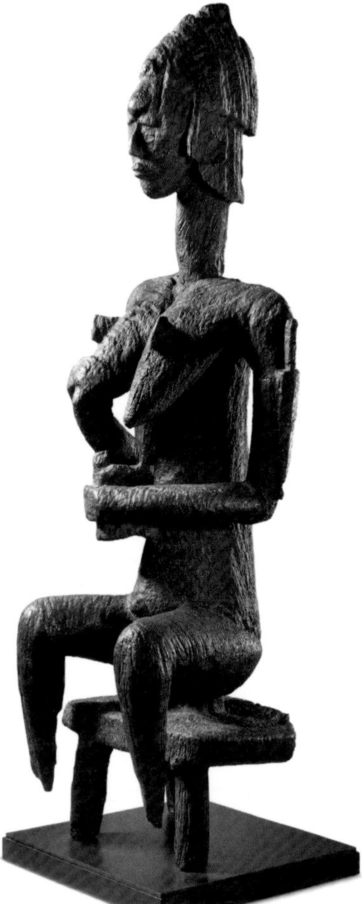

El Anatsui (Ghana, b. 1944, active Nigeria)
*Fading Scroll*, 2007 (detail)
Aluminum liquor-bottle caps, wrappers, and copper wire; 136 × 472 in.
LACMA and the Fowler Museum, UCLA, purchased jointly with funds provided by The Broad Art Foundation, Phil Berg, Mary and Robert Looker, and Margaret Pexton Murray, M.2008.110

El Anatsui transforms discarded bottle caps into shimmering textile-like sculptures that reference Ghanaian woven traditions while addressing themes of consumption, labor, and globalization. Composed of intricately linked metal fragments, *Fading Scroll* exemplifies his evolving practice of sourcing materials from distilleries and recycling centers and working with a collaborative studio team. The work's flexible structure allows it to be draped or folded in multiple configurations, emphasizing its fluid, ever-changing form and dynamic relationship to architectural space.

The Power of Objects in West and Central Africa

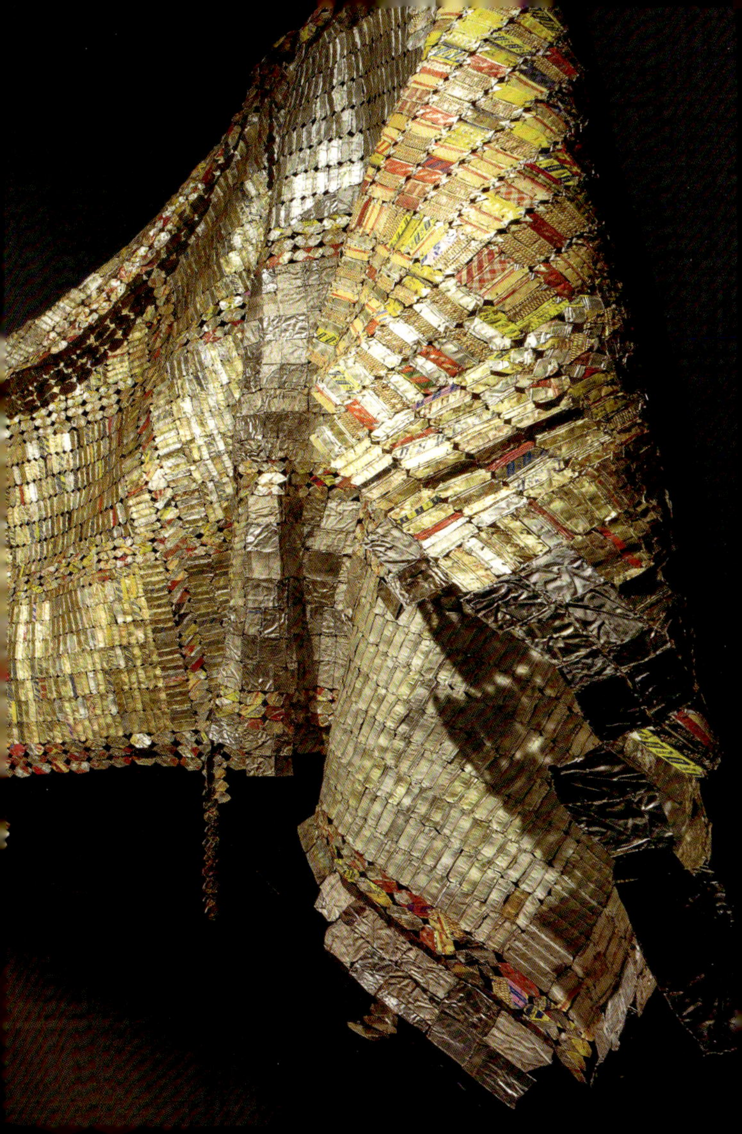

Rosie Lee Tompkins (United States, 1936–2006)
*Hit and Miss Strip*, 1983 (detail)
Silk and rayon velvets and cotton velveteen, pieced and quilted;
109¾ × 73 in.
Gift of the 2019 Collectors Committee, M.2019.219.5

California Bay Area artist Rosie Lee Tompkins collected velvet and velveteen clothing from stores, then deconstructed and cut the garments into unmeasured cloth fragments. As her hands assembled each unique piece into irregular strips of cloth, her mind managed the variations that provided additional opportunities for improvisation when combining the strips into a dynamic quilt-top composition of various shapes, with shifting color tones due to the cut-pile nap direction of each textile.

Textile Conversations: Africa and Black America

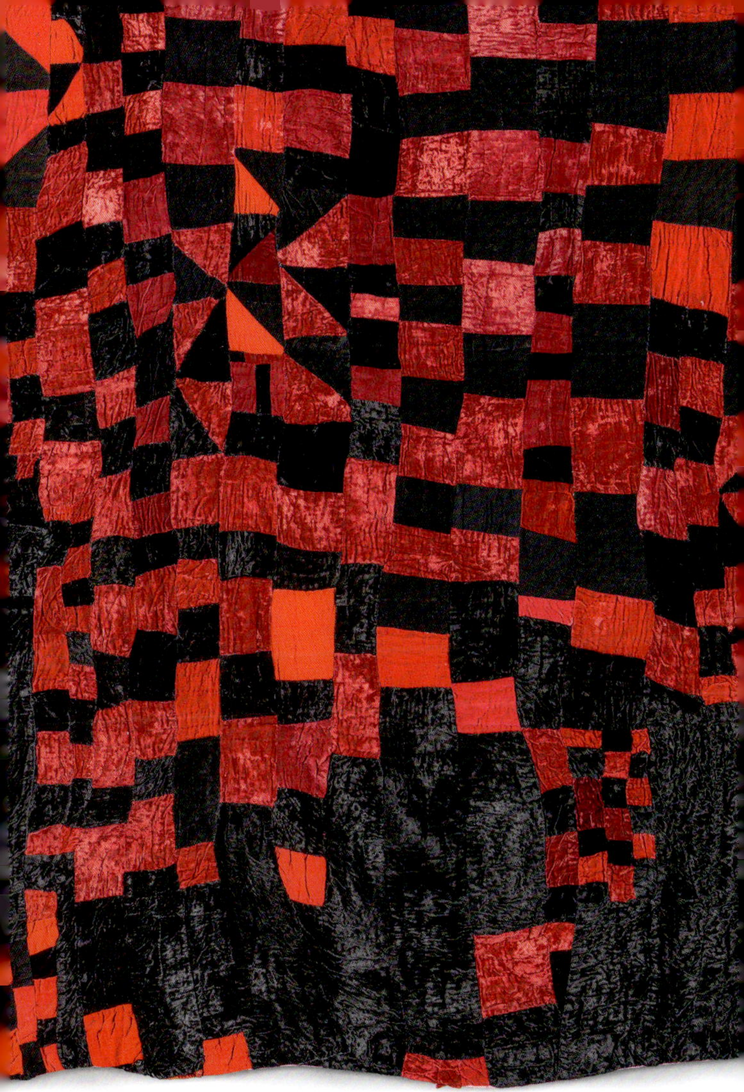

Kuba people, Shoowa group (Democratic Republic of the Congo)
Ceremonial Textile Panel, late 19th–early 20th century
Raffia, woven, with raffia cut-pile embroidery; 26 × 28 in.
Gift of the 2009 Collectors Committee, M.2009.43.5

In an activity considered as crucial as hunting, Kuba men wove raffia palm fibers into cloth panels in sizes determined by the length of the fronds. After being cut from the loom, the panels were handed to women, who embellished them with raffia embroidery and cut-pile techniques. Through the repetition of motifs, shifts in scale, and directional interruptions of lines, Kuba women created free-form visual compositions akin to those of modern African American improvisational jazz musicians.

Textile Conversations: Africa and Black America

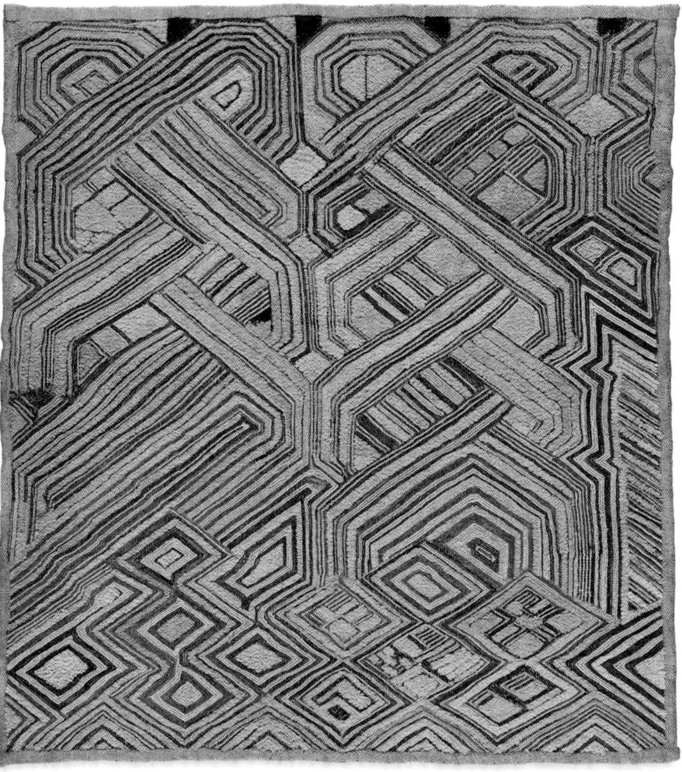

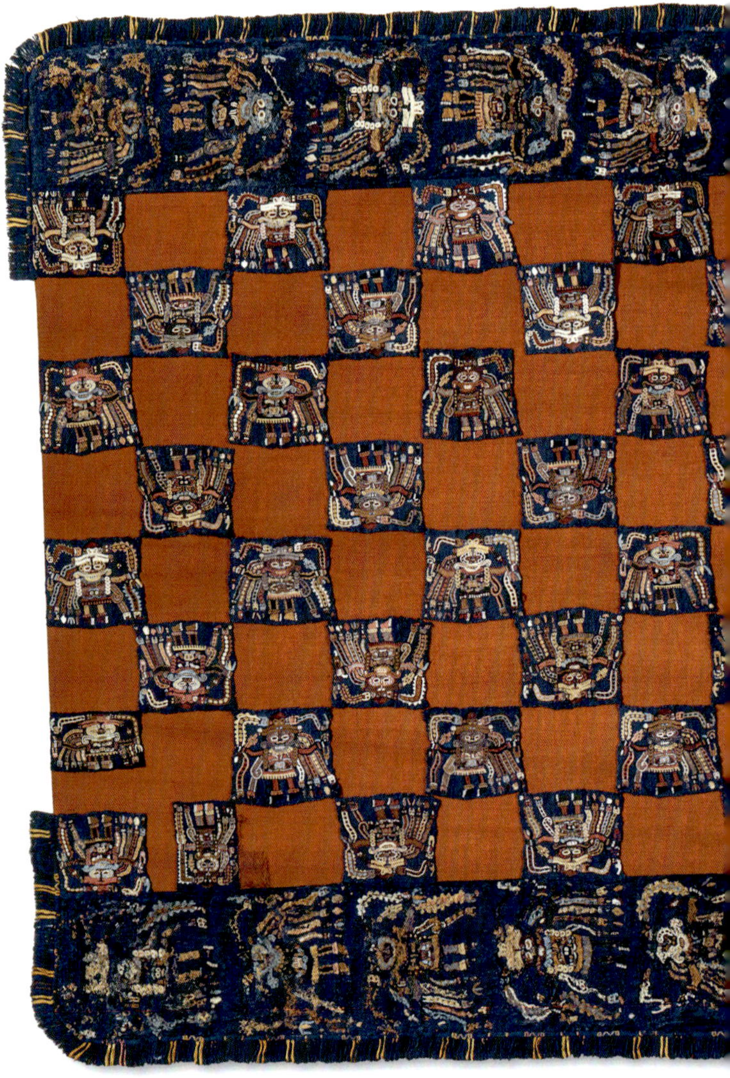

Paracas artists (Peru)
Mantle, made c. 100 BCE–200 CE (detail)
Camelid fiber, woven and embroidered; 59 × 101 in.
Costume Council Fund, M.72.68.7

Paracas weavers developed the earliest sophisticated textile tradition in South America. They often embellished woven color-blocked designs with embroidered motifs that reference the physical environment: plants, animals, and people. Floating figures like these—shown standing upright or flying downward—may depict supernatural beings or ritual performers. The garments and adornments worn by the figures, including necklaces, ear danglers, and tunics, are identical to some recovered from ancient burial sites.

South American Symbolic Universes

Guaraní artists, Franciscan missions (Paraguay)
Cabinet and Writing Desk, 18th century (detail)
Wood, mother-of-pearl, and bronze; open: 91 × 105½ × 30¾ in.;
closed: 91 × 59¾ × 30¾ in.
Gift of the 2022 Collectors Committee with additional funds provided by Ryan Seacrest, Ann Colgin & Joe Wender, and the Bernard and Edith Lewin Collection of Mexican Art Deaccession Fund, M.2022.11.1–.28

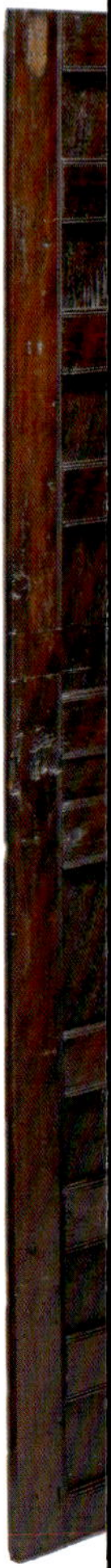

This exuberant cabinet inlaid with tropical woods and freshwater shells was created by Indigenous Guaraní artists, likely in a Franciscan mission in Paraguay. The amphibious creatures may relate to Guaraní cosmology, and figures of Indigenous chieftains, one wearing a lip ornament that symbolizes virility, recline nearby. Local birds, flowers, and stylized geometric motifs combine with elements associated with the Spanish world (bulls, lions, horses, and angels), demonstrating a remarkable degree of Indigenous artistic agency under Spanish rule.

South American Symbolic Universes

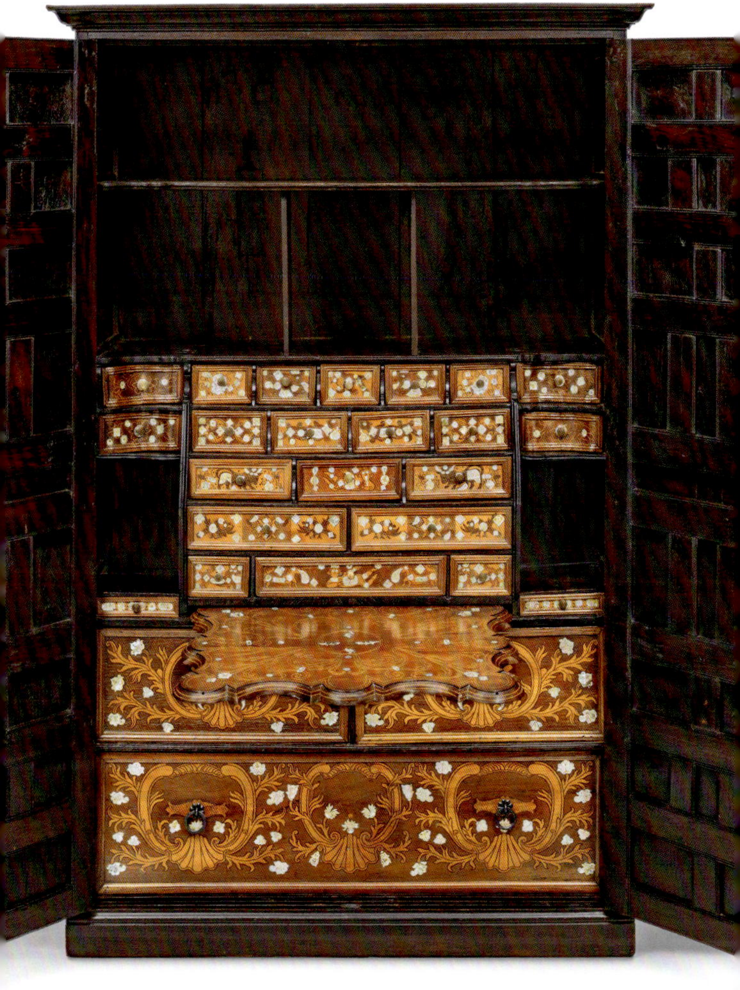

Maya artists (Guatemala)
*Birth of Huk Siip*, made c. 650–800 CE
Engobe-painted earthenware; height: 6½ in.; diameter: 5⅝ in.
Anonymous gift, M.2010.115.3

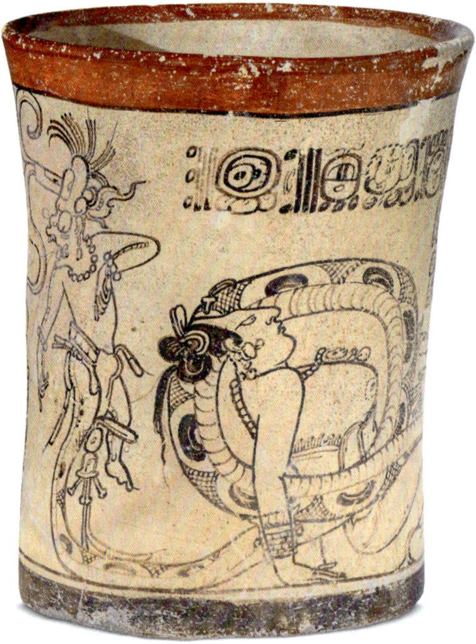

Enveloping the surface of this drinking cup, rendered in a limited palette of black and cream, a serpent extends from the leg of the lightning deity K'awiil and wraps its gargantuan body around a bare-chested woman. She sits facing an old man who emerges from the serpent's maw, reaching for her. The glyphic text describes the enigmatic scene as the birth of Huk Siip, an old deity of the hunt.

Stonework from Mesoamerica and the Caribbean Coast

Olmec artists (Mexico)
Crouching Man with Jaguar Features, "Transformation Figure," made c. 900–400 BCE
Serpentine with cinnabar; height: 4¼ in.
Gift of Constance McCormick Fearing, M.86.311.6

This figurine, posed in an eternal crouch, has a protruding upper lip, like that of a snarling jaguar, and the furrowed brow of the Olmec rain deity, as if his feline nature were emerging from beneath a human form. In Mesoamerican societies, jaguars can influence the health and sickness, protection and destruction of both individual and community. Sculpted from unyielding serpentine, a stone associated with agriculture and abundance, the figure embodies the power necessary to provide for humankind.

Stonework from Mesoamerica and the Caribbean Coast

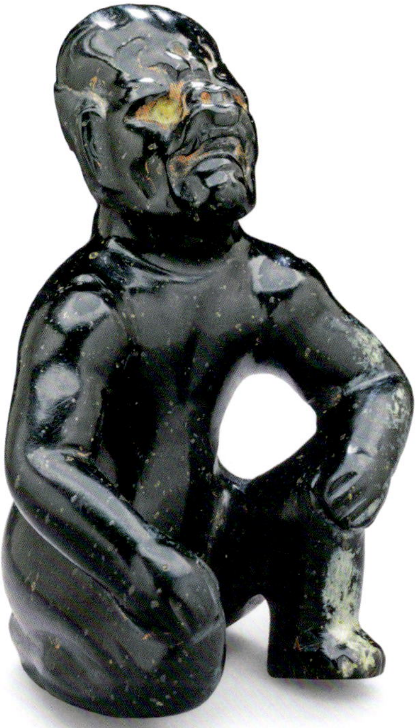

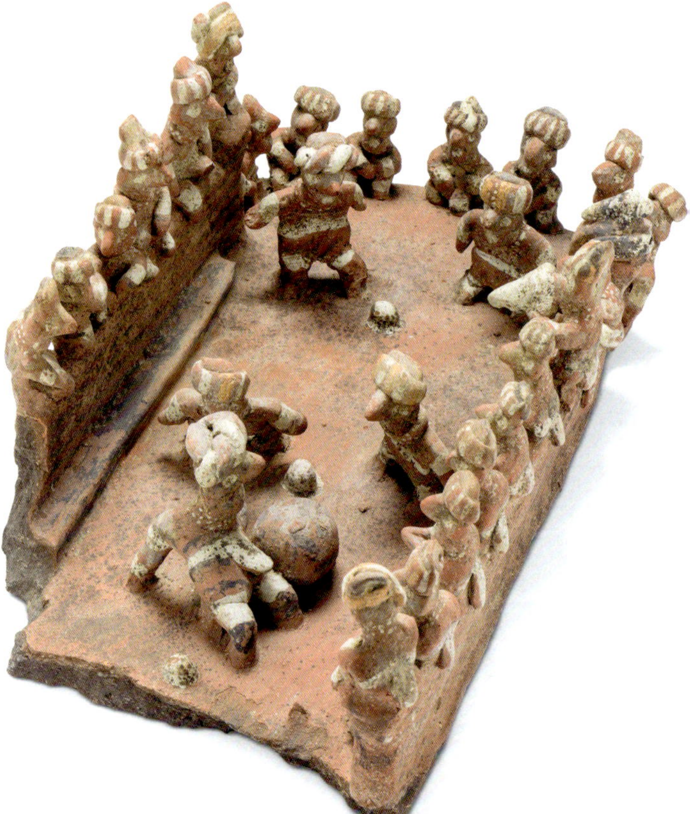

Artists working in the Nayarit tradition (Mexico)
Ballgame Scene, made c. 200 BCE–500 CE
Slip-painted earthenware with postfire pigment; 6 × 8½ × 13½ in.
The Proctor Stafford Collection, purchased with funds provided by Mr. and Mrs. Allan C. Balch, M.86.296.34

The Mesoamerican ballgame has been played since around 1500 BCE, and this ceramic model captures the sport's athletic intensity in miniature form. A player prepares to strike the oversized ball with his hip while spectators and musicians line the court. Garments draped on the wall likely represent the players' clothing, removed before the game. Rulers, warriors, and gods engaged in the ballgame, and its outcome and meaning had great religious and political ramifications across Mesoamerica.

Stonework from Mesoamerica and the Caribbean Coast

Artists working in the Macaracas style, Greater Coclé tradition (Panama)
Pedestal Plate with Dancing Figure and Stingray Spines, made c. 800–1100
Engobe-painted earthenware; 10⅝ × 6¾ in.
Gift of Drs. Alan Grinnell and Feelie Lee, M.2024.204.5

Pedestal plates were produced in the thousands for burial alongside what we assume were elites of ancient Panamanian society. Compositions featuring hybrid human-crocodilian creatures are ubiquitous, often shown in dynamic twisted or dancelike poses. Stingray spines, used for ceremonial bloodletting, radiate from the body of the main figure. Their depiction may signal a bleeding ritual that resulted in visions of, or transformation into, a composite animal spirit, or function as a design device used to convey the life force emanating from the central being.

Ancestral Ceramics from Panama and Colombia

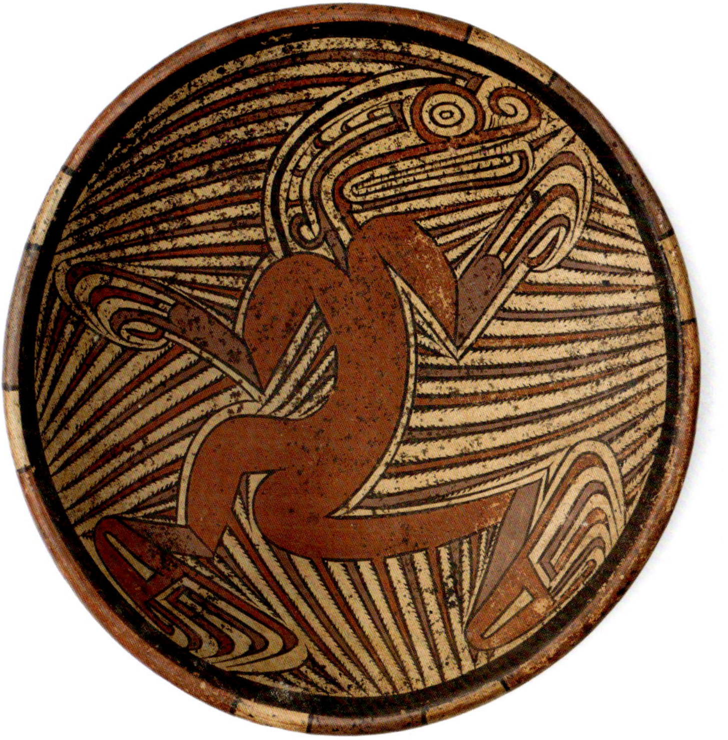

Tairona artist (Colombia)
Ocarina of Seated Chief with Extended Tongue, made c. 900–1600
Slip-painted earthenware; $3\frac{1}{2} \times 3\frac{3}{8} \times 1\frac{3}{4}$ in.
The Muñoz Kramer Collection, gift of Jorge G. and Nelly de Muñoz and Camilla Chandler Frost, M.2007.146.448

A figure with an enormous extended tongue occupies the center of what appears to be a throne flanked by serpent or crocodilian heads. The exaggerated tongue may signal supernatural characteristics associated with Tairona chiefs and religious leaders who mediated between human and spiritual realms. Finely incised lines filled with whitish pigment detail elaborate clothing, earspools, and a headdress that conceals this functional ocarina's mouthpiece. Two finger holes on each side allow pitch variation.

Ancestral Ceramics from Panama and Colombia

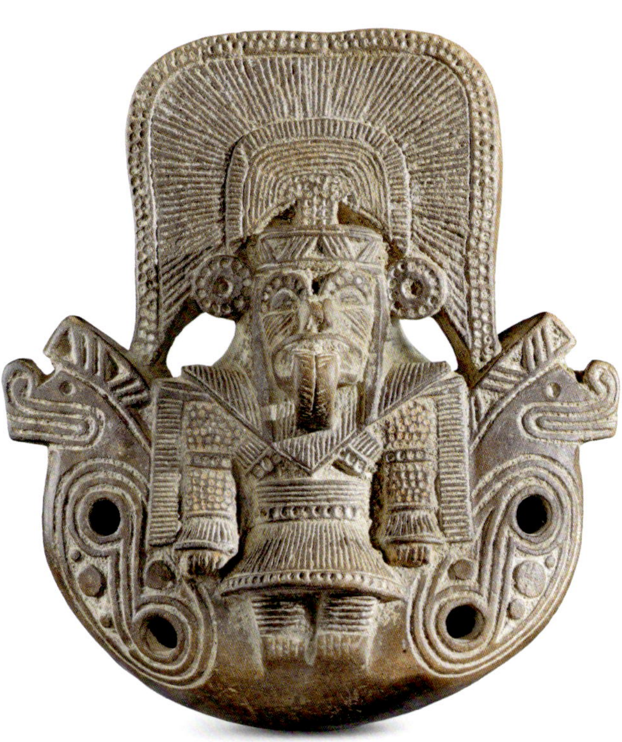

Artists working in the Macaracas style, Greater Coclé tradition (Panama)
Burial Urn with Supernatural Anthropomorphic Beings,
made c. 800–1100 (detail)
Engobe-painted earthenware; height: 19½ in.
Gift of Drs. Alan Grinnell and Feelie Lee in memory of Dr. Virginia Fields, M.2013.223.1

Among the densely packed polychrome designs covering this enormous vessel, two front-facing anthropomorphic beings emerge from swirling patterns. Their wide-set eyes—rendered in concentric circles of black paint—suggest trance or supernatural vision, while red-lipped mouths filled with sharp teeth grin outward. With arms extended wide, the figures appear to float or fly as their slender torsos dissolve into surrounding motifs. This design likely represents shamans in transformation or ritual flight, reflecting beliefs about powerful ritual specialists who could transform into or communicate with other beings.

Ancestral Ceramics from Panama and Colombia

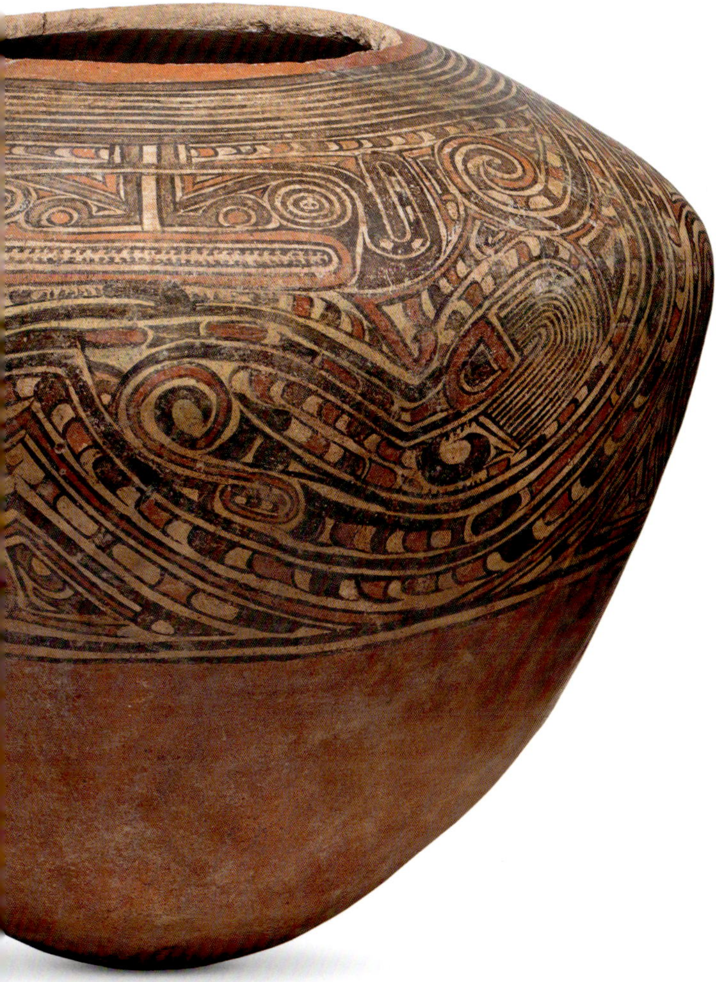

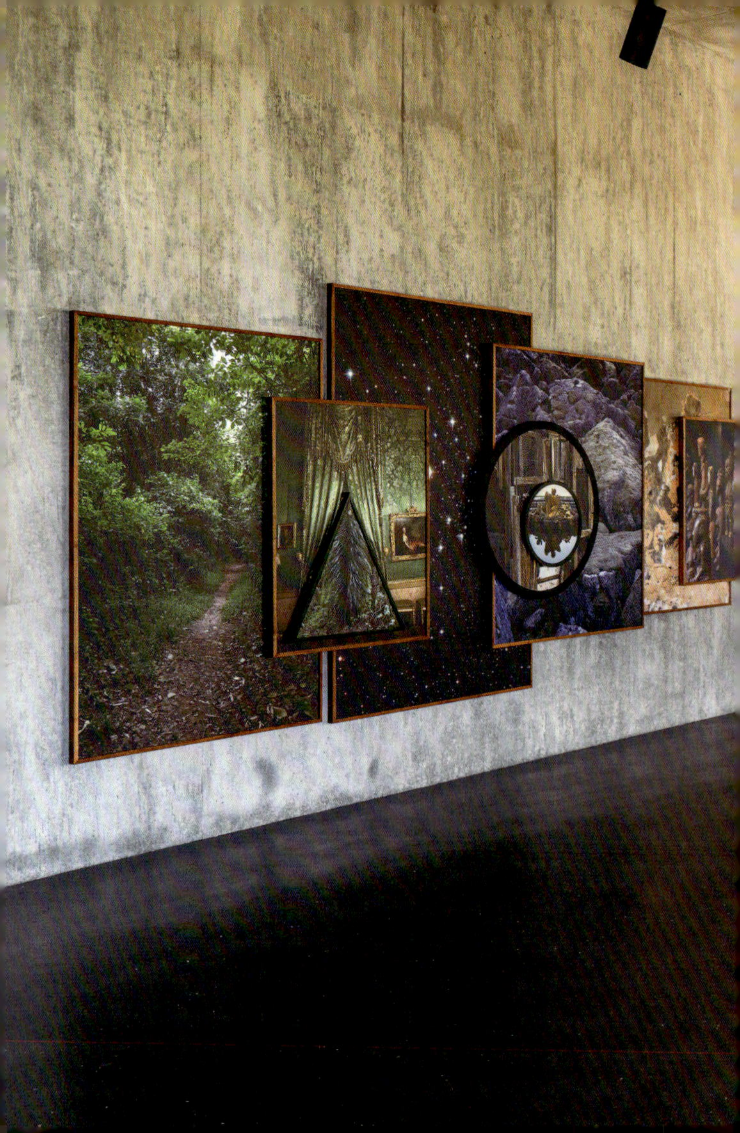

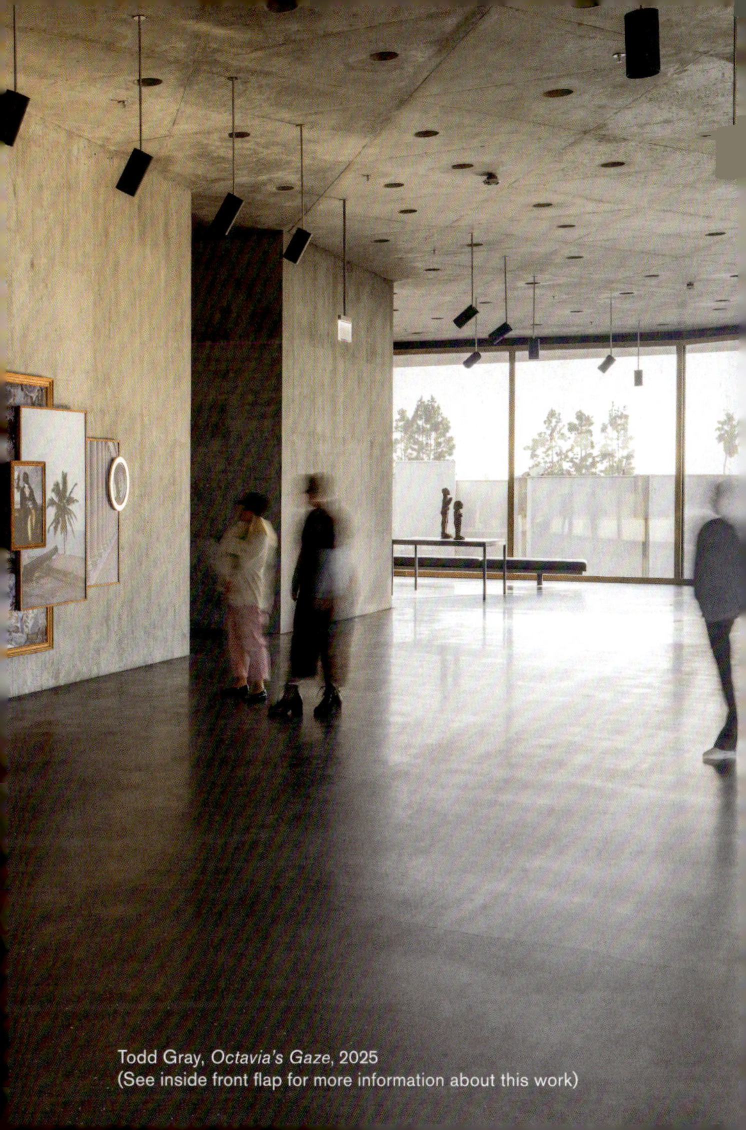

Todd Gray, *Octavia's Gaze*, 2025
(See inside front flap for more information about this work)

## Glossary

adobe
Building material made from earth and organic materials.

amate
Type of bark paper produced in Mexico since pre-Hispanic times.

amphora
Two-handled storage jar from ancient Greece with a narrow neck.

Art Nouveau
Decorative style that flourished from roughly 1890 to 1920, characterized by flowing, organic forms.

Arts and Crafts movement
Design reform movement (c. 1860–1915) that championed handmade objects over industrial production.

Baroque
17th-century European art style characterized by dramatic intensity and dynamic movement.

batik
Wax-resist dyeing technique for creating patterned textiles, originating in India and perfected in Indonesia.

bodhisattva
In Buddhism, an enlightened being who delays their own nirvana to help others achieve salvation.

*casta* paintings
18th-century Mexican painting genre documenting racial mixing among Indigenous, Spanish, and African populations.

celadon
Glaze with a distinct green or blue-green color, or a term for ceramics bearing that glaze.

chiaroscuro
Artistic technique that uses strong contrasts between light and dark to model three-dimensional forms and create dramatic effects.

coiling method
Pottery-building technique where long ropes of clay are stacked in spirals and smoothed together.

Cubism
Revolutionary early 20th-century art movement that abandoned single-point perspective, breaking subjects into geometric planes.

earthenware
Type of pottery fired at relatively low temperatures, leaving the body porous.

engobe
Liquid clay slip, often colored, applied to earthenware pottery before firing to coat or decorate the surface.

engraving
Printmaking technique using tools to incise an image into a metal plate; ink is held in the grooves and transferred to paper when passed through a press.

*estofado*
Technique consisting of painted and incised patterns made to emulate fine fabrics.

etching
Printmaking technique using acid to incise an image into a metal plate; ink is held in the grooves and transferred to paper when passed through a press.

fritware
Artificially created ceramic body combining silica, glass frit, and fine white clay.

gelatin silver print
The most common 20th-century black-and-white photograph type, made using light-sensitive paper.

gilding
The application of thin gold leaf or gold paint to a surface.

glaze/underglaze
A glaze is a glassy coating fused to ceramics during firing, while underglaze is decoration applied before the glaze.

glyph
Symbolic character or sign used in writing systems, such as that of the ancient Maya.

handscroll
A horizontal East Asian scroll format, viewed in sections by unrolling right to left.

*huipil*
Traditional loose blouse or tunic typically worn by Indigenous women in Mexico and Guatemala since the pre-Conquest period.

Impressionism
19th-century French movement that sought to capture the fleeting nature of modern life and the immediate effects of light.

inlay
Decorative technique where one material is set into the surface of another.

kinetic art
Art that depends on motion for its effect.

kufic
An early, angular form of Arabic script.

lost-wax method
An ancient metal-casting technique in which a wax model is encased in clay, the wax melted out, and molten metal poured into the cavity.

maiolica
Italian tin-glazed earthenware, typically featuring colorful painted decoration on an opaque white ground.

mantle
A large sleeveless garment worn draped on the body.

Mingei
Japanese folk art movement that celebrates the beauty of functional, everyday crafts. The word *mingei* means "craft of the people."

missal
Liturgical book used in the Catholic Mass.

netsuke
Small carved objects from Japan, typically wood or ivory, used as counterweights for hanging containers on kimono sashes.

ocarina
A small wind instrument, often made of earthenware.

Op art
Mid-20th-century style using abstract geometric patterns to create visual vibrations or optical illusions.

pax
Small devotional object featuring Christian imagery, used in the Catholic Mass.

Pictorialism
Early 20th-century photography movement emphasizing artistic interpretation over documentary realism.

porcelain
Hard, white, translucent ceramic fired at very high temperatures.

raffia
Fiber derived from the leaves of the raffia palm for weaving, native to Africa, Southeast Asia, and South and Central America.

red-figure
Ancient Greek pottery technique depicting figures in the clay's natural red-orange color against a black background.

Rinpa (Rimpa)
Japanese art lineage originating in the early 17th century, known for its decorative style and use of precious materials.

Romanesque
Architectural style of medieval Europe characterized by rounded arches and barrel vaults.

schist
Metamorphic gray rock that splits easily into layers.

slip
Fluid suspension of clay in water, used for coating or decorating pottery. Unlike glaze, slip is clay-based.

stoneware
Durable, nonporous ceramic fired at high temperatures (higher than earthenware, lower than porcelain).

stupa
Dome-shaped Buddhist monument used to house the Buddha's relics.

Symbolism
Late 19th-century movement that rejected realism in favor of emotion, dreams, and spiritual meaning.

tapa
A nonwoven textile made from beaten tree bark, traditional throughout the Pacific Islands.

tempera
Painting medium where pigment is mixed with a water-soluble binder, typically egg yolk.

terracotta
Literally "baked earth," this is a type of fired clay, often unglazed or painted.

triptych
An artwork divided into three sections or panels.

vernacular forms
Design elements drawn from local, traditional, or folk building and craft practices.

*wadjet*
Ancient Egyptian symbol depicting a stylized falcon eye, associated with protection and healing.

warp/weft
In weaving, warp elements are the lengthwise (or vertical) threads through which the weft elements are woven. Weft elements pass crosswise over and under the warp elements to create a fabric.

## Also at LACMA

In addition to the artworks on view in the David Geffen Galleries, visitors will find other collection works and temporary exhibitions in the Broad Contemporary Art Museum (BCAM), the Lynda and Stewart Resnick Exhibition Pavilion, and the Pavilion for Japanese Art (currently under renovation).

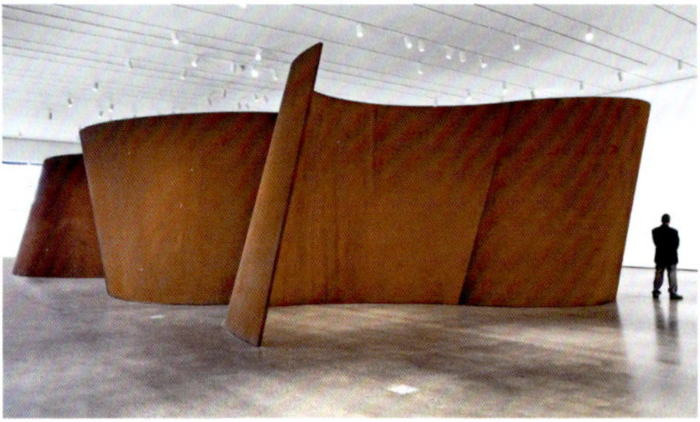

Richard Serra (United States, 1938–2024)
*Band*, 2006
Steel; 153 × 846 × 440 in.
Purchased with funds provided by Eli and Edythe L. Broad, M.2007.122

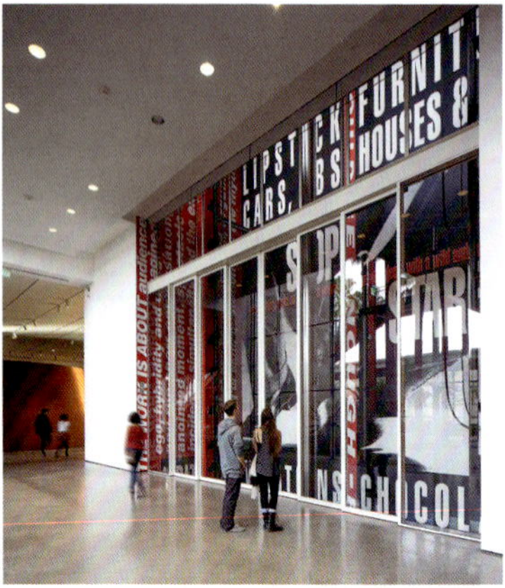

Barbara Kruger (United States, b. 1945)
*Untitled (Shafted)*, 2008
Digital-print installation; 94 × 18 × 12 ft.
Gift of Carole Bayer Sager, commissioned by the Los Angeles County Museum of Art for the opening of the Broad Contemporary Art Museum, M.2012.20

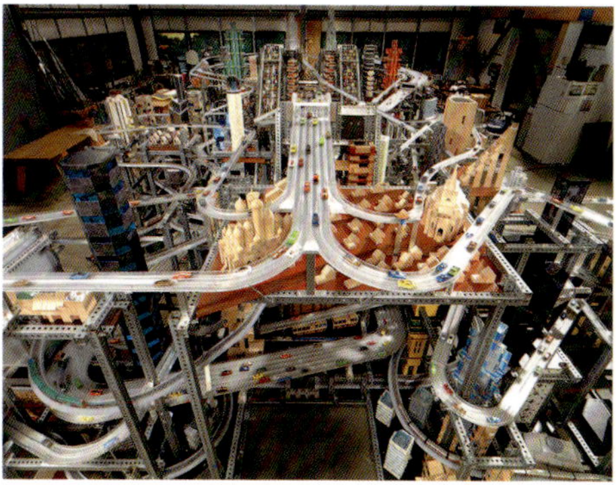

Chris Burden (United States, 1946–2015)
*Metropolis II*, 2010
DC motors, electronic controls and sensors, custom die-cast cars, HO-scale train sets, neodymium magnets, steel, aluminum, copper wire, copper sheet, brass, plastics, assorted wood products, tiles, acrylic and oil-based paints, rubber, and adhesives; 117 × 339 × 230 in.
Courtesy of Berggruen Charities

Robert Irwin (United States, 1928–2023)
*Miracle Mile*, 2013
Lightwork; 72 × 432 in.
Gift of Hyundai Motor as part of The Hyundai Project: Art + Technology at LACMA in honor of the museum's 50th anniversary, M.2016.113

Henri Matisse (France, 1869–1954)
*Tea*, 1919
Oil on canvas; 55¼ × 83¼ in.
Bequest of David L. Loew in memory of his father, Marcus Loew, M.74.52.2

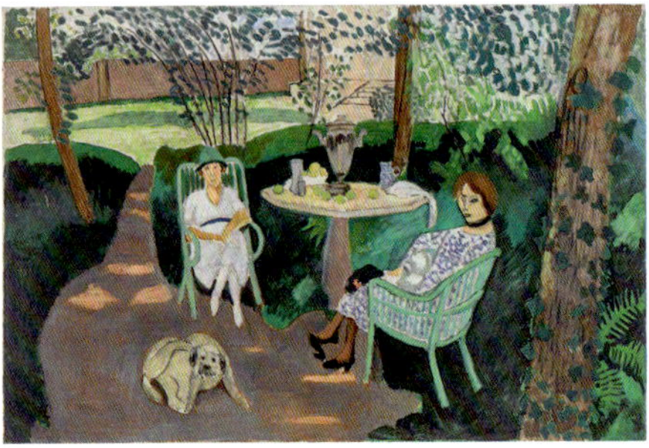

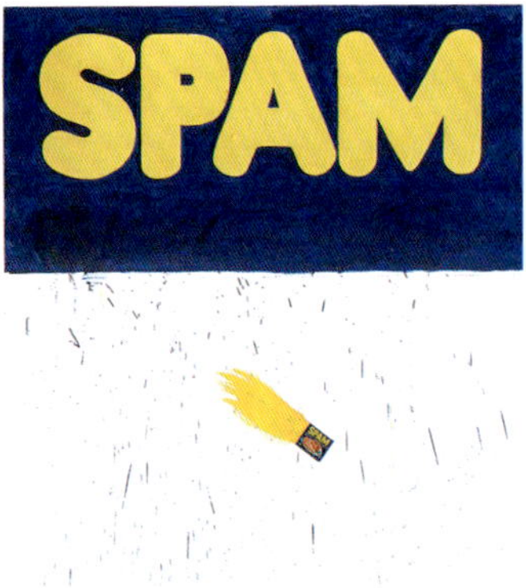


Ed Ruscha (United States, b. 1937)
*Actual Size*, 1962
Oil on canvas; 67⅛ × 72⅛ in.
Anonymous gift through the Contemporary Art Council, M.63.14

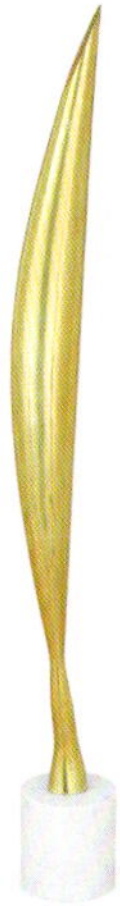

Constantin Brâncuși (Romania, 1876–1957, active France)
*Bird in Space*, 1927, cast later
Polished bronze; height: 73 in.
Partial, fractional and promised gift of Janice and Henri Lazarof, M.2005.70.13

René Magritte (Belgium, 1898–1967)
*The Treachery of Images (This Is Not a Pipe)*, 1929
Oil on canvas; 23¾ × 32 × 1 in.
Purchased with funds provided by the Mr. and Mrs. William Preston Harrison Collection, 78.7

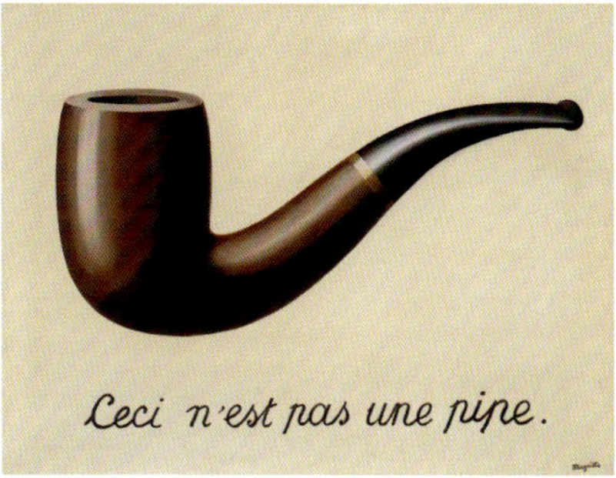

Matta (Chile, 1911–2002, active France, Italy, Mexico, and United States)
*Burn, Baby, Burn*, 1965–66
Oil on canvas; $117\frac{3}{8} \times 386\frac{1}{4} \times 2$ in.
Gift of the 2009 Collectors Committee with additional funds provided by the Bernard and Edith Lewin Collection of Mexican Art Deaccession Fund, M.2009.42

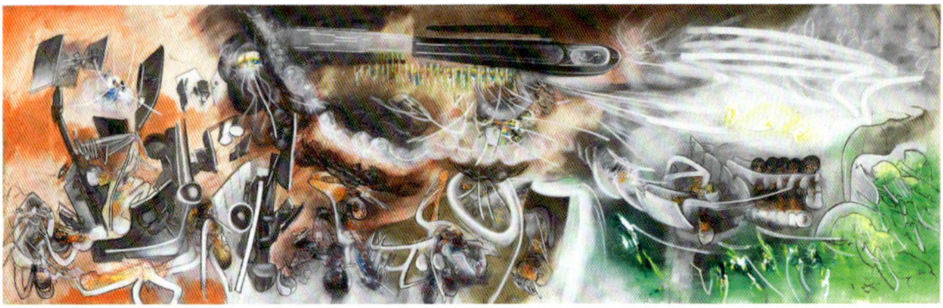

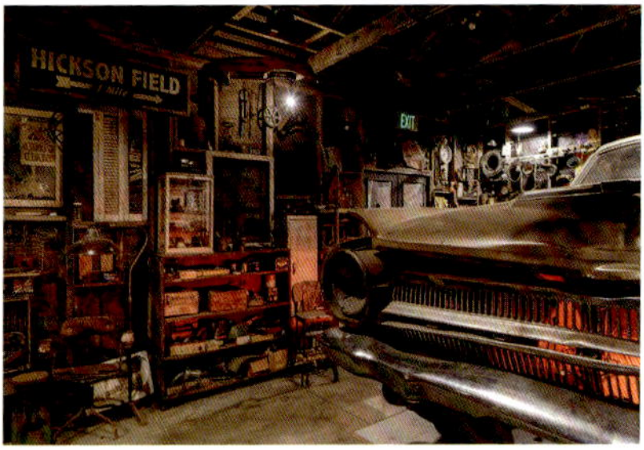


Michael C. McMillen (United States, b. 1946)
*Central Meridian (The Garage)*, 1981
Mixed media, audio component; dimensions variable
Art Museum Council Fund, M.2005.17

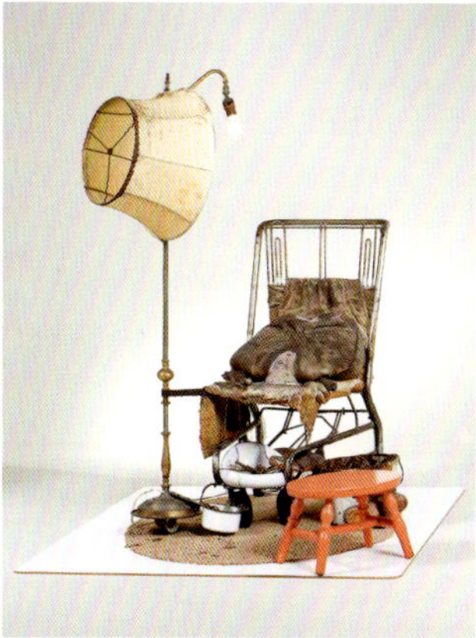

Edward Kienholz (United States, 1927–1994)
*The Illegal Operation*, 1962
Polyester resin, pigment, shopping cart, wood stool, concrete, lamp, fabric, basin, metal pots, blanket, hooked rug, and medical equipment; 59 × 48 × 54 in.
Partial gift of Betty and Monte Factor and purchased with funds provided by the Art Museum Council, Daniel Greenberg and Susan Steinhauser, the Modern and Contemporary Art Council, Dallas Price-Van Breda and Bob Van Breda, the Robert H. Halff Fund, David G. Booth and Suzanne Deal Booth, Virginia Dwan, Elaine and Bram Goldsmith, The Grinstein Family, Ric and Suzanne Kayne, Alice and Nahum Lainer, Frederick R. Weisman Art Foundation, Mrs. Harry Lenart, The Robert Gore Rifkind Foundation, Philippa Calnan and Laura Lee Woods, M.2008.107a–d

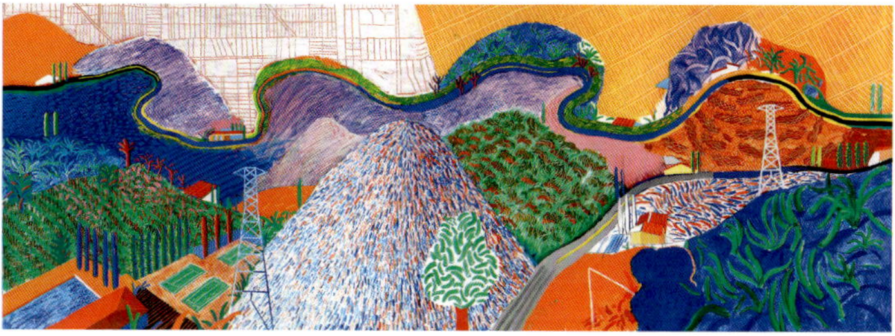

David Hockney (England, b. 1937, active United States)
*Mulholland Drive: The Road to the Studio*, 1980
Acrylic on canvas; 86 × 243 in.
Purchased with funds provided by the F. Patrick Burns Bequest, M.83.35

# Outdoor Art

Outdoor sculpture is a highlight of LACMA's 20-acre campus. During 2026, many old favorites will return from storage, joined by new commissions and acquisitions. Scan the QR code for an up-to-date map of outdoor artworks currently on view.

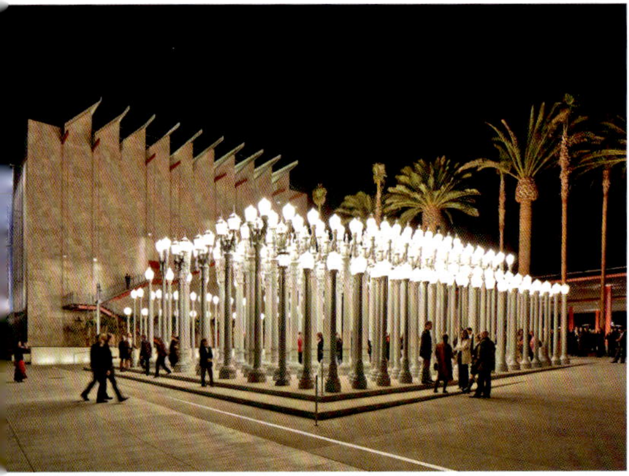

Chris Burden (United States, 1946–2015)
*Urban Light*, 2008
202 restored cast-iron streetlamps; 320½ × 686½ × 704½ in.
*Urban Light* is made possible by Willow Bay and Bob Iger, and is open 24 hours a day thanks to their generosity. Special thanks to the Brandon-Gordon family for their founding support of the 2008 installation, M.2007.147

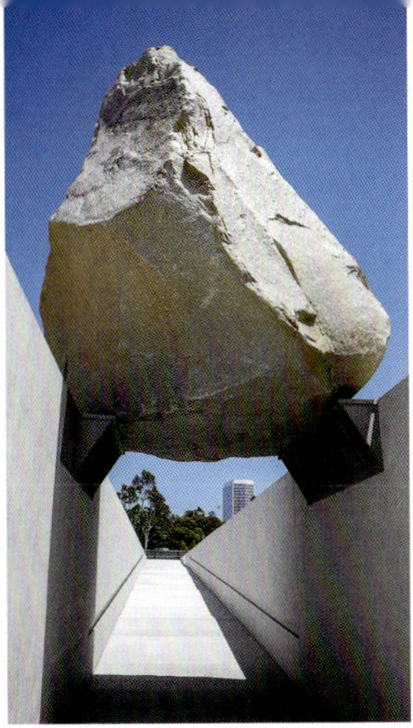

Michael Heizer (United States, b. 1944)
*Levitated Mass*, conceived 1969, realized 2012
Diorite granite and concrete;
35 × 456 × 21⅝ ft.
Purchased with funds provided by Jane and Terry Semel, Bobby Kotick, Carole Bayer Sager and Bob Daly, Beth and Joshua Friedman, Steve Tisch Family Foundation, Elaine Wynn, Linda, Bobby, and Brian Daly, Richard Merkin, MD, and the Mohn Family Foundation, and dedicated by LACMA to the memory of Nancy Daly. Transportation made possible by Hanjin Shipping Holdings Co., Ltd., M.2011.35

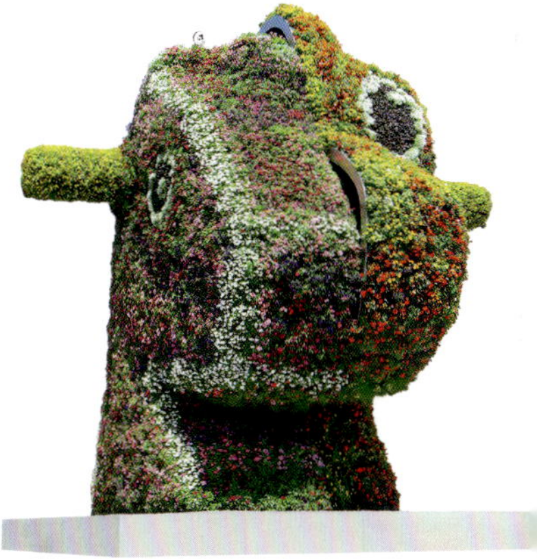

Jeff Koons (United States, b. 1955)
*Split-Rocker*, 2025
Stainless steel, soil, geotextile fabric, internal irrigation system, and live flowering plants;
446⅞ × 483⅛ × 427⅝ in.
A gift from Lynda and Stewart Resnick,
M.2017.103

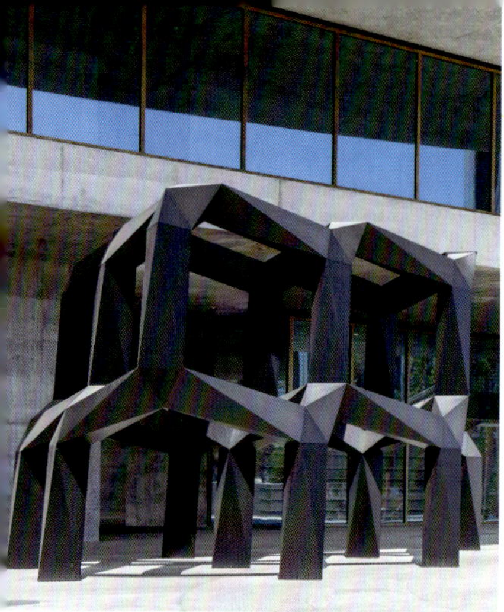

Tony Smith (United States, 1912–1980)
*Smoke*, 1967, fabricated 2005
Painted aluminum; 290 × 564 × 396 in.
Made possible by The Belldegrun Family's gift to LACMA in honor of Rebecka Belldegrun's birthday, M.2010.49.1–.66

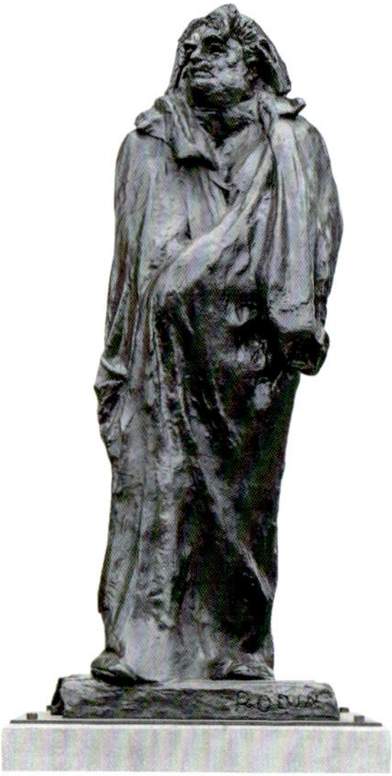

Auguste Rodin (France, 1840–1917)
*Monument to Honoré de Balzac*, modeled 1897, this cast 1967
Bronze; 117 × 47¼ × 47¼ in.
Gift of the B. Gerald Cantor Art Foundation, M.85.267

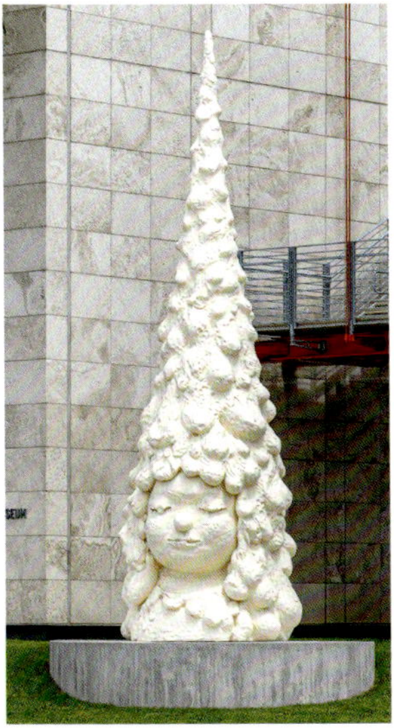

Yoshitomo Nara (Japan, b. 1959)
*Miss Forest (LACMA Version)*, 2020
Urethane on bronze; 307 × 93 × 87 in.
Purchased with funds from an anonymous donor, M.2020.282

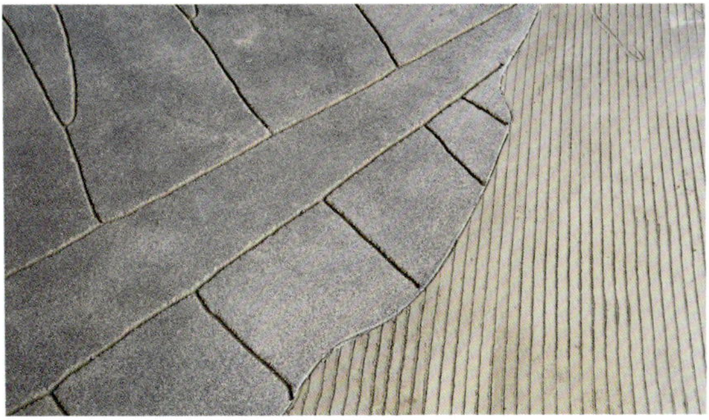

Mariana Castillo Deball (Mexico, b. 1975, active Germany)
*Feathered Changes*, 2025 (detail)
Reinforced concrete; 207,000 sq. ft.

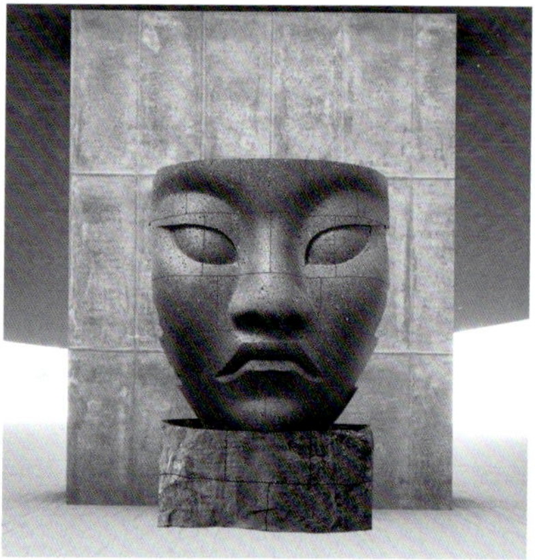

Pedro Reyes (Mexico, b. 1972)
*Tlali*, 2025
Volcanic stone; 215⅜ × 155½ × 80¾ in.
Purchased with funds provided by the David and Meredith Kaplan Foundation, M.2026.5

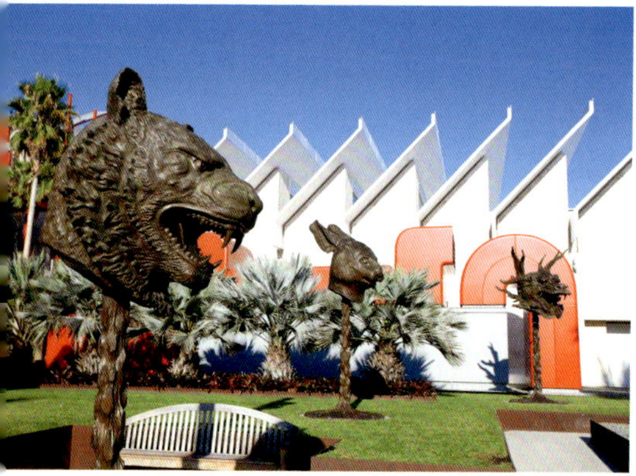

Ai Weiwei (China, b. 1957)
*Circle of Animals/Zodiac Heads*, 2010
Bronze; height: 118⅛ in.
Gift of Budi Tek and the Yuz Foundation, M.2020.95.1–.12

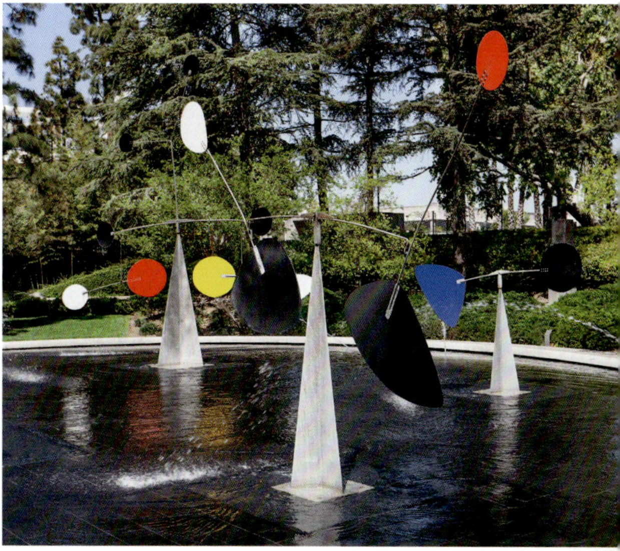

Alexander Calder (United States, 1898–1976)
*Three Quintains (Hello Girls)*, 1964
Sheet metal and paint with motor; 275 × 288 in.
Art Museum Council Fund, M.65.10

# Board of Trustees

## Image Credits

Works and photographs are reproduced courtesy of the creators and lenders of the materials depicted. The following images, keyed to page number, are those for which additional or separate credits are due. Unless otherwise noted, all photos are © Museum Associates/LACMA. We have made every effort to contact rightsholders to obtain all necessary permissions to publish images and text materials, and to provide accurate credit information. Please contact the publishers with any corrections.

4: © Andreas Gursky/courtesy Sprüth Magers/Artists Rights Society (ARS), New York, 2025; 8–9, 422 left: © Tony Smith Estate/Artists Rights Society (ARS), New York, photo © Iwan Baan; 11: photo © Iwan Baan; 14, 404–5: © Todd Gray; 16: © Succession H. Matisse/Artists Rights Society (ARS), New York; 18–19, 124–25, 196–97, 290–91: map © Museum Associates/LACMA; 31: © Banco de México Diego Rivera Frida Kahlo Museums Trust, Mexico, D.F./Artists Rights Society (ARS), New York; 32: © Tamayo Heirs/Mexico/Artists Rights Society (ARS), New York; 50: © Graziella Laffi; 52: © William Spratling; 54: © Lisa Reihana, photo courtesy of the artist; 66: © Satoru Hoshino; 68: © Kawai Kanjiro; 77: © June Wayne/Artists Rights Society (ARS), New York; 79: © Ed Ruscha; 80–81: © Catherine Opie, courtesy Regen Projects, Los Angeles; 82–83: photo © Museum Associates/LACMA Conservation, by Yosi Pozeilov; 84: © Judy Chicago/Artists Rights Society (ARS), New York; 86: © John Mason; 89: © Craig Kauffman Estate; 91: © Helen Pashgian; 93 top: photo by Kerry Taylor Auctions; 93 bottom: © Robert Mapplethorpe Foundation; 95: © Roni Horn; 96: © Larry Bell; 99: © 2026 Ruth Asawa Lanier, Inc.; 101: © Dora De Larios, photo by Dale Strumpell; 102: © Scherezade García & Praxis, 107: © Estate of Jane Coper; 110: © Wendy Red Star, image courtesy Sargent's Daughters; 112–13: © 2017 Richard Prince, photo courtesy of the artist; 115: © 1979 Amon Carter Museum of American Art; 117: © Kimsooja/Artists Rights Society (ARS), New York, courtesy of Studio

Kimsooja; 119: © Shizu Saldamando, photo by yubo dong photography; 120–21: © rafa esparza, photo by Kaelan Burkett; 122–23, 420: © Chris Burden/licensed by The Chris Burden Estate and Artists Rights Society (ARS), New York; 135: photo courtesy Atlantic Art Partners LLC; 145: © Han Youngsoo Foundation; 146: © Henri Cartier-Bresson/Magnum Photos; 155: © Do Ho Suh; image courtesy of the artist; 160–61: © Manjunath Kamath; 177: © Haji Ehsan; 187: © Hiroshi Sugimoto, courtesy Lisson Gallery; 217: © Vera Lutter, photo courtesy of Gagosian Gallery; 229: © Nasser Al Salem; 285: photo courtesy of Colnaghi, Madrid; 299: © Betye Saar, courtesy of the artist and Roberts Projects, Los Angeles; 313: © James Van Der Zee Archive, The Metropolitan Museum of Art; 314–15: © The Estate of Francis Bacon. All rights reserved, DACS Images 2025, photo: Prudence Cuming Associates Ltd; 317, 318: photos © Fredrik Nilsen; 321: © C. Herscovici, Brussels/Artists Rights Society (ARS), New York, photo © Fredrik Nilsen; 322–23: photo by Bruce White; 329: © Artists Rights Society (ARS), New York/ADAGP, Paris; 346: © Frank E. Cummings III; 361: © Ladi Kwali; 367: © 1981 Center for Creative Photography, Arizona Board of Regents; 368–69: photograph by Ansel Adams © 2015 The Ansel Adams Publishing Rights Trust; 370: © Eggleston Artistic Trust; 373: © Thomas Joshua Cooper, photo courtesy of the artist; 377: © Julio Le Parc/Artists Rights Society (ARS), New York/ADAGP, Paris; 378–79: © 2026 Artists Rights Society (ARS), New York/AUTVIS, Sao Paulo; 383: © El Anatsui; 385: © Rosie Lee Tompkins; 414 top: © Richard Serra/Artists Rights Society (ARS), New York; 414 bottom: © Barbara Kruger, photo © Fredrik Nilsen; 415 top: © Chris Burden/licensed by The Chris Burden Estate and Artists Rights Society (ARS), New York, photo courtesy E. Koyama; 415 bottom: © Robert Irwin/Artists Rights Society (ARS), New York; 416 top: © 2026 Succession H. Matisse/Artists Rights Society (ARS), New York; 416 bottom: © Ed Ruscha; 417 left: © Succession Brancusi—All rights reserved (ARS) 2026; 417 right: © 2026 C. Herscovici/Artists Rights Society (ARS), New York; 418 top: © Artists Rights Society (ARS), New York/ADAGP, Paris; 418 bottom: © Michael C. McMillen; 419 top: © The Edward and Nancy Kienholz Foundation, Inc., courtesy of L.A. Louver, Venice, CA; 419 bottom: © David Hockney; 421 left: © Michael Heizer, photo by Tom Vinetz; 421 right: © Jeff Koons; 423 top: © Yoshitomo Nara; 423 bottom: Art by Mariana Castillo Deball; 424 top: © Pedro Reyes, photo courtesy of the artist; 424 bottom: © Ai Weiwei Studio; 425: © 2026 Calder Foundation, New York/Artists Rights Society (ARS), New York. Calder® is a registered trademark of Calder Foundation, New York, NY

The inaugural edition of *Wander: Exploring LACMA's David Geffen Galleries* is published in conjunction with the opening of the David Geffen Galleries at LACMA, April 2026.

The opening presentation of the David Geffen Galleries was made possible by the generosity of members of LACMA's Inaugural Exhibition Fund: The Blanchard Nesbitt Family, The David & Meredith Kaplan Foundation, Ezra and Lauren Perlman, The Michael Silver Family, and Marietta Wu and Thomas Yamamoto.

Text contributions by David P. Bardeen, Stephanie Barron, Robert L. Brown, Julia Burtenshaw, Jennifer Cernada, Alyce de Carteret, Claudine Dixon, Christine Drosse, Carol S. Eliel, Clarissa M. Esguerra, Susanna Ferrell, Rita Gonzalez, Michael Govan, Tushara Bindu Gude, Rika Hiro, Alexandra Kaczenski, Rachel Kaplan, Wendy Kaplan, Ilona Katzew, Cynthia Kok, Linda Komaroff, Nicole LaBouff, Dhyandra Lawson, Leah Lehmbeck, Stephen Little, Diana Magaloni, Arvin Maghsoudlou, Stephen Markel, Erin Maynes, Thomas Michie, Rebecca Morse, Danielle Pesqueira, Polly Nooter Roberts, Stephanie Rouinfar, Britt Salvesen, Eve Schillo, Shadi Shafiei, Cambra Sklarz, Claire Spadafora Baes, Staci Steinberger, Sharon S. Takeda, Nancy Thomas, Bobbye Tigerman, Shannon Vittoria, Sandra Williams, Katia Zavistovski, and Diva Zumaya



Library of Congress Control Number: 2026933588

ISBN: 978-1-943042-99-9

Artificial Intelligence (AI) Disclosure
Anthropic's Claude (Sonnet 4.5) supported the production of this guide. Claude was used to summarize existing texts originally authored by LACMA staff; it identified terms for the publication glossary; and suggested cultural, political, migratory, and trade connections linking works by ocean. No original texts or images were generated by AI, and all texts were edited, proofread, and fact checked by humans, whose names are included on this colophon.

Published by the Los Angeles County Museum of Art

Los Angeles County Museum of Art
5905 Wilshire Boulevard
Los Angeles, CA 90036
www.lacma.org

Trade edition distributed by Angel City Press at Los Angeles Public Library
www.angelcitypress.com

For LACMA
Senior Deputy Director for Art Administration and Collections:
Nancy Thomas
Publisher: Susan Chun
Creative Director: David Karwan
Editorial Director: Sara Cody
Managing Editor: Dawson Weber

Editors: Philomena Mariani with Susan Chun, Sara Cody, Claire Crighton, and Dawson Weber
Designers: David Karwan and Green Dragon Office (Lorraine Wild and Xiaoqing Wang with Thomas L. Huang)
Digital Strategy: Bruce Wyman
Rights and Reproductions: Piper Severance and Emma Crow
Proofreader: Jean Patterson
Photographers: Kristina Simonsen, Charles Powers, and Jonathan Urban
Photography Coordinator: Sarah Applegate
Production: Janet Klein
Project Management: Charlie Kang
Administrative Support: Charlene Wesley
Curatorial Consultants: Leah Lehmbeck, Britt Salvesen, and Ilona Katzew

For Angel City Press
Editorial Director: Terri Accomazzo

Color Separations: Echelon Color, Los Angeles

Typeset in Akzidenz Grotesk Pro
Printed and bound in China by Artron

Notes